PLATINUM SPONSORS

adventz
MW Corp

GOLD SPONSORS

ACC
kcp
Nestlé Good Food, Good Life
Punj Lloyd GROUP
xproindia

SILVER SPONSORS

ALSTOM
APEEJAY Stya
Fortis HEALTHCARE
GODFREY PHILLIPS INDIA LIMITED
GREAT EASTERN ENERGY CORPORATION LTD.
imfa
JUBILANT BHARTIA Caring Sharing Growing
KCI
ROLTA
The India Cements Limited

ADVERTISERS

ADITYA BIRLA GROUP
apollo
BRITANNIA Eat Healthy, Think Better
GHCL
kerala God's Own Country
MSD Be well
ओएनजीसी ONGC
RANBAXY Trusted medicines. Healthier lives
TATA
TATA CAPITAL We only do what's right for you

We gratefully acknowledge the assistance of our sponsors and promoters for the book.

AN ILLUSTRATED HISTORY OF INDIAN ENTERPRISE

FICCI

FICCI

AN ILLUSTRATED HISTORY OF INDIAN ENTERPRISE

OXFORD
UNIVERSITY PRESS

OXFORD

Oxford University Press is a department of the University of Oxford.
It furthers the University's objective of excellence in research, scholarship, and education by publishing worldwide. Oxford is a registered trademark of Oxford University Press in the UK and in certain other countries

Published in India by
Oxford University Press
YMCA Library Building, 1, Jai Singh Road, New Delhi 110001, India

First published in 2013

ISBN-13: 978-0-19-808981-0
ISBN-10: 0-19-808981-3

Designed by Roopali Jain and Vivek Sahni
Vivek Sahni Design, 3 K Commercial Circle, Jangpura Extension, New Delhi 110 014
Printed in India by Lustra Print Process, New Delhi 110 028

ACKNOWLEDGEMENTS
Anjana Rajwar, Secretarial Assistant, Special Projects, FICCI
P.L. Joseph, Marketing Consultant, Special Projects, FICCI

Views expressed in the book are those of the individual authors and do not reflect those of FICCI.

CONTENTS

VI Messages from Past Presidents, FICCI

XI Introduction
R.V. KANORIA

01 Origins of Indian Enterprise from Ancient Times to 1947
DWIJENDRA TRIPATHI

46 Trade and Commerce in Early India
R. CHAMPAKALAKSHMI

56 Trade and Merchants in Mughal India
SHIREEN MOOSVI

64 The Indian Merchants of Astrakhan
PURUSHOTTAM AGARWAL

73 Indian Enterprise since Independence
FROM TRADE TO INDUSTRY
ASHOK V. DESAI

175 India Inc.
POLICY IMPACT ON BUSINESS (1947–2012)
T.C.A. SRINIVASA-RAGHAVAN

231 Multinationals in India
A DYNAMIC PERSPECTIVE
VIKRAM SINGH MEHTA

281 Conclusion
HOPES AND CHALLENGES
OMKAR GOSWAMI

287 Profiles
EDITORS AND CONTRIBUTORS

290 Acknowledgements and Picture Credits

294 Index

A LEGACY OF PIONEERING AND TRUE GRIT

Voices from the Federation of Indian Chambers of Commerce and Industry's Past Presidents

As we tread the footprints of Indian business over the decades, we cannot but take pride in our past. It is heartening that the new generation of business people continues the Indian legacy of excellence, and the future that it weaves together will certainly bring greater prosperity and stature to our nation.

I have great pleasure that FICCI is bringing out this volume and I am confident that it will provide a deeper insight into the history of Indian enterprise.

1971 S.S. KANORIA

Chairman, Ludlow Jute & Specialities Ltd

The J.K. Organisation and FICCI were born at a time of turbulence. My grandfather had ventured into industrial entrepreneurship in 1921, a few years before the birth of FICCI in 1926. My uncle, Sir Padampat Singhania, was involved in the process of the formation of FICCI, of which he became President in 1935-6. FICCI has played a stellar role in furthering business and industry, and I remain confident it will carry on its role as the leading torchbearer of Indian entrepreneurs.

1979 HARI SHANKAR SINGHANIA

President, J.K. Organisation

Business has a fascinating history in our country from time immemorial. It is more than a calling and bigger than 'buying cheap and selling dear to make some profit'. It has been my privilege to have a ringside seat in India to watch the growing importance of commerce and industry and its emergence across the world. Business today deserves the commitment and involvement of the country's best minds.

1986 R.P. GOENKA

Chairman (Emeritus), RP-Sanjiv Goenka Group.

FICCI's history is closely joined with the emergence and development of independent India and its industry and trade., to now emerge as one of the most rapidly growing economies. I have the privilege of being closely associated with FICCI and its initiatives over decades, and share my great happiness as we memorialize Indian enterprise and its spirit in this volume.

1990 SUDARSHAN KUMAR BIRLA

Director (Emeritus), Birla Brothers Pvt. Ltd

For eight and a half decades, FICCI has represented the best face of India's industry and commerce, all the while basing its activity profile on its inspiration, Mahatma Gandhi's keyword—service.

FICCI's leadership has always been drawn from India's finest business talent and has invariably been the consul-in-chief for the Government on economic, industrial, and trade issues. This illustrated volume on Indian enterprise will be a much read, referred to, and retained publication for anyone interested in India's modern history.

2002 A.C. MUTHIAH

Chairman, SPIC Ltd

India's greatest asset is its inherent entrepreneurship. Historically, this has given India its fabulous riches, and its fine textiles have dominated global markets.

In the 21st century, it is entrepreneurship that will give direction to the economy. I am confident that of the future global corporations, many will be Indian in origin, guided by Indian entrepreneurs. It is already happening.

FICCI, ever since its inception, has articulated and nurtured the growth of Indian entrepreneurship. I feel proud of my association with FICCI.

2003 YOGENDRA KR. MODI

Chairman & CEO, Great Eastern Energy Corporation Ltd

Intertwined with the growth and development of corporate and commercial India for the last eight and a half decades, FICCI today is increasingly more relevant to not just the business community but to the nation as a whole. The emergence of the economic super-power that India is destined to become is helped by the leading role that FICCI continues to play in this evolution. I wish it, and all those associated with it, many more years of path-breaking guidance in the forefront of the economy.

Onkar Kanwar

2004 ONKAR S. KANWAR

Chairman & MD,
Apollo Tyres Ltd

India's pre-eminent position, as one of the world's fastest growing economies, owes much to the pioneering spirit, inspired vision, missionary zeal, and storied legacy of our nation's entrepreneurship and enterprise.

A saga of true grit and determination in the face of overwhelming odds, the many splendoured achievements of Indian business and industry continue to resonate, providing inspiration and leadership for a better tomorrow.

It is, therefore, extremely gratifying and in the fitness of things that FICCI, the country's leading industry association, which I have had the honour to be associated with for many productive and fulfilling years, is commemorating the history of Indian enterprise through this beautifully produced, authoritative, and richly illustrated volume. It is a magnificent and befitting tribute, indeed, and I am confident that it will serve as a beacon and inspirational guide to many, for generations to come.

2005 **SAROJ KUMAR PODDAR**

Chairman, Adventz Group

Decades ago, the father of the nation, Mahatma Gandhi had said, 'A man is but the product of his thoughts. What he thinks, he becomes.' This should be an inspiration to transform India. FICCI has been playing this role proactively, pushing new boundaries of change to transform India.

We live in turbulent times. India has enormous intellectual and human potential, and there is great opportunity in the coming decades for it to become an economically and politically significant voice in the world.

2006 DR HABIL KHORAKIWALA

Chairman, Wockhardt Ltd

Indian businesses and entrepreneurs have played a vital role in shaping India's economy and contributed immensely to its growth story. It is their efforts and vision that have given us the platform to build a modern India and global enterprises.

FICCI has had the privilege of being associated with some of these stalwarts, and I am delighted at this timely initiative that will throw light on the rich legacy of Indian enterprise

2010 RAJAN BHARTI MITTAL

Vice Chairman & MD, Bharti Enterprises Ltd

An entrepreneur's journey is always an interesting one. I have seen that entrepreneurs who are ambitious, innovative, and eager to learn share and collaborate to succeed in their journey. I believe a successful entrepreneur should follow a conscious capitalist approach. I am glad that FICCI is coming out with this illustrated publication showcasing the entrepreneurial journey of Indian enterprises.

FICCI as an organization has really emerged as the thought leader and voice of Indian business and industry over the years.

2011 HARSH MARIWALA

Chairman & MD, Marico Ltd

Organized law was one of the gains India received under the Raj. Open courts administered to people's needs often in distant districts, as in Meerut. Though the Mughals and other princely kingdoms were known for their quality of justice, one uniform business law for the country was introduced under the British.

Introduction
THE INCREDIBLE JOURNEY OF INDIAN ENTERPRISE

R.V. KANORIA

Trade and enterprise were important activities in India well before the start of the colonial period. India's external trade made a significant contribution to the world economy. The large size of the country also evolved an extensive trade network within it. Any analysis of India's trade must keep in perspective the large volume of trade that happens within the country. India's engagement with the rest of the world is limited because of the large domestic market, which is complex owing to the typicality of the interplay between constituent states and regions. By AD 1000, India's estimated share in the world economy was over 30 per cent, the largest in the world. This reduced to about 25 per cent by the year 1500. During the colonial period, by the end of the 18th century, the Indian economy witnessed large-scale exploitation of domestic resources. It became a captive supplier of raw materials. Investments in the economy fell sharply, severely dampening growth. A study by Cambridge University historian Angus Maddison showed that India's share of world income fell from 22.6 per cent in 1700 to 3.8 per cent in 1952.

Kuber, the treasurer of the gods, is a pot-bellied dwarf who, according to mythology, lives in the Himalayas from where he watches over the riches of the world.

Rashtrapati Bhawan, formerly the Viceregal Lodge, marked the movement of the seat of government from Calcutta to New Delhi. The shift has seen New Delhi become the hub of business while Calcutta, British India's capital of commerce, has still to recover from the twin misfortune caused by the loss of opportunity, and compounded by a siege of refugees following Partition.

British systems became ingrained during its two centuries of rule in India. The legal and political systems developed in a way that 'a few could control the destiny of many'. Political power was vested with the bureaucracy which became the most powerful institution in the governance of the country.

With the emergence of Indian business, a collective voice for industry became desirable. In 1927, the Federation of Indian Chambers of Commerce and Industry (FICCI) came into being with the blessings of Mahatma Gandhi, who advised that industry and business should act as trustees of the poor. Since then, FICCI has extended support to Indian industry in different areas of public policy, creation of capacity, and imparting training for professional excellence. It has also continued to channelize contributions from industry towards socially useful investment.

'I cannot forget the services rendered by commercial classes, but I want you to go a step further. I want you to make the Congress your own and we would willingly surrender the reins to you. The work can be better done by you. But if you decide to assume the reins, you do so only on one condition. You should regard yourselves as trustees and servants of the poor. Your commerce must be regulated for the benefit of the toiling millions.'

– Mahatma Gandhi, at the fourth annual session of FICCI held in April 1931.

National Thermal Power Corporation's gas plant at Dadri. Public sector concerns have laid a strong foundation for industrial development, and pioneered activities, often in the country's hinterlands.

Following Independence, India adopted a socialistic model of self-reliance. The task of national reconstruction fell to the government of independent India. With a fragmented and weak private sector, the role of government was not limited to social development and redistribution of income, but extended to manufacturing and the provision of basic services to citizens. In trying to become self-reliant, the country built barriers around itself, particularly in areas of industrial licensing, tariffs, and controls. This prevented its integration into the world economy and abetted the governance practice of 'a few managing the rest'.

This restrictive economic environment remained in place for the next four decades. India became relatively isolated from the rest of the world. It was not until the mid-1980s, when Rajiv Gandhi was prime minister, that the seeds of reforms and liberalization were sown. Rajiv Gandhi had the opportunity and the mandate of the people to usher in contemporary economic principles of free enterprise and to undertake Constitutional amendments, if necessary. His background and sudden entry into politics constrained him from taking major decisions during office, yet I believe that reforms would have taken off much earlier had his life not been cut short in 1991.

It was in the early 1990s that the process of economic reforms, liberalization, and structural adjustments were initiated in the wake of an unprecedented balance of payments crisis. The process began with a stutter, under compulsion, and lacked a holistic approach. *The Economist* magazine editorial in May 2001 commented that 'India's variety and vagueness conspire to frustrate anyone who tries to be objective in charting the effects of economic reforms over the past decade. The place is all subplots and no plot.'

Another factor that prevented the reforms process from gathering steam was the emergence of coalition governments represented by both national and regional political parties. With specific reference to the Indian polity based on democratic governance and a multi-party political structure, several areas of governance have languished because of short-term measures. Policies sometimes are not issue-based but are a result of reactive thinking influenced by factors that make political parties popular and help them stay in power. Populist rhetoric and political exigencies have overshadowed hard economic reality.

FACING PAGE, *top*: Congress leader Rajendra Prasad, who subsequently became the first President of Independent India, laying the foundation stone of the first Indian Chambers of Commerce, FICCI.
Middle: Prime Minister Rajiv Gandhi arriving at a FICCI seminar, flanked by R.P. Goenka *(left)* and D.N. Patodia *(right)*. Rajiv Gandhi was a pioneering reformist whose role in opening the economy was critical.
Bottom: Finance Minister Pranab Mukherjee — now President of India—presides over the 84th annual general meeting of FICCI. With him are, *from left*, Rajiv Kumar, former secretary-general, FICCI; Harsh Mariwala, past president, FICCI; R.V. Kanoria, president, FICCI and Naina Lal Kidwai, president - elect, FICCI

BELOW: Pt Jawaharlal Nehru at the inauguration of Guwahati Refinery.

A fundamental distortion in the delivery of good governance is often because of populist policies devoid of socio-economic imperatives. Even partisan ideologies are sometimes sacrificed to stay popular. In the words of Lee Kuan Yew, prime minister of Singapore from 1959 to 1990, '…I do not believe that popular government means you have to be popular when you govern.'

In 1991, the choice of a non-political financial technocrat to spearhead the reforms process was one of the best political decisions taken, and under Manmohan Singh's deft leadership, coupled with his deep understanding of the subject, some semblance of direction was imparted to the liberalization and globalization process that helped the growth of the Indian economy .

After two decades of economic reforms, India can look back to commendable achievements in the unshackling of its economy, the dismantling of barriers, globally benchmarked tariff reduction, de-licensing industry, removal of restrictions in trade and investment, and so on. Indian industry has been supportive of these measures and has responded by enhancing efficiency and productivity.

The journey is still incomplete. The share of manufacturing in India's GDP is only about 16 per cent. India needs to take several measures and internal reforms to boost trade by developing a robust manufacturing sector. These measures include the creation of infrastructure, simplification of fiscal structures, and the development of social infrastructure, particularly in education and health.

Prime Minister Manmohan Singh, who oversaw the liberalization of the country's economy as its finance minister in 1991, seen here with present and future FICCI presidents: (*from left*) Siddharth Birla, president-designate, 2014; Naina Lal Kidwai, president-designate, 2013, and R.V. Kanoria, president, FICCI.

On the path to prosperity—India's economy remains heavily dependent on agriculture, and both government and industry are working to ensure that their produce reaches the market and cold-chains to avoid wastage and gain fair price while eliminating middlemen.

I believe that an important aim for India in future is to become a truly homogenous entity. Historically, the country has been a federation of provinces, states, and regions, bifurcated on cultural, ethnic, and linguistic barriers. This has meant federalism with a multi-government, multi-policy system. What we need is an Indian Economic Union with seamless movement of goods and services. The impact on transaction costs would be tremendous. Inter-state differences prevent a common approach. More specifically, inter-state movement of goods and services, legislative issues in setting up and operating industrial enterprises, documentation requirements of various governmental and municipal authorities, and lack of 'co-operative competition' among states are issues that prevent India from becoming a single 'common market'.

The future course of India's development would depend on its ability to build systems that retain its diverse socio-cultural fabric and yet ensure a cohesive and integrated nation. I believe that the citizens of India have the ability to shift away from parochial sectorism.

The contentious issue of agriculture should be kept in perspective. The past rounds of discussion at WTO repeatedly brought this issue to fore. About 65 per cent of India's population depends directly on agriculture. One needs to be conscious of this aspect while making an effort at evolving a rule-based, multilateral trading system. It is also true that agriculture in developing countries could languish without a competitive environment. This is being denied through the persistence of trade-distorting and price- distorting subsidies.

In India, policymakers still appear to be in a state of denial. A penchant for popularity often obfuscates real needs. Unless corrected, such a stance could create problems and even jeopardize food security, throwing trade into a downward spiral. In 1991,

India was forced by external pressures to liberalize its industrial economy. Similar internal pressure that would force the government to aggressively initiate an agriculture-driven internal reform programme is required. Such a transformation is necessary to unravel the true economic potential of the country and to ensure that the food needs of a still-rising population are met.

The seamless global movement of goods and services, as well as financial capital, is today more or less a way of life. The world has, however, failed to develop a system to absorb the movement of human capital, which will become critical to true globalization. The systems needed for such change are amorphous and subjective and based on the tenets of tolerance and understanding. Countries need to move away from nationalism and inculcate these values. Education systems need transformation to create positive alignment, with shifts in global demographic patterns, to prepare the 'global citizen' to face this reality.

In addition, the developed countries need to move away from old beliefs and recognize the demographic and economic power of Asia. The current global power structure is a relic from the post-Second World War era.

An Illustrated History of Indian Enterprise by FICCI, with contributions from eminent authors who have closely studied Indian enterprise for several years, maps this incredible journey. We expect it to provide the reader a closer insight into the development of different industry and business sectors in India, along with their strengths and weaknesses. Undeniably, it is the spirit of enterprise in the country that will propel economic growth and define the characteristics of the Indian economy in the years to come.

2012 R.V. KANORIA
President, FICCI

The rock-cut caves at Ajanta, Maharashtra, were built in two phases: the first between the 2nd and 1st centuries BC, and the second during the 5th and 6th centuries CE. Executed on a scale that would have nurtured entire families of artisans for probably their lifetimes, the sculptures and murals here and at Ellora recreate mythic and historic scenes that depict gods and people robed in expensive raiments and jewelled accoutrements—a comment on the extraordinary heritage of textile weaving and jewellery making in ancient India. The Ajanta and Ellora caves are now a UNESCO World Heritage Site.

Maritime traders undertake a journey by sea in this terracotta temple sculpture; Indian merchants have a long history of mercantile relationships with neighbouring countries.

1 Origins of Indian Enterprise from Ancient Times to 1947

DWIJENDRA TRIPATHI

LEFT: The 8th century rock-cut caves of the Kailashnath temple complex, Ellora, combine the richness of fables with the astounding skill of masons and sculptors, and provide a glimpse of the architect's ability to think on a large scale.

ABOVE: Scenes from the Buddha's life enrich this wall painting at Ajanta.

It is customary to periodize various aspects of Indian history—trade included—into ancient and early medieval, late medieval, and modern periods, even though this classification does not strictly apply to business and social developments. Business, in its essential features, was marked by remarkable continuity until the emergence of British colonial rule. Changes undeniably occurred in scope and scale, but the basic character of business during this long span of time remained almost unchanged. And, the defining feature of it was trade.

ANCIENT AND EARLY MEDIEVAL TIMES

Our only source of information for ancient India almost up to the beginning of Buddhist times is archaeology, and this provides only fragmentary insights. However, it points to vigorous commercial interaction between western India and West Asia, with Lothal in Gujarat being an important port of call as early as the 3rd millennium BC. Evidence suggests that a variety of household industries and internal trade fed this external commerce and trade in that hoary past.

By the middle of the 1st millennium BC, trade and commerce had developed into a significant element in the socio-economic fabric of the subcontinent. The Buddhist texts mention several classes of merchants such as Vanik (ordinary merchant), Shreshthin (big merchant), and Sarthavaha (leader of caravans, or long distance trade). These sources contain references of urban centres which could not have developed without a dynamic commercial life. Although barter was the most common method of exchange, archaeological evidence suggests that silver and copper coins were also in circulation. Literary sources refer to at least two major trade routes: Uttarpatha (northern route) and Dakshinpatha (southern route). The rise of the Mauryan empire in the 4th millenium BC that extended over almost the entire subcontinent and lasted for about a century and a half must have expanded the size of the market, providing an added impetus to commercial pursuits.

By the beginning of the Christian Era, Indian commerce had developed sufficient maturity to have international linkages. The migration into India of several ethnic groups such as the Greeks, the Sakas, and the Kushans from West and Central Asia further strengthened this process.

LEFT: Coin depicting Kanishka, the 2nd century ruler of the Kushan dynasty, who was a major patron and promoter of textiles and the arts.

FAR LEFT: The lion capital of the Mauryan kingdom is today the national symbol of India.

BELOW: Emperor Ashoka's empire, spread across much of the continent; note the tiny segment in the south that comprised the small, but rich, Chola empire at the time.

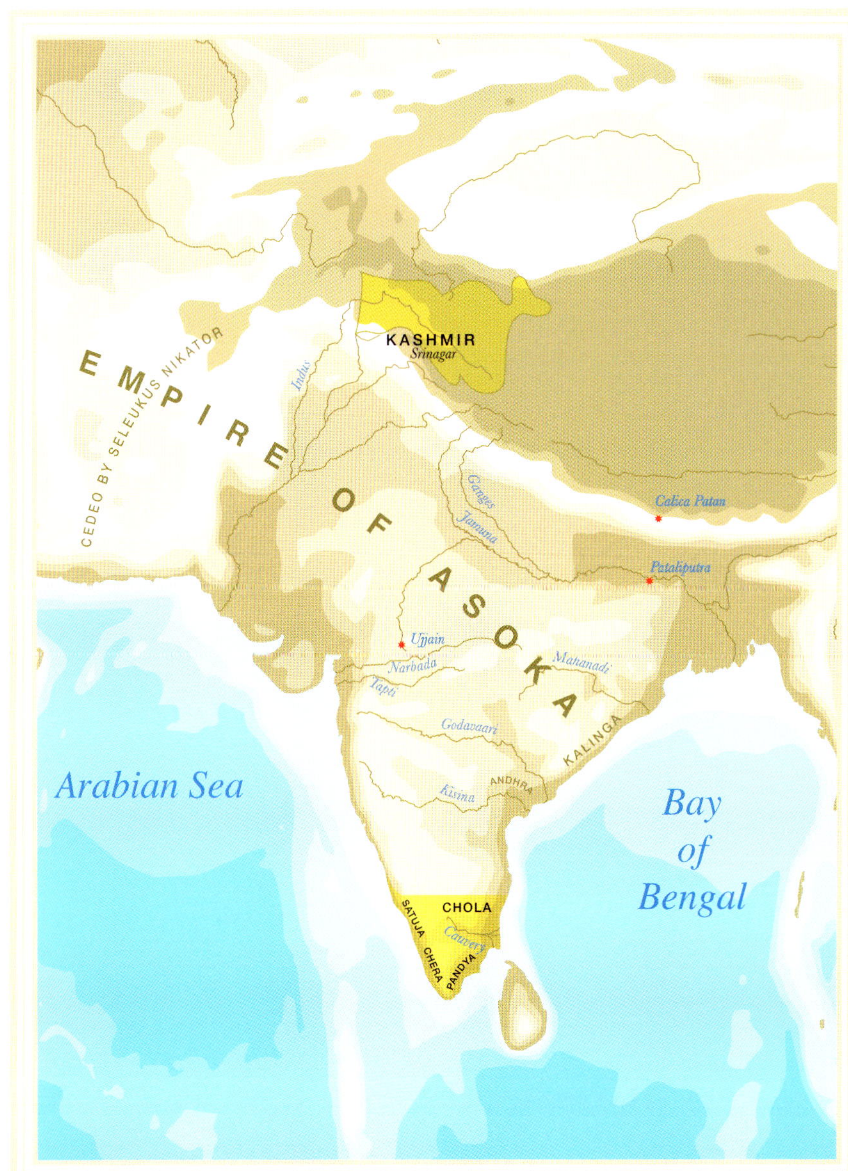

FACING PAGE, *Top, left*: Gold ear-pendant, Takshila, 1st century CE. Indians have always used gold for jewellery as well as for financial security, then as now.
Top, middle: Terracotta statue, Harappa, 2500 BC. The river civilization had a thriving business climate made possible by the deep harbour that was put to use by sea-going vessels.
Top, right: Painted earthen jar, Mohenjodaro. The quality of pottery testifies to the sophistication of the Indus Valley Civilization.
Bottom: Bronze dancing figure, Mohenjodaro. Sophistication in metallurgy, evidence of which has been unearthed from all parts of the subcontinent, is among the distinguishing traits of a developed society.

Both Indian and Chinese sources have established that Indian merchants were engaged in trade with the Roman empire through the so-called Silk Route that ran across Afghanistan and Central Asia and connected the Chinese and Roman empires. Stories in the Buddhist Jatakas refer to Indian merchants undertaking voyages to Suvarna Bhumi and Suvarna Dweep, usually identified with Southeast Asia. References in literary sources to ports such as Bharuch on the Gujarat coast, Sopara on the Konkan coast, Muziris on the Malabar coast, Kaveripatnam on the Coramandel coast, Dantapura in Orissa, and Tampralipiti in Bengal also testify to India's well-developed maritime contacts. Java seems to have been one of the regions in Southeast Asia that attracted a large number of Indian merchants, many of whom settled there. An old Gujarati proverb about 'One who goes to Java never returns, but if he does he brings so much wealth that it lasts for generations' is a reminder of the attraction that the island held for Indian traders.

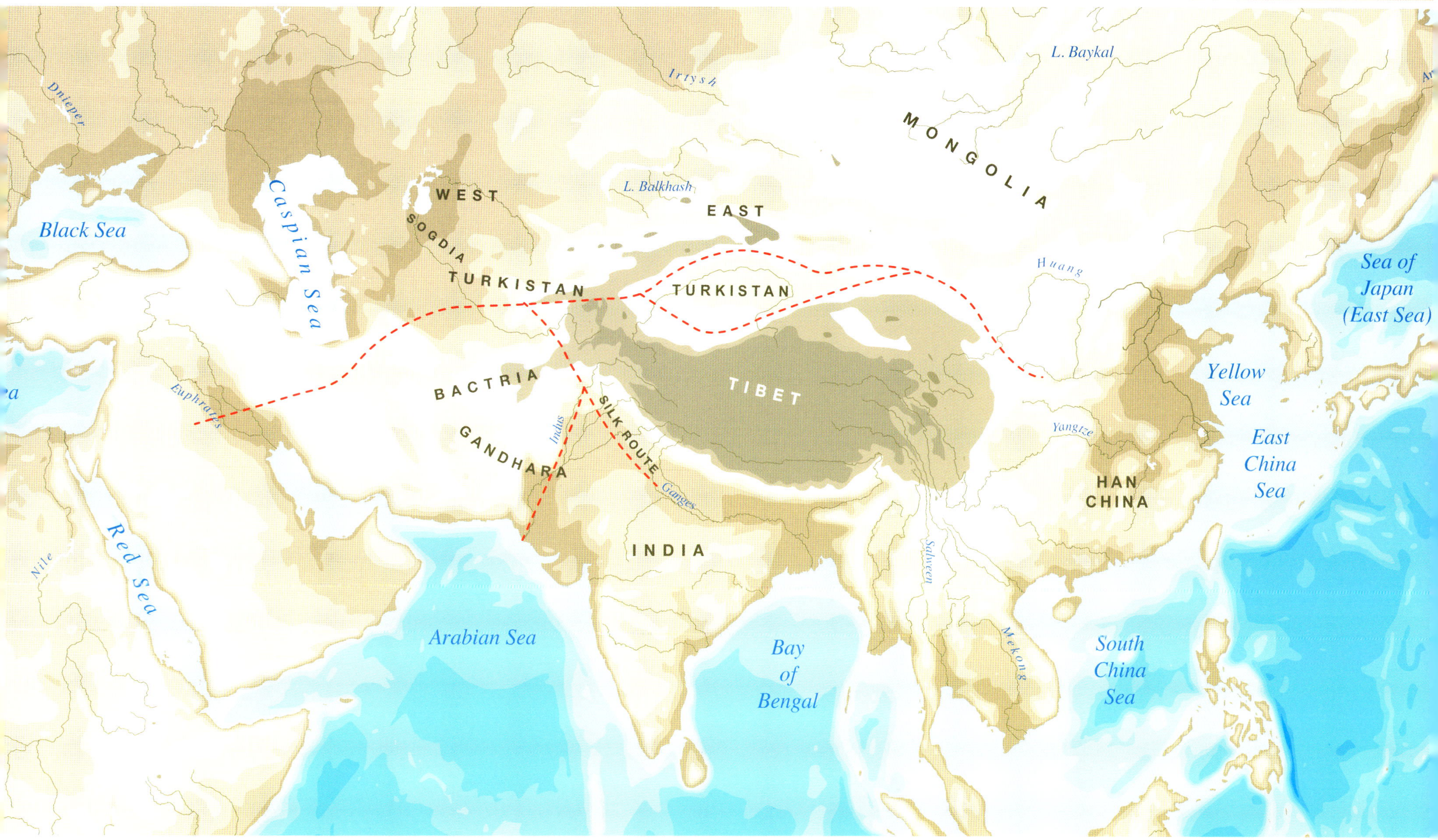

ABOVE: The Silk Route bound continents and stretched all the way, from China, where it originated, to Europe and Africa, with the Indian subcontinent forming a critical part of the trade that was generated along the different highways.

FACING PAGE, *left:* A Chinese painting depicting the traveller Xuan Zang returning from India to China accompanied by a white elephant gifted by the Indian king, Harsha. Accounts by Chinese travellers have provided fascinating glimpses into the commercial and cultural history of and between the two civilizations.
Right: A relief from the Ramayana detailing the legend of Garuda, king of the birds, Java, Indonesia. The Pallava and Chola ports were hubs for trade and influenced the culture of Southeast settlements.

LEFT: Relief depicting the fight between Ram and Ravana, Angkor Wat, Cambodia. While Indian literature abounds in stories about ships sailing to Southeast Asia, a vibrant trade and cultural links also helped to spread Hinduism and Buddhism throughout the region. There is almost no evidence to show that this was done by way of conquest, while enough proof abounds that spiritual beliefs were spread by merchants, many of whom were domiciled in these outposts.

India, in turn, too attracted traders from other lands. A first century Greek text, *Periplus of the Erythrean Sea*, contains details about several ports in the country and the goods and merchandise traded. The text was probably intended as a guide for sailors coming to India. Some epigraphical sources belonging to this period refer to a special class of traders, called Yavanas, sailing to Indian ports in search of spices and other items. The Yavanas are normally identified with people from the Graeco-Roman and West Asian regions. Some Yavanas had apparently settled in India, for their names appear among the patrons of Buddhist cave monasteries that were located in the Western Ghats.

Map showing the ancient spice route from China to the islands of Indonesia, and from Arabia to India and then to the Spice Islands, as well as the Mediterranean routes to Europe, and the old route across North Africa is shown (red lines). Also included in the map is the Silk Road (grey lines) extending from China via Central Asia which went all the way to Europe.

FACING PAGE, *left*: A Buddha like head found in Takshila in north-west India, depicting Greek influence. This region emerged as a highly developed centre of learning and commercial activity.

Right: Chaitya Hall, late 5th century, Ajanta. Such cavernous meeting places were used for discourses, but it cannot be ruled out that they had a purpose beyond just the spiritual. The majesty of the space could also have been used to promote trade and entrepreneurial activities which were linked with the cultural spread of both Hinduism and Buddhism much beyond thier places of origin.

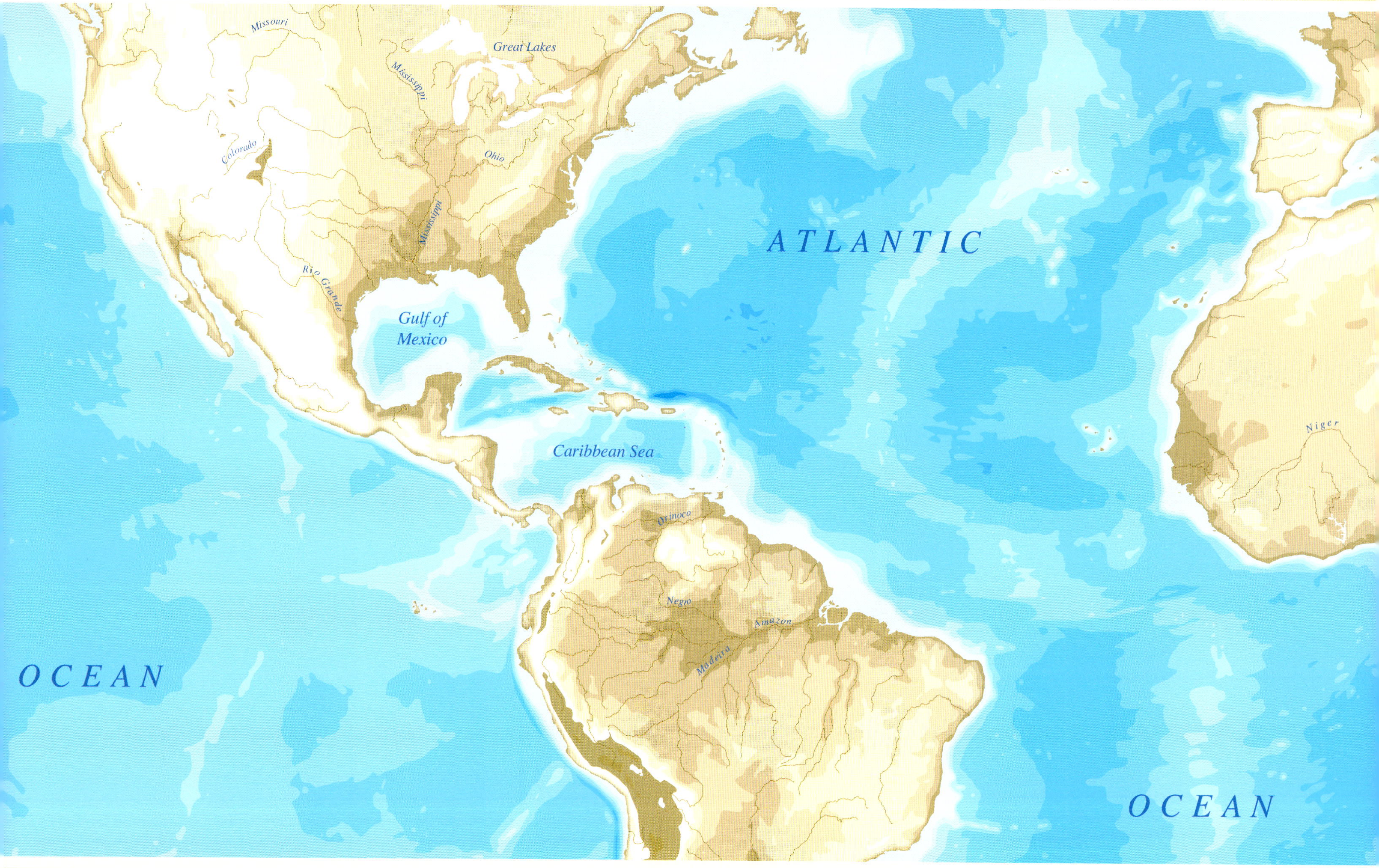

RULER
Cities
COUNTRIES
PEOPLE
Location

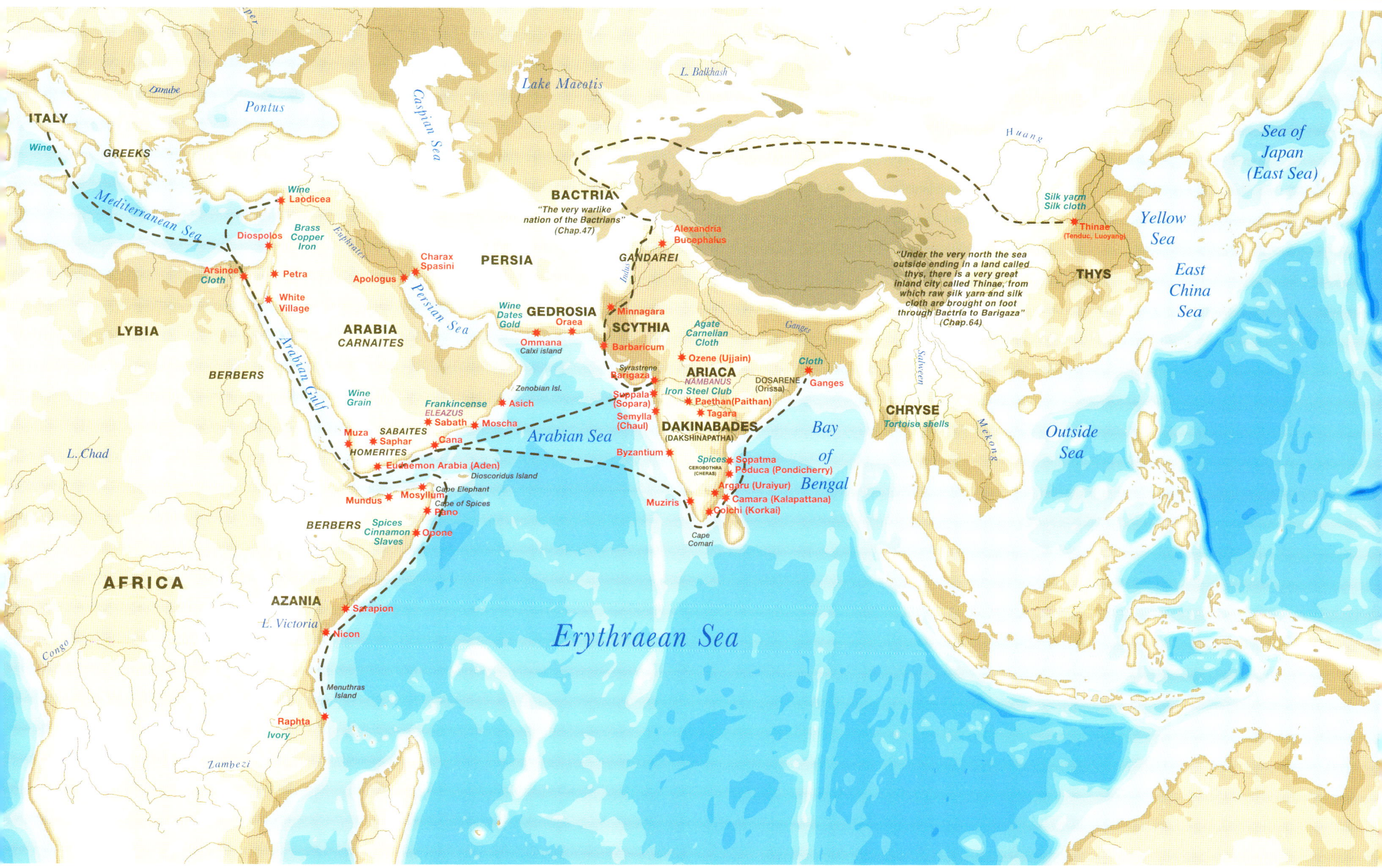

Elaborate maps were prepared by seafarers as early as 1st century CE (*Periplus of the Erythrean Sea*), detailing the ports that were in use along the routes between India, Africa, and the European cusp in between the continents. These were accompanied by texts that detailed the Yavanas— probably of Graeco-Roman and West Asian origin—who frequented Indian ports.

Indus Valley seal, Harappa, 2500 BC, National Museum. These seals, which also bear an indeciphered script, were in all likelihood used for trade.

Elephant Copper tablet, Harappa, 2500 BC, National Museum. The seal tablets of the Indus Valley Civilization featured other animals such as the tiger, gaur, water buffalo, rhinoceros, and bull.

Punch marked coin, silver, 600–100 BC, Jnana Pravaha. Made of silver of a standard weight, they were imperfect and of irregular size.

Head of Alexander on obverse side of coin, 4th century BC, Jnana Pravaha. Coins such as this were in all likelihood issued by one of his successors.

Nahapana, silver coin, obverse, *c.* 119–24 BC. A descendant of the Indo-Scythians, Nahapana established kshatrapa coinage based on the Indo-Greek model with a thunder bow and arrow on the reverse, and the ruler's image on the obverse.

Coin depicting Kanishka, the legendary 2nd century ruler of the Kushan dynasty. His coins portray images of Indo-Aryan, Greek, Iranian, and Sumero–Elemite deities in keeping with his spread of empire and syncretic beliefs.

Samudra Gupta gold coin 335–375 BC, National Museum. The Gupta period, an era of great Empire builders and warriors, is considered a golden period in Indian history for its rich achievements in art, sculpture, and classical literature.

Akbar gold seal, National Museum.The authority of the Mughals empire over the Indian dominion was absolute and based as much on managing regional interests as on the economy.

Jahangir coin, National Museum. Though the Mughals had minted coins in Kabul during Jahangir's rebellion against his father, those issued when he was emperor were known for their aesthetic quality and weightage.

Shahjahan gold coin, National Museum. Minted in gold and silver, Shah Jahan had the Kalima placed within a circle or square, with the mint's name on the obverse, indicating Mughal authority.

References to trade associations in literary and epigraphical sources suggest that by the early centuries of the Christian Era, commercial life had become sufficiently variegated and vigorous to warrant the emergence of such formations. Called Sreni and Nigama, these bodies were probably meant to regulate trade and commerce in some ways, perhaps because of the inability or unwillingness of the state to play a meaningful role in this respect. Some of these associations minted coins and also participated in the administration of the city. Some cities had a Nagarshresthin (chief merchant) who, apart from being the leader of the trading community, performed some administrative and ceremonial functions.

Although trade and commerce seem to have suffered some setback in the 5th and 6th millenias AD, Indian business by that time had developed sufficient strength and resilience to gather fresh momentum. Inscriptions of the 8th and 9th centuries, and of later periods, refer to busy market centres of various sizes, operating at different levels, and guild-like organizations mobilizing businesses in specific areas. Such organizations were particularly active in peninsular India that held a key position in Indian maritime trade extending from Europe to China.

Inscriptions also refer to a number of Arab settlements along the Malabar coast, which also had a few Jewish settlements. Some business instrumentalities that would play an important role in the expansion of business in later times had also started taking shape by the 14th century. One of these was *hundika* (*hundi* in later times) that facilitated the dispatch of large sums of money over long distances.

Our knowledge of business situations in ancient and early medieval India, however, is still confined to its bare outlines. Little is known about its methods, instrumentalities, and the trade–industry nexus. With the exception a few stray, indirect references, our sources tell us nothing about the role of the state in promoting or retarding business. Even the names of prominent merchants remain unknown, except in a handful of cases covering a long period of at least three millennia. Scanty details about businessmen and their exploits in literary sources—and we have little else to depend on—could be due to the fact that as a profession business was held in low social esteem. Kautilya's dictum that 'merchants…are all thieves in effect, if not in name', and that 'they shall be prevented from oppressing the people', seems to sum up the general attitude of the society towards the vocation. Although rulers occasionally offered protection to traders, and in regions like Gujarat merchants enjoyed a relatively higher social status, Indian society, in general, appeared to disapprove of business—an ideology that remained in currency till very recent times.

LEFT: Gold bracelet, Takshila, 1st century CE. The elegance and refinement of jewellery in the Indian subcontinent speaks of a highly evolved civilization that attracted craftsmen and artisans from surrounding regions.

BELOW: *Torana* or carved lintel from Mathura. The depiction of a cart flanked by horsemen is a reference to goods that were transported often over long distances. Protection for these caravans was considered necessary.

FACING PAGE: Detail from Chitragupta temple, Khajuraho, 9th–10th centuries. The medieval age saw the Chandela kings undertake a major temple building programme —in all, 85 temples have been excavated in Khajuraho—that were extensively sculptured, pointing to a treasury replete with funds for such activities.

MUGHAL INDIA

Our knowledge of the business situation in medieval times is somewhat better, thanks to the records maintained by the European East India Companies, particularly the English, from around the beginning of the17th millenium CE. As trading companies they had numerous dealings with Indian merchants. Apart from normal business contacts, these companies often had to borrow funds from Indian merchants because the economic philosophy in their countries discouraged the export of bullion, and the demand for European goods in India remained too low to generate sufficient funds to acquire Indian merchandise, particularly textiles, that were very popular in Europe. Virji Vora was one such merchant whose name occurs frequently in the 17th century records of the English East India Company. We have no idea when he started his business career, but by the beginning of the second decade of the 17th millenium he had already built up a colossal business in wholesale trade comprising a vast variety of goods—coral, spices, precious metals, ivory, quicksilver, vermillion, opium, cotton goods, tea, et cetera.

LEFT: This 17th century miniature of a Mughal military market depicts the commercial activities surrounding such encampments. While, typically, horses and even camels were traded here, it was clear that armament traders as well as bakers (top of the picture) had a role to play in these activities.

RIGHT: Indian chintzes and textiles were particularly popular in Europe in the 18th century, but Indian disinterest in European goods meant merchants found it difficult to monetize the largely one-way trade between the continent and India.

Spices, jewellery, and textiles may have sparked mercantile interest in India, but as a major centre for crafts, the subcontinent was considered a treasure-trove with its artistic heritage that had begun in ancient times and been sustained into the medieval and modern ages.

LEFT: Talismanic bowl, Bidar, Karnataka, *c.* 1800.

BELOW: Krishna and Radha, 17th century ivory carvings, Orissa.

BOTTOM, *left*: Glass hubble-bubble, 17th century, probably Mughal; it was during the Mughal reign that the use of glass had developed into a fine art.

LEFT: A supervisor oversees the dispatch of cotton bales. The cotton trade drew the attention of traders in western India who saw in the business an opportunity better than moneylending which was the traditional practice. In time, it was to provide the region with much of its revenue.

BELOW, *left*: The use of damascene steel for making swords and daggers had developed during the medieval age, and the arrival of the Mughals and the Europeans refined the technology available in the making of personal weapons. At left is a Mughal innovation of a steel *jamadhar* cum pistol; at right is an elephant goad made with ivory and steel.

R*ight*: Gold Salabhanjika, or tree goddess, Gupta period, 6th–7th CE, eastern Uttar Pradesh or Bihar. Stone carvings of these goddesses were a popular architectural concept, used to hold up ledges and lintels, particularly in temples.

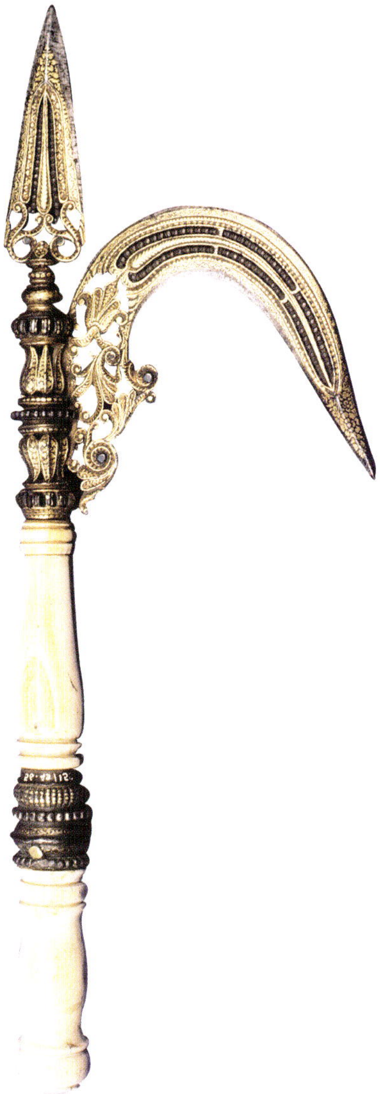

A Jain by religion, Virji Vora also lent huge sums of money to the Europeans, often charging exorbitant rates of interest. On occasion he bought up entire stocks of commodities to sell at monopoly prices to European traders. With Surat as his headquarters, Vora had branches at several commercial centres in the country and agents in the port cities of the Persian Gulf, Red Sea, and Southeast Asian countries. With his awesome financial powers, he would intimidate European traders into conceding to his terms, howsoever unfair. Not surprisingly, the English looked upon him as a 'most injurious man' to their trade 'in all the Mogulls dominions', And yet, the English as well as other European companies had no option but to deal with him.

ABOVE: Seventeenth-century East India Company factory, Surat. Businessmen in Gujarat had at least initially welcomed foreign traders because it helped restore their eroded position in society.

RIGHT: A Kayasth accountant depicted in a painting in James Skinner's *Tashrihu'l Aqwam*, 1825. The account papers shown here are in Persian, but in Hindi accounts, too, the same procedure was followed—daily income and expenditure following each other (not in parallel columns) with the totals stated not at the bottom but on the top of the page.

Apart from Vora (who seems to have died around 1680), Surat had several other prominent business families such as Haji Zahid Beg, Abdul Ghafur (who is reputed to have owned over 20 ships), the Chellabys, the Parekhs, the Rustomjis, and the Travadis. Beg was a general merchant who sometimes joined hands with Vora to corner the market for specific commodities; the Chellabys were primarily shippers like the Ghafurs; the Parekhs and the Rustomjis were engaged in brokerage; and the Travadis, who claimed to be the first bankers to the East India Company, had a flourishing business as moneylenders.

One of the reasons for Surat being home to a large number of prominent businessmen was because of its importance as a port and India's window to the outside world. Ahmedabad, linked to Surat by a major trade route, was another prominent business centre in Mughal India. Shantidas Zaveri, who dealt in precious metals and jewellery, had almost the same position in the Ahmedabad market as his contemporary Virji Vora had in Surat.

RIGHT: Berries of the rudraksha tree, common across South and Southeast Asia, have traditionally been used for the making of rosaries in India. This Chettiar necklace consists of an ornate gold pendant depicting Shiva, strung using gold links and rudraksha beads.

FACING PAGE, *left:* Early Company painting depicting village women selling fruits, vegetables, grains, and pottery. Women hawkers were quite common in pre-colonial times in both towns and villages.
Right: A bazaar scene at Fatehpur Sikri, Akbar's capital close to Agra, 16th century. Note the masonry row of shops which have been discovered following excavations here. Apparently, these were built by Akbar's administration and rented out to shopkeepers. One can identify the shops of a cotton-carder and a potter.

The Zaveris too had banking as part of their business portfolio, and on occasions obliged the English East India Company with loans. Shantidas Zaveri's grandson, Khushalchand, saved the city from Maratha plunder in early 18th century, paying a huge ransom from his personal pocket. Apart from the Zaveris, Ahmedabad had other large merchants and a thriving class of brokers. The presence of a number of guild-like trade associations, known as Mahajans, was a conspicuous feature of Ahmedabad's business life. These Mahajans regulated trade and commerce in specific lines. The city also had a Nagarseth—a position that became hereditary in the Zaveri family beginning with Khushalchand. Surat, and probably other cities too, had their own Nagerseths and Mahajans. The existence of Nagarseths and Mahajans in medieval times apparently represented a continuation of similar institutions in more ancient times.

European sources have referred to other powerful merchants in regions such as Malaya Chetti, Kasi Viranna, and Suncaram Chetti on the Coromandel coast, and the all-powerful Jagat Seth family in Bengal whose ancestors had migrated from the Marwar (Jodhpur) region of present-day Rajasthan in the last decade of the 17th century. Although European sources do not mention the merchants operating in the interior—understandably, because the European companies operated largely from the coastal towns—but the existence of a large number of upcountry urban centres like Multan, Agra, Patna, Murshidabad, and Burhanpur, point to a thriving business life in the Mughal dominions. The growing use of hundi, drawn on merchants belonging to different parts of the country, reinforces this conclusion.

European companies were not the only foreign participants in Indian commerce during Mughal times. Arab and Egyptian merchants, operating largely from the West coast, were active in

export trade with countries of the Red Sea. A particular class of merchants operated in most Indian ports and their hinterlands and had among them some very powerful business figures. These were Armenians whose national origin still remains obscure. Reputed to be 'the most ancient merchants of the world', they were highly skilled arbitrage dealers. Operating in Asian as well as European markets, they claimed a large share of trade between India and the Persian Gulf. How powerful they were is clear from the fact that one of them, Khoja Wajid, was among the chief conspirators along with the Jagat Seth family and another Indian merchant, Amirchand, who helped the English East India Company in the events leading to the British victory in the Battle of Plassey. The followers of Islam, the Armenians, are now indistinguishably assimilated with the Indian population. Also assimilated are the Banjaras, another class of traders who moved from place to place, carrying their merchandise and personal effects on oxen, and had no fixed abode.

Although trade was the dominant feature of Indian business in Mughal times, India was also known for its textile products—cotton, silk, and wool. Silver and gold brocades produced in Ahmedabad, Dhaka muslins, and Patan sarees were noted for the manual dexterity of their weaves, as were gold and silver jewellery. Other industries included dyeing and bleaching, embroidery and needlework, inlaying of precious stones, and paper making. All these were produced in household establishments as the available technology based on manual labour and traditional equipment was incapable of high volume production. Naturally, sole proprietorships, and occasionally partnerships, were the dominant form of business organizations.

It was the Europeans who commissioned ethnographic drawings and, later, lithographs such as these, depicting the different trades, skills, and crafts processes that were followed in India.

LEFT: A weaver weaving cloth on a rudimentary loom.

TOP (*from far left*): A more sophisticated version of the handloom in a weaver's home; spinning cotton yarn using the charkha, a simple device that Mahatma Gandhi later popularized; a printer prints a pattern on a piece of fabric.

ABOVE: An 18th century Mughal amulet pendant. Set in gold and encrusted with diamonds and gemstones, the flourishing jewellery ateliers recorded both Mughal and Rajput patronage. India remains a major centre for the manufacture of gold jewellery and the cutting and polishing of gemstones.

LEFT: Printed cotton cloth, most probably part of a tent, 18th century. Printed textiles often depicted complex narratives, reminiscent of a tradition of painted scrolls, dating to the medieval ages when they were exported as far as Egypt. The absence of human figures in this pattern indicates Mughal origin, though Europeans too favoured similar designs, later developed and marketed as Indian chintz.

This 17th century *Pahari* (Himachal school) illustration depicts a town bazaar with well-built shops selling (left to right) drums, scents, knives, wines, grain, eatables, and liquor. Evidence of thriving markets and the availabilty of a variety of goods is well documented in different regions of India through history.

Although Mughal stability must have been a positive factor in the overall business environment, the empire was not overly dependent on merchant princes for funds. A well-organized treasury and revenue system greatly reduced their political relevance for the Mughal rulers. The disintegration of the empire after the death of Aurangzeb in 1707 brought about a radical change. As most of his successors lacked the financial solvency of the Great Mughals and had no efficient revenue collection machinery, they turned to the rich merchants and bankers for funds, granting them the right to collect land revenue from specified areas in exchange. The merchant moneylender also emerged as an indispensable medium for safe transfer of funds through the traditional hundi network. The growing dependence of the successor regimes on the merchant class for funds greatly enhanced their social position. Not only did money-lending operations receive a boost, but the moneylender also emerged as the central figure in the unending vortex of power games witnessed in every part of the subcontinent with the fading of Mughal glory in the 18th century. Never in the long sweep of India's past did the merchant occupy such a central place in the socio-economic system as he did during the interregnum between the decline of Mughal might and the rise of British power. Although the merchants often changed sides, depending on their assessments of the winning party, their overt or covert support to the alien power against the successor regimes in most parts of the country proved decisive to the eventual success of the British. By way of poetic justice, as it were, the British ascendancy marked the end of the brief period of glory of the Indian merchant class.

COLONIAL PERIOD

The British control over India produced two contradictory results for Indian business. While it destroyed traditional Indian industries, particularly cotton textiles, the mainstay of India's export trade, it also pointed to new vistas of profitable opportunities that Indians had neglected so far. The destruction of the textile industry was a result of the industrial revolution because of which machine-made goods produced in Britain enjoyed substantial price advantage over manually produced Indian ones. To add to the plight of the Indian weaver, his country was in no position to save him from this foreign onslaught through tariff protection because of political fragmentation followed by the loss of sovereignty altogether.

Madras in the 19th century as seen by a European artist. These early depictions tended to emphasize the exotic nature of Indian settlements, here characterized by a skyline consisting of the domes and minarets of mosques and the towers and spires of temples. A pond in the foreground, an elephant with a howdah, and a palanquin suggest the presence of people of noble personage being attended to by their bearers.

TOP: The seal of the East India Company came to signify the change in the seat and exercise of power, first as an important trading body, and later as the power that became the government. The imperial lions would roar over India for two centuries as a British colony before the country won its independence.

BOTTOM: Calcutta was the imperial seat of government in India, and it is here that the earliest Indians began to subscribe to Western ideology and ethos. Dwarkanath Tagore was one such visionary who hoped to see Indians enjoying not only freedom, but also the liberty of choice in developing personal and professional relations with the British.

The opening of new vistas of business was due mainly to the indirect effect of the growing presence of British nationals on the Indian business horizon. Operating independently of the English East India Company, many British nationals, including those Company servants who resigned from their jobs, formed partnership firms, known as agency houses, or functioned as independent merchants. Avoiding business lines in which Indian merchants were already firmly established, they engaged themselves in activities of which the Indians had taken little notice, such as indigo plantation, coal mining, river navigation using steamships, leather manufacturing, and even steel making. The agency houses overstretched themselves and practically disappeared from the scene by the beginning of the 1830s, but their initiatives pointed to new avenues of profit waiting to be exploited by the Indians. Unsurprisingly, on the ashes of the agency houses rose a number of Indo-British partnerships in Bengal, a principal theatre of agency house endeavours between 1830–50 with business portfolios similar to those of the agency houses. Significantly, the Indian partners in these ventures—Dwarkanath Tagore, Muthylal Seal, Rustomji Turner, and others—were sufficiently exposed to Western ways through education or personal contacts and had great admiration for the British enterprising spirit.

The European conquest of India was defined by superior technology, and it was clearly nuanced in the huge ships that began calling on the ports of the country. This early photograph shows the bustle of activity surrounding the ships that sailed up the Hooghly to Calcutta.

RIGHT: Pirojsha B. Godrej was the younger brother of Ardeshir B. Godrej, the founder of the Godrej group. He consolidated the Godrej business and made it a household name. The group has been at the forefront of self-sufficiency and is known for its range of FMCG and home products.

MIDDLE: Cowasjee Nanabhai Davar signed an agreement in 1854 with the Bombay Spinning and Weaving Company for the export of cotton from India to America which, in the 1860s, was the first hurdle Indian industrialists experienced.

FAR RIGHT: Sir Jamsetjee Jeejebhoy was the son of a Parsi weaver who was able to seize opportunity in the export and import trade. His business revolved around Chinese tea, opium, and cotton, and he became one of the most prominent businessmen in 19th century Bombay.

Ahmedabad, in Gujarat, developed a reputation as a textile centre because of a group of promoters such as Ranchhodlal Chhotalal who confined their operations to the city and the establishment of cotton spinning mills.

Modern industries too owe their origin and early development in India to persons of similar exposure and cultural orientation. The process began around mid-19th century with the cotton textile industry as a forerunner. Cowasjee Nanabhai Davar, the founder of the Bombay Spinning and Weaving Company, the first successful industrial venture in the country, was a Parsi with close connections with British business houses in Bombay. Those who followed him in the industry over the next two decades came from a similar background and had a progressive outlook. Even the early promoters of the cotton mills among conservative caste groups such as the Kuchchi Bhatias belonged to the reformist sections of the community. Ahmedabad, which would emerge as the second-largest textile centre in the country, presented a similar scenario. The founder of the first textile mill, registered in 1858, was Ranchhodlal Chhotalal, a well-educated, high-ranking civil servant of the Nagar Brahman caste with extensive contacts with British officialdom in Gujarat. His dreams to set up a cotton mill, in fact, antedated the birth of the first Bombay mill by about seven years. But with no funds of his own and no support from the moneyed merchants, he had to wait for over a decade to realize his dream.

With the success of these early experiments, many traders and merchants shed their caution and took to cotton manufacturing. The industry also attracted a few enterprising individuals previously unconnected with the business, or at least on its periphery. The result was the emergence of a number of powerful business groups generally identified with founding families.

The exploitation of industrial opportunities required much larger financial resources and entailed a greater risk for which the hitherto joint family structure was wholly inadequate. Consequently, a sort of corporate management gradually evolved which in its fully developed form came to be known as the managing agency system. This revolved around an enterprising family creating a business jointly with other individuals, or families, and managing it under a set of terms and conditions agreed upon in advance among them. The originator of the idea, or the 'managing agent', provided a substantial part of the start-up capital, which entitled him to a dominant voice in the management of the enterprise. The enterprises so created were usually joint stock companies with limited liability, in which the managing agents, by virtue of their controlling interest, had the same kind of powers that the owners of proprietary businesses had with regard to their concerns. This form of management was ideal for the promotion of industrial undertakings in a society where investible capital was in short supply and the will to invest in modern industries promised no certain returns. The ability to manage relatively complex business systems was also in short supply. The result was the emergence of a host of companies engaged in diverse product lines under the managerial control of a single family, termed business house or business group. A preponderant proportion of all industrial enterprises set up in colonial India were the handiwork of these houses or groups. So suitable was the managing agency system to the Indian conditions that it was adopted even by British nationals to manage the enterprises set up by them in India, some of which grew into large business conglomerates.

With the growth of modern industries, traders and moneylenders lost much of the prominence that they had enjoyed when commerce was dominant. Traders, however, continued to remain a significant link in the distribution network for industrial products throughout the colonial period. Significantly, the period that witnessed the consolidation of modern industries also witnessed the rise of chambers of commerce in different parts of the country, comprising a large number of trading organizations. And when the apex body of Indian business interests was formed in 1927, it was originally named Federation of Indian Chambers of Commerce. 'Industry' was added a year later to make it the Federation of Indian Chambers of Commerce and Industry (FICCI). Industry, however, defined the contours of Indian business at the end of the colonial era.

The end of the colonial period saw the rise of Indian industry. As early as 1927, the Federation of Indian Chambers of Commerce was established, and the word Industry was added to it in 1928, signalling the growing importance of manufacturing in the 20th century.

Jamsetji Tata laid the foundations of one of India's most powerful industrial houses in the early 19th century with the establishment of a few modern cotton mills. Today, Tata is a well-known name not just in India but also respected around the world, where it has been making important acquisitions. In the picture, seated, from left to right: Heerabai (Jamsetji's wife), Meherbai (Dorab's wife), founder Jamsetji Tata, and Navajbai (Ratan's wife); standing, from left: elder son Dorab and younger son Ratan.

Brief accounts of the most dominant business groups on the eve of Independence will bear this out. The Tatas were the largest of them all. Having started out as traders in Bombay under the leadership of Jamsetji N. Tata, they entered modern industries with the establishment of a few cotton mills in the latter half of the 19th century. Their claim to pre-eminence in Indian business, however, rests on their capital intensive ventures, involving a great deal of risks, in iron and steel, hydroelectric power generation, air transport, heavy chemicals, and transport vehicles. To begin with, Tata Hydro Electric Power Supply Company was floated on 7 November 1910. It started production from Khopoli on 11 February 1915. In 1916, Andhra Valley Power was promoted and, by 1922, its six generating sets were ready to be commissioned at Bhivpuri. Tata Power Supply Company was registered in 1919. It put up another plant in Bhira in 1927. While their steel and hydroelectric companies resulted from the entrepreneurial vision of the founder, air transport, heavy chemicals, and transport vehicles were added to the business portfolio under the leadership of J.R.D. Tata, who headed the empire at the end of the colonial era.

TOP: A batch of vehicles bearing the familiar 'T' logo rolling out of the Tata Engineering and Locomotive plant (now Tata Motors Limited) at Jamshedpur.

BOTTOM: A view of the Bhira power generating station. The scheme visualized by Jamsetji Tata was to supply cheap and clean electric power for the growing needs of Bombay. With the supply of hydroelectric power, it was hoped Bombay would become a 'smokeless city', free from the soot and grime of coal-burning textile mills and other factories.

Mahatma Gandhi played a critical role in the nascent stages of the development of Indian business, even though he confined himself to its philosophical practice. An enthusiastic follower of science and scientific discoveries, he nonetheless believed in self-sufficiency and was opposed to materialism. He accepted the role of technology in the advancement of mankind though he preferred a spartan lifestyle for himself.

The Birlas, the second-largest group, also started out as traders, first in Bombay and, later, in Calcutta, which became the major theatre of their activities. Under the leadership of Ghanshyam Das (G.D.) Birla, they earned huge profits during the First World War, which helped them debut in industry, in 1916, with the acquisition of a cotton mill in Delhi. In subsequent years, they set up a number of companies to produce a large variety of consumer goods such as cotton textiles, sugar, soap, chemicals, paper, and bicycles. They also promoted an insurance firm, a bank, a company to produce textile machinery, and another to produce passenger cars. The last two, however, did not become operational until after the Second World War.

TOP: The Birlas migrated to Calcutta from Rajasthan and launched among the largest business and industrial conglomerates within the confines of what was then a hostile business environment. In the picture, the Birla brothers: (*from left*) Jugal Kishore, Rameshwar Das, Ghanshyam Das, and Braj Mohan.

BOTTOM: Braj Mohan Birla takes his son Chandrakant on a ride in a favourite old car that was handmade for him in 1928. The Birlas' Hindustan Motors continues to manufacture the Ambassador brand of cars and is currently headed by Chandrakant Birla.

TOP, *left*: In Delhi business circles, Lala Shri Ram became one of the earliest entrepreneurs across a spectrum of industries with DCM. The family, continues to have varied interests.
Right: Kasturbhai Lalbhai laid the foundations for a thriving enterprise in cotton and textiles in 19th century Ahmedabad, a business with which the family has remained associated since.

MIDDLE, *left*: Seth Ram Krishna Dalmia came to Calcutta from Rajasthan's Shekhawati and cornered the market for silver, becoming for a while the richest Indian in the bargain. He later shifted to New Delhi from where he ran diverse businesses.
Right: Sir Rajendra Nath Mookherjee launched the Indian Iron & Steel Company in 1918 along the path first laid more ambitiously by TISCO.

BELOW: Inside a jute spinning mill in eastern India. The British created a monopoly by discouraging Indians from entering the business; they later sold their enterprises to Indians when exiting the country.

BOTTOM, *right*: Another Ahmedabad promoter of textile mills, Mafatlal Gagalbhai soon expanded the network of his mills to other parts of Gujarat and Bombay and, finally, even Uganda.

The Dalmia–Sahu Jains were a much younger group in comparision to the Tatas and the Birlas. The founder, Ram Krishna Dalmia, started as a minor trader but made a small fortune through stock market speculation in Calcutta. He then set up a cluster of sugar mills in Bihar in the early 1930s around which developed a fairly diversified group known as Rohtas Industries. Then followed a succession of enterprises during the late 1930s and early 1940s that included two banks, an insurance firm, a colliery, a biscuit company, an airline, and a paper manufacturing unit. The complex included a large number of companies controlled by Dalmia's brother Jaidayal, and son-in-law Sahu Shanti Prasad Jain. The meteoric rise of the group aroused great public suspicion, but occupying the fourth place in Indian business towards the end of the colonial era, they appeared unstoppable on their upward course.

India's third-largest group around this time was Martin Burn, an expatriate house that represented an amalgamated entity of two groups of companies, Martin & Co. and Burn & Co. The former had been founded by an Englishman, Acquin Martin, jointly with an Indian, Rajendra Nath (R.N.) Mookerjee, in 1892; the latter, founded in 1781, was one of the oldest British trading firms in India. Starting as a firm of builders, engineers, and contractors, they had by the end of the colonial era at least 25 companies under their control, including Indian Iron & Steel Co., the only manufacturer of iron and steel in the country apart from Tata Iron and Steel Co. Engineering, power, construction, and light railways were other areas of their interest. By the time of Independence, Sir Biren Mookerjee, son of R.N. Mookerjee, was head of the group, as Martin's successor, though holding the controlling block, preferred to stay home in Britain, away from active management.

Bird & Heilger and Andrew Yule & Co., two other expatriate groups, were among the largest in the country. Bird & Heilger arose out of labour contracting operations mounted by two brothers, Sam Bird and Paul Bird, in 1858. They started their industrial career with coal mining, but later moved into jute, engineering, insurance, and tea. Their acquisition of a German firm, F.W. Heilger & Co., during the First World War, brought to them several new lines of business such as lubricating oil, paper, shipping, and forestry. At the time of Independence, the leadership of the group was in the hands of Edward (Tom) Benthall, perhaps the most influential among the European business operators in India, who presided over an empire of more than 40 companies. Bollywood superstar Amitabh Bachchan's first job was in Orissa Mineral Development Company, a subsidiary of Bird & Heilger, in 1967. Andrew Yule, set up by Scotsman Andrew Yule and his brother George Yule, in 1863, entered the industrial field 10 years later. Starting with a coal company, they added jute, tea, cotton, insurance, inland navigation, jute pressing, flour and oil milling in quick succession with the result that, on the eve of Independence, the house could boast of as many as 57 companies under its managerial umbrella.

Much smaller and less variegated in their business portfolio were four groups which had cotton textile as the mainstay of their operations. Of these, the Lalbhais, the largest mill owners in Ahmedabad, and the Khataus of Bombay, had very little presence in any other line. In contrast, the Mafatlals and the Shrirams had other industrial interests apart from cotton manufacturing, although cotton manufacturing dominated their operations too. Founded by Mafatlal Gagalbhai, a cloth peddler, in 1905, the Mafatlal group had, besides several textile mills in Ahmedabad, Surat, Navsari, and Bombay, a jute company in Calcutta, a number of ginneries, and minority interest of varying degrees in sugar, shipping, and timber. Somewhat larger than the Mafatlals in terms of gross physical assets in 1947, the Shrirams were virtually unknown to the Indian business world until 1921, when Lala Shri Ram and his father, Madan Mohan, acquired controlling interest in Delhi Cloth and General Mills (DCM), founded by a group of Punjabis in 1898. The growth of the house thereafter was swift under Shri Ram's leadership, leading to the emergence of DCM as the largest diversified company in the country. Though DCM was still the identifying emblem of Lala Shri Ram's business power in 1947, the house also had interest in lines such as sugar, chemicals, vanaspati, light engineering, and the Shrirams had their operations spread large parts of India, from Punjab in the north to Bengal in the east.

The Walchands, the Kirloskars, the Thapars, and the Seshasayees were other major groups by the end of British rule in India. The Walchands owed their origin to the restless energy of Walchand Hirachand Doshi. Starting his business career in construction around the turn of the 20th century, he rose to fame when he launched a shipping company in 1919, challenging British monopoly in Indian waters, in collaboration with two prominent businessmen of Bombay—Narottam Morarjee and Kilachand Devchand. He also set up an aircraft producing concern and an automobile company in association with others. While these gigantic ventures brought little revenue (his Premier Automobiles started production when Independence was round the corner), what sustained Walchand was a civil engineering enterprise, Premier Construction, and a highly diversified and technologically equipped sugar farm near Bombay, known as Walchandnagar Industries. Laxmanrao Kirloskar, the creator of the Kirloskar group, was no less patriotic than Walchand but more down to earth. Starting his career around the same time as Walchand as a producer of improved varieties of agricultural equipment like ploughs and chaff cutters, he built up a sizeable business through the production of sophisticated farm equipment, engine oil, machine tools, and electric motors in colonial India.

ABOVE, *left and right*: The old and new Kirloskar factories at Kirloskarwadi, Poona

FACING PAGE, *Top, left:* Seth Walchand Hirachand (extreme left) at the completion of the Bhor Ghat tunnel between Bombay and Poona. The tunnel still serves traffic between the two cities.
Top, right: At the plough yard at Kirloskarwadi, Poona, in 1914, from left: Shankarrao Kirloskar, Shambharao Kirloskar, Nagudada Ogale, Bhaurao Patel, and Laxmanraoji Kirloskar.

LEFT and FACING PAGE, *bottom:* Kirloskar's new and old pumps, respectively, were among the earliest farm equipment and electric motors in India.

Like the Walchands and the Kirloskars, the Thapars too began modestly in early 20th century. Having made handsome profits during the First World War as a coal merchant in Calcutta, Karamchand Thapar, the founder of the group, emerged as a prominent figure in Indian business in the 1930s with a number of collieries, a paper mill, two sugar mills, a cotton textile company, a bank, and an insurance firm under his control. Unlike Thapar, Seshasayee's founders (R. Seshasayee and his brother-in-law V. Seshasayee) were highly trained engineers. Starting as road transport operators in and around Trichinopoly during the First World War, they took to power generation in the mid-1920s and then moved into chemicals and fertilizers in the 1940s. With an enviable reputation for their managerial efficiency, the Seshasayees were counted among the 20 largest business groups in the country—and the only one from south India in the haloed list—by the end of the colonial era in India.

Others were prominent at local and regional levels and these included the Sarabhais of Ahmedabad, Juggilal Kamlapat of Kanpur, the Wadias of Bombay, and the Amins of Baroda. A few other business families such as those of the Godrej, Modi, Mahindra, and Bajaj clans were also emerging on the horizon, but they were yet to develop a distinct identity at the time of Independence. In the same class was T.V. Sundaram in the south. Perhaps the most influential Indian industrialists in the south were Kurumuthu Thyagaraj Chettier and three Naidu families of Coimbatore—G.K. Naidu, V.R. Naidu, and P.S.G. Naidu. Chettier was among the first Indians in the south to enter modern industry, and the Naidus played a critical role in developing Coimbatore as a major centre of cotton production. In the Delhi–Punjab region, perhaps the most important were the Lahore-based Narangs, the producers of the largest quantity of sugar in the country. A large number of expatriate enterprises were mostly located in the three Presidency cities, but some operated from upcountry towns as well. Sales agencies or branches of a few multinationals such as Imperial Chemical Industries, Imperial Tobacco Company, Unilever, and Standard Oil Company, too dotted the business firmament in India in 1947.

TOP ROW, *left*: Seth Walchand Hirachand pioneered shipping and aircraft making factories in India, and was the founder of Premier Automobiles Ltd.
Right: Karam Chand Thapar developed interests in textiles, chemicals, sugar, and finance.

SECOND ROW, *left*: The popular Bombay Dyeing brand owes its genesis to Nowrosjee Nusserwanjee Wadia who made the shift from dyeing to textile manufacturing in late 19th century. His heirs have since achieved great success in the business.
Right: Ardeshir Burjorji Godrej (1868-1936), founder of the Godrej enterprise.

THIRD ROW, *left*: Keshub Mahindra, who retired recently as chairman of Mahindra & Mahindra, oversaw the company's shift from the auto industries to information technology, under the supervision of his nephew, Anand Mahindra.
Right: Jamnalal Bajaj created the Bajaj group of industries but is well regarded as a freedom fighter and a close supporter of Mahatma Gandhi.

BOTTOM ROW, *left*: Dewan Bahadur P. Somasundaram Chettier was among the first Chettiers who dabbled in banking and finance, but who shifted to lay the foundations of a modern textile industry in the south while continuing to extend institutional credit.
Right: G. Kuppuswamy Naidu who provided a thrust to Coimbatore's textile industries.

FACING PAGE, *top*: Coimbatore in Tamil Nadu enjoys premier status on account of its cotton and hosiery mills. Its eminence owes a good deal to the Kamma Naidus who diverted their profits from speculation during the war years to the ginning and milling industries.
Bottom: One of several coal factories started by Karam Chand Thapar.

Towards the end of colonial rule, trade and money-lending formed an important constituent but no longer covered the entire canvas of Indian business. Though dominated by a few business communities, an all-embracing business class was already in the making, thanks to the emergence of a national market and growing occupational mobility during the colonial era. Modern industries had made considerable headway, investing India with the distinction of being the most industrialized country in Asia with the exception of Japan. But industrialization had touched only the fringes of the Indian economy as only a few industries—cotton, jute, sugar, coal mining, tea, and coffee plantations—had registered a noticeable presence. As the industrial firms were completely dependent on imported technology, they were ill-equipped to embark upon major innovation—a critical instrument of sustained industrialization. Despite a century of development behind it, India at the time of Independence was still, at best, a proto-industrial society. Indian business, like Indian society in general, presented a strange mixture of continuity and change at the dawn of freedom.

RIGHT: Jawaharlal Nehru's tryst with destiny. India gained independence on 15 August 1947, a watershed moment that saw undivided India torn asunder to create Pakistan. Under colonial rule, India had moved from having one of the highest GDPs in the world to an extremely low one. Nehru supported a mixed economy for the nation's development, though his socialist leanings led to the public sector commanding the heights of the Indian economy, one among the reasons that created the Hindu growth of rate before it was dispelled by the economic reforms of 1991.

Trade and Commerce in Early India

R. CHAMPAKALAKSHMI

ABOVE: An artist's rendering of what the harbour at Lothal, Gujarat, might have looked like at the height of seafaring activities during the course of the Indus Valley Civilization. The harbour has been excavated. In the subsequent millennium, Gujarat has continued to be at the forefront of maritime activities in the subcontinent.

FACING PAGE: *Above, left*: Obverse and reverse of a tribal Kuninda silver coin from the 2nd–1st century BC.
Above, right: Obverse and reverse of Roman silver coin dating to Emperor Livvia, 2nd century CE.
Below, left: Obverse and reverse of Satavahana Gautamiputra Satakarni coin, 2nd century CE.
Below, right: Obverse and reverse of a copper Pandya coin, 2nd–3rd century CE.

Trading activities in the Indian subcontinent date back to the 3rd millennium BC with the Indus Valley region providing archaeological evidence of commercial encounters between India and West Asia in which Lothal on the Gujarat coast served as the main port of entry. However, the archaeological evidence is confined to India's west and mid-north, the other regions remaining outside the Harappan culture zone. A millennium-long hiatus saw the mid-Ganga valley emerge as the epicentre of trade and commerce from the mid-1st millennium BC. The Mauryan period (3rd–2nd century BC) saw the opening up of the subcontinent with trade routes and political control over areas rich in mineral and other resources crucial to the development of large scale exchange and movement of trade. Trade networks emerged connecting the inland centres of politico-economic importance to the coastal towns and ports that developed.

Coins issued by trade guilds (Sreni and Nigama), local ruling families (Satavahana, Chera, and Pandya), and tribal chieftains (Kuninda and Taudheyas) in north and south India, a large number of Roman coins in hoards, apart from archaeological data from important ports and inland towns, and craft centres, form the source for evidence of this activity. The wide variety of coins and the inflow of Roman gold and silver coins point to a fairly high degree of monetization in inter-regional commerce, and the direct participation of ruling families in such exchange. Commerce was a major resource potential for the ruling elite (Chera, Chola, and Pandya), who patronized poets and bards and kin groups through their control over the movement of luxury goods in and out of major ports.

The early medieval centuries—the 6th to 13th centuries AD—saw a shift in emphasis to agrarian development under ruling families like the Guptas in north India, the Vakatakas, Chalukyas, and Rashtrakutas in the Deccan, and the Pallavas, Pandyas, and the Cholas in south India, establishing institutions like the Brahmadeya and the temple to which land grants led to the expansion of agrarian activities through irrigation and advanced farming methods. Trade became incidental or secondary as a resource. In the pre-Chola period (that is, before the 10th century CE), commerce had principally been oriented to the commercial needs of the royal patronage in Kanchipuram and Madurai. The pattern changed in the Chola period as markets and exchange centres emerged in the peasant regions. The *nagarattar* or members of the *nagaram* as an organized body maintained local markets *(angadi* and *perangadi)* supervising the flow of goods, providing a regular link between the *nadus* (peasant regions) and itinerant traders bringing into existence a unified economic exchange. These nadus and *kurrams*, as the agrarian regions were known, saw trade assume greater importance once again from the 9th to the 13th centuries, facilitating the local and regional exchange of goods and increased diversification.

The Vaniya Nagaram of the Tamil region, and Teliki of Andhra, were large organizations of oil mongers. The Kudirai Chettis dealt with trade in horses brought in by Arab traders. While the Saliyas and Kaikkolas were weavers who were also suppliers of textiles to the itinerant traders, the Chilai Chettis dealt only in textiles. Thus, the nagaram promoted by the ruling families provided a network and intersection points for the movement of itinerant trade. *Mahanagarams* like Kanchipuram and Thanjavur, which were ceremonial centres as well as cities where trade and commerce was brisk, served as convergence points.

LEFT: Meenakshi Sundareshwar temple, Madurai, Tamil Nadu, said to be 2,500 years old though the current structure was completed in the 17th century CE.

In the early medieval centuries, the temple was the centre of agrarian activities and reform, as well as of learning and education. Scholars would congregate to these centres, and temples became opulent repositories of the arts.

ABOVE: Chola gold coins with figures on the obverse. It was during the Vijayanagara period that the currency system was ushered in and monetized trade provided the impetus for organized commerce.

TOP, *right*: The 1,000-year-old Thanjavur temple has been a popular centre of pilgrimage and learning associated with music and dance in the tradition of Shiva, the Cosmic Dancer.

RIGHT: A UNESCO World Heritage Site, the rock-cut temples of Mahabalipuram—or Mamallapuram—was once a major port city during the rule of 7th century Pallava king Narasimhan Varman I.

Inter-regional trade within the subcontinent, and more particularly in the peninsular regions, also developed, and supra-regional merchant organizations like Ayyavole came into existence in Karnataka as corporate trading communities interacted with local nagarams and merchant bodies of specific regions like the Manigramam, and trading organizations of foreign merchants like the Anjuvannam Chola embassies to China, and expeditions to the Southeast Asian countries, were meant to establish a trading presence in those regions.

To enable the free movement of itinerant trade, protected merchant towns called Erivirappattana came up along major trade routes within the peninsular regions, the merchants moving along with their armed protectors through different areas and inhospitable tracts. Their presence in distant lands is attested by 12th and 13th century inscriptions in Sri Lanka and parts of Southeast Asia. As a result, beside itinerant traders, even the Nagarattar (or the Chettiers, as they are now known) moved there to establish permanent trading interests in these countries. Their movement was facilitated by the Chola expeditions of the 11th century CE to Srivijaya, the Malaysian archipelago, the expeditions being intended more for establishing trade contacts than for conquest and political control. The Tamil traders built temples in Takua Pa (the Malay peninsula), Pagan (Myanmar), and in Canton and Chu'an Chou (Zayton) in China.

In the 12th–14th centuries, the merchant guilds acted jointly with other large, supra-local organizations like the Chittirameli in making gifts to temples, and exercised joint authority in levying and granting cesses and tolls to local temples. Dominant agricultural organizations like the Chittirameli had commercial transactions with the Ayyavole and exchanged their produce for exotic and non-agricultural commodities from distant lands. For the assignment of brokerage and monopolies to individuals and groups of traders on specific items of trade, the Ayyavole acted jointly with the local nadu, nagaram, and Chittirameli.

TOP: Sculpture from Brihadeshwar temple, Thanjavur, built by Rajraj Chola in the 11th century. Many merchants visited the temple.

ABOVE: Panel of a 9th century memorial stone in southern India illustrates ships with banks of oars which would have carried India's seaborne trade with the east and southeast Asia.

Brihadeshwar Temple, Thanjavur, a UNESCO World Heritage Site, is the world's first complete granite temple and an example of the major heights achieved by the Cholas in temple architecture. The Chola kingdom was a major centre of the arts, particularly religious painting and music.

LEFT: Bronze sculpture of Shiva as Nataraja, the Cosmic Dancer with the power to destroy the world. This iconic image from the 9th–13th century CE is part of Chola bronzes that are celebrated for their elegance and restrained beauty. The rich treasuries of the Chola and Pallava kings fostered a tradition in nurturing artisans, and their skill was held in high esteem.

BELOW: A figure of Kali from the late-Chola period, 12th century.

The list of regions traversed by itinerant traders covered Persia, Nepal, north India, the Malay peninsula, Cambodia, Java, and Sumatra. Guild inscriptions from Shikarpur (Karnataka) and Piranmalai (Tamil Nadu) provide an interesting insight into the nature of goods brought in and taken out of especially south India—superior elephants, well-bred horses, sapphires, moonstones, pearls, rubies, diamonds, lapis-lazuli, topaz, carbuncles, myrobalan, aloe, sandalwood, rose water, camphor, musk and saffron, cotton, metals like copper, zinc, lead, and iron, and tin from Southeast Asia used in the remarkable bronze images of the Cholas. The *matha*, hospital and educational institutions attached to temples, created a continuing demand for spices and herbal medicinal plants. Silk weaving became a major industry in Karnataka and Tamil Nadu (Kanchipuram).

ABOVE: Sarassa fragment of a resist and mordant dyed fine handspun cotton from a south Indian hanging exported to Sulawesi, Indonesia, 15th–16th century. The fragment is in the south Indian style with interlocking mandala-shaped repeat.

RIGHT: An exquisite Chola bronze. The spare elegance of the statuary is matched by the excellent quality of metallurgy used in its making.

South Indian textiles continued to be in demand in all these countries, while spices, camphor, and other items were imported from Southeast Asia and Sri Lanka to serve the ritual needs of the temples.

Though no direct parallels can be drawn with the medieval European guilds, the Hang of China, or the Karimi of Egypt, yet the south Indian guilds were described as Samayam, meaning a convention or organization born out of an agreement or contract with a code of conduct called the Bananju Dharma, or conventional set of rules and regulations. It was a forum for commerce and as a corporate organization its members came from different regions and castes including the Brahmans, the Jains, and different religious affiliations.

Craft production was more intensive in the Kongu (Coimbatore and Salem) region and increased during the 12th–13th centuries. Special privileges were extended to the artisanal community, as their commercial importance had increased. That the merchants were a powerful and economically influential force was evident from the size of their grants to temples.

Monetization remained on a low key till at least the 12th century. The barter system remained in use in most local and regional transactions, with money being used only occasionally. Interest rates were mainly calculated in kind in the pre-Vijayanagara period, although Arab coins were in circulation from the 8th century onwards, and Chinese coins have been found in hoards dating back to the Chola period. The Cholas too issued coins in gold, silver, and copper. The rise of Vijayanagara in the 14th century ushered in important changes in the degree of monetization, with regular currency systems and foreign and native coinages finding constant use. Interest rates increasingly came to be calculated in terms of money, and money as a medium of exchange acquired a greater salience from the 13th–14th centuries onward.

Around the same time, the hub of the trading network shifted westwards to Cairo and the Red Sea. Jewish and Muslim traders took over a large part of the trade movement from the west coast of south India. The Jewish traders carried on a flourishing trade in spices and aromatics and procured other goods from Southeast Asia through Indian merchants in the eastern circuit. Muslim traders acquired control of coastal towns, and Chinese trade increasingly moved to the west coast (Kerala and Konkan). With the establishment of the Vijayanagara state in the 14th century CE, large-scale Western trading ventures led to the ultimate European domination of South Asian commerce.

LEFT: Ramanathaswamy temple in Rameshwaram, Tamil Nadu, is known for its 1,212 pillars and dates to the Chola empire between 9th–13th centuries CE. The grandeur of the architecture is a reference to the vaulting ambition of the Chola kings, but also to provide the people of the kingdom with a place they could congregate to gain scholarship, learn the arts, and nurture spiritual experiences.

Trade and Merchants in Mughal India

SHIREEN MOOSVI

LEFT: Emperor Akbar's new capital, Fatehpur Sikri, was a measure of his ability and confidence to create a city the like of which had not been known before in the world. Built entirely of sandstone, it had to be abandoned soon after it was occupied because of a shortage of water, forcing the Mughal capital to return to Agra and Delhi. But for a brief while, Fatehpur Sikri enjoyed the importance of being at the heart of what was the most powerful kingdom during the 16th and 17th centuries CE.

FACING PAGE, *left*: Chintz-sellers in a Delhi market, detail from a painting from *Akbarnama*, 16th century. *Right*: Walnuts being gathered at Farghana for export to India. Image taken from the *Baburnama*. Trade between Central Asia and India received a boost with the ascendancy of the Mughals in India.

It is difficult to visualize today the position India occupied in world commerce during the times of the Great Mughals. Its cotton manufactures, silk, and spices dominated East–West commerce, and large quantities of silver and gold flowed into the country. Bernier, the famous French traveller, noted in the 1660s that 'gold and silver, after circulating in every other quarter of the globe, came at length to be swallowed up, lost in some measure, in Hindoustan'. Sebastian Manrique in the 1630s spoke of the 'immense wealth of fortunes' of the merchants at Agra. At the great port of Surat, even the English East India Company found itself dwarfed by local merchants such as Virji Vora and Zahid Beg, and, later, Mulla Ghafur.

By 1619, Virji Vora was so well established that the factors of the English East India Company were obliged to provide 'corteous usage of all English ships' to his agent. His trading network had branches at Bharuch, Baroda, Ahmedabad, Burhanpur, Golconda, Agra, and Malabar, apart from the port towns of the Persian Gulf, Red Sea, and Southeast Asia. Virji Vora virtually monopolized the pepper trade and dealt in a wide range of commodities. Such was his domination of the market that 'no merchants in the towns dare displease him by coming to our howse to look uppon our commodities', commented the English factors. Virji Vora exploited his position as banker (sarraf) to assist his trade.

The English bitterly described him as a 'costly creditor'. Virji Vora conducted his commercial activities in an environment of 'free trade' with little use of administrative support and was influential enough to even get the Mughal governors of Gujarat transferred.

Of other Surat merchants we know less, but the operations of many of them were on no mean scale. In the last quarter of the 17th century, Mulla Ghafur was said to own 20 ships and to drive a trade equal in size to that of the English East India Company.

The inland towns were populous and had large markets: Agra, Delhi, and Lahore had estimated populations of over half a million each, and Ahmedabad, Thatta, Patna, Dhaka, and Masulipatam were thought to contain 2,00,000 people each. These towns depended on supplies from the countryside for their food as well as raw materials for manufacture; and the merchants were an important cog in the wheel necessary for such transfer of resources. In the Mughal empire, land revenue was largely realized in cash and production was, therefore, keyed to the market. How well-entrenched money transactions were in villages can be gauged from the French traveller Tavernier's statement (1666) that 'in India a village must be very small indeed, if it has not a money changer, called Shroff [sarraf], who acts as a banker to make remittances of money and issue letters of exchange'.

LEFT: A scene of celebration on Akbar's return to Fatehpur Sikri, *c.* 1590, from the *Akbarnama*. The artist has taken pains to paint regular scenes from everyday life, including *pan*-sellers, showing how little has changed here since Akbar's time!

FACING PAGE, *top*: Detail from a 17th century painting showing a well-built town bazaar.
Bottom: A Bania grain-seller *(ghalla farosh)* painted in the tradition of the late Mughal school to accompany a chapter on the Vaishya caste in *Tashrihu'l Aqwam* (Gazetteer of castes), written in Persian by, or for, James Skinner at Hansi, Haryana, 1825.

Long-distance trade in bulk goods was carried out by Banjaras or nomads who lived with their families in camps known as *tandas*. A large tanda might contain as many as 600–700 persons and 12,000, 15,000, or even 20,000 oxen. The English factor Peter Mundy (1630s) reported of the Banjaras that 'they are sometimes hired by merchants, but most commonly they are the merchants themselves'. But the most important merchant caste in India was that of the Banias who controlled practically the entire inland trade and credit system and to the impecunious, God and the Bania were virtually synonymous. So the poor weaver and great monotheist Kabir (*c.*1510) could envision God as a just Bania: 'My Lord is a Bania. He so well conducts his business. Without scales and balances, he weighs the entire Universe!'

The Banias did indeed dominate the commercial world in most parts of India; but there were analogous mercantile castes, like Khatris, holding sway in the Punjab and Chettiers ('Chettys') in south India. In Andhra, it was said, *c.*1620, of the Komatis ['Committeys'] that they seemed to be 'Banias transplanted and grown up in this country by another name'!

Bernier (1660s) describes merchants' shops in the cities as being well-ventilated buildings with residences on top and shops on the ground floor. The wheels of commerce were oiled by a system of brokerage *(dalali)*. The Banias often employed their own capital to act for their principals and operated as commission agents on behalf of anyone who wished to employ them. Much of the capital for trade was raised through the issue and discounting of *hundis* or bills of exchange. In major marts, such as Ahmedabad in 1761, practically all payments were made in such bills, and coins were seldom used. Sarrafs were not only money-changers but also specialized in the issue and discounting of hundis. In order to obtain or reinforce their capacity to discount bills, Sarrafs accepted deposits, and lent money obtained through deposits to others at higher rates, thus becoming almost full fledged bankers. In 1645, the English factors reported on the operations of these bankers in terms that could apply to modern banks: 'Those that are great monied men in the towne, and live onely uppon interest receive from the sherrofs [Sarrafs] noe more than 5/8 per cent, month. The sherrofs they dispose of it to others [at] from 1 to 2.5 per cent, running some hazzard for same, and that is their gaines'.

The hundis, like bills of exchange in contemporary Europe, were used for safe transmission of money from one place to another as well as to raise short-term credit repayable usually at another place. They bore no seal or signature of witnesses but were always honoured and the payment punctually made by the drawees. Their reliability made both the Mughal administration and foreign companies use them for practically all their money transfers. There were customary links between bill markets, so that from a small place a hundi could directly be drawn only on a major mart nearby. According to Tavernier, Agra was the main bill market of the Mughal empire with almost all important marts drawing bills directly on it. The discount rates seem high, but this was due, says Tavernier, to the fact that they were more secure: unlike Europe, all persons who discounted and then sold a bill in India, became, in their turn, responsible for payment to the buyer if it was not honoured by the drawee. The Sarrafs also instituted a well-developed insurance (*bima*) system that made India the sole country outside Europe where such a system existed in the 17th century. Ships and their cargo could be insured; and there was an indigenous practice of bottomry called 'avog'. Even the English East India Company took the precaution of insuring its ships with the Surat Sarrafs on voyages within the Indian Ocean, especially in troubled times.

There were, of course, limits to the capacity of bankers to meet their obligations. In India, as a famous lexicographer, Tek Chand Bahar, tells us (1740), 'when a sarraf loses his money and nothing remains in his till, he lights a candle [in day-time] as if he is searching for his lost money. Such a person is called a diwaliya ("candle-holder")' — a Hindi word still in use for a person gone bankrupt.

Though the institution of joint-stock companies was alien to the Indian commercial world, business partnerships were not always confined within the family or within the caste. For example, we find a Jain merchant from Jaunpur, Banarasidas, forming a partnership with Dharmdas, a merchant from Agra, in Jahangir's time. After the latter's death, Banarasidas had to stay for a long period at Agra to settle accounts with the heirs of Dharmdas who showed no interest in the partnership; yet Banarasidas could not leave the city for fear that if accounts were not settled, he could be held guilty of evading debt.

ABOVE: The Mughal empire reached its peak by the time Shah Jahan ascended the throne. This is amply supported by the discovery of rich gold coins that were minted during his reign.

RIGHT: A scuffle breaks out at a bread and kebab shop in a busy market with residences on top, taken from a *Kulliyat-i-Sa'di* painting, 1604.

FACING PAGE: Bakers, hawkers, beggars—a hub of commerical activity taking place in the Mughal empire. Book Illustration, 17th century.

When they loaned money to artisans, merchants were also able to control production by converting the artisan into a wage-worker in the merchant's *karkhana* ('workshop'). A 'Cor Conna', employing nearly a hundred workmen to wind silk at Patna in 1620, was established by two visiting factors of the English East India Company, obviously following local custom. Francois Bernier, reporting on conditions in Delhi in the early 1660s, speaks of 'rich merchants and tradesmen who pay the workmen rather higher wages' in comparison to what Mughal nobles paid in their private karkhanas. But such general statements do not tell us about the degree to which merchants had come to control the actual production process—a step regarded as crucial in studies of the rise of modern capitalism. It is best perhaps to remind ourselves that the merchants' workshops were probably confined to work in high-value goods like silk or gold, silver and jewellery, which could not be 'put out' to artisans for work in their huts. The germs of true capitalism were, therefore, still far away.

The notion of a 'market rate' of interest however did exist, this being the rate at which bankers lent to trustworthy merchants. At Surat, the interest rates on loans fluctuated between 1 and 1.5 per cent per month from 1624 to 1650; thereafter, there was a considerable fall from 1651 to 1703. At Ahmedabad, a fall of the same magnitude appears to have occurred in or by 1647; and in Agra, during the course of 1647. In the Deccan, interest rates were higher than in Gujarat and Agra. A great fall in commercial interest rates appears to have occurred here too, between 1639 and 1642. In Europe too, a decline in interest rates occurred around the mid-17th century. The difference was, indeed, large enough for the English factors in India to argue with their principals that if money raised on loan in England was sent as bullion to India, it could be lent here at advantage. Such a situation may in fact suggest that bullion imports into India might have been concealing a real transfer of capital (by indirect routes) into India right through the 17th century; and this could be why the declines in interest rates in Europe and India broadly synchronized around the middle of that century.

When friction occurred between merchant and state, a major weapon of the trader was the *hatt-tal* ('market-closure'), which we now know so well as '*hartal*'. In 1616, when a leading Bania merchant at Surat took affront at the conduct of the local customs official, 'the whole multitude [of "Bannyanes"] asembled, shutt up their shoppe and (as their custome), after a generall complaynt to

FACING PAGE: A 17th century *sarpech* or turban ornament of Mughal origin. The Mughal court was synonymous with some of the finest jewels of the time, including the Kohinoor diamond, while its Peacock Throne was celebrated as the seat of the most powerful kingdom in the world.

RIGHT: Cotton and silk masnad, 18th century, Mughal. The spread of the Mughal empire, the most powerful since the Mauryan empire, brought with it consolidation and offered patronage that helped craftsmanship to flourish and reach a level of excellence.

the Governor lefte the cittie, pretending to goe to the courte for justice'. In 1669, again, 'the Bannians having bound themselves upon severe panalties not to open any of their shops without orders from their Mahager [Mahajan] or Generall Council, there was not any provisions to be got; the tanksall [mint] and customs house shut; no money to be procured'. That such grievances were partly settled by official concessions and assurances would suggest that a 'constitutional' weapon to secure redress was available to the merchants in an otherwise despotic empire.

Theories that attribute stagnation to the unchanging traditions of 'indigenous' commerce, or propositions that Indian merchants were mere 'peddlers' compared to the foreign companies, are scarcely tenable. It was the English conquest that, by throttling much of internal trade and drawing off India's resources through the notorious 'Tribute', did so much to constrict Indian merchant capital. As European firms moved in and European-dominated banks were established, the analogous institutions within the indigenous sector were forced into a process of decline and subordination, so that some of its striking elements, such as its own systems of insurance and bottomry, became mere memories. The Indian merchant was then, contra C.A. Bayly, not an ally or collaborator, but a major victim, of modern colonialism.

The Indian Merchants of Astrakhan

PURUSHOTTAM AGARWAL

The city of Astrakhan (known as Haji Al Tarkhan prior to the 15th century) in the Volga basin, off the Caspian Sea, was an important trade centre linking the East and the West. The Indian traders from Marwar, Multan, and Gujarat played an important role in the mercantile significance of the city. Astrakhan was annexed into the Russian empire in 1556, as Ivan the Terrible realized its commercial and strategic importance.

India had a flourishing domestic and foreign trade in the pre-colonial period. Indian merchants and traders had a powerful presence and thriving network in Iran and neighbouring territories. In the early 17th century, the Indian diaspora extended its activities to Astrakhan and, for a brief period, Moscow itself.

From mid-16th century onwards, Moscow adopted a policy of encouraging international traders, particularly Indians, to create their establishments in Astrakhan. Having the advantage of active networks in the region, and a good knowledge of trade routes, the Indian traders responded enthusiastically and several of them settled in Astrakhan though they did not cut off ties from their homeland. In 1625, the local governor had the Hindi Serai (an inn for Indians) built for their convenience.

In 1747, the local authorities undertook a survey of Indian businessmen settled in Astrakhan. All of the 51 surveyed families were Vaishnava Hindus or Jains from Multan, Marwar, and Gujarat; their names were Russianized not only in this survey but also in other official documents. In this context, Stephan Dell has noted, '(for Russian authorities), Muslim names were usually not a problem. Not only were Russians more familiar with Muslims, but few Indian Muslims were present in [the] Astrakhan settlement'.

In 1735, when the city of Orenburg was coming up as a possible alternative to Astrakhan as a centre of trade with India, the Orenburg authorities relied on a prominent Indian merchant from Astrakhan, Marwari Barayev, for a description of trade routes from India. Describing himself as a resident of Delhi, Barayev gave the details of all four routes used by Indian merchants to reach Astrakhan from Delhi. These were: via Kandahar; via Bukhara, crossing the Caspian after Xiba; from Tatta (near Karachi) to Bandar Abbas by sea, and then Isfahan by land, en route to Astrakhan; and via Karat, Kerman, and Isfahan.

Marwari Barayev's description should lead to a re-think about the notion of the so-called Hindu taboo about seafaring. These Vaishnavas and Jains did not cross sea just once in their life-time, but maintained a to-and-fro movement over the waters. It is noteworthy that the Astrakhan Hindus actively maintained their religious identity, and frequently invited Brahmin priests and Jain Munis to Astrakhan. They even 'imported' Ganga-*jal* and poured it into the Volga, thus symbolically turning it into the Ganga for everyday rituals and practices. Given their importance in foreign trade, the Russian authorities allowed, or at least tolerated, their religious practices despite pressure from conservative Christians who felt 'threatened' by these 'Pagans'. P.S. Pallas, professor of natural history in the Russian Imperial Academy who visited Astrakhan in 1793–94, has described the social and religious practices of Hindu merchants living there. His companion, Y.M. Kernev, drew a sketch of regular evening puja in Hindi Serai. During my research trip to the Astrakhan city archives in September 2011, I was able to obtain a photograph of this sketch. Pallas's description and Kernev's sketch undoubtedly document a standard Vaishnava puja.

The religious intolerance shown by a section of the local Christian population towards Astrakhan Hindus was naturally connected with the ethnic Russian traders' dislike of Hindu merchants who, due to their business acumen and extensive network, offered them tough competition. On several occasions, the Russian traders petitioned the local authorities, and even the Tsar, to curb the business activities of the Indian traders. It is a testament to the importance of these Indian traders that the authorities were called in to play the balancing act in matters relating to both religious and commercial matters. The Astrakhan Hindus mixed well with the local citizens, particularly with Tatars. Some even married Tatar women and their offspring were known as Agrizans.

By the mid-19th century, the Astrakhan Hindus lost regular contact with India as well as their specific cultural identity, and submerged in the Russian Orthodox Church. How this happened and what role the British consolidation in India played in this process, and also in the creation of the myth of the 'insular' Hindu who observed taboos on seafaring, needs careful research and analysis.

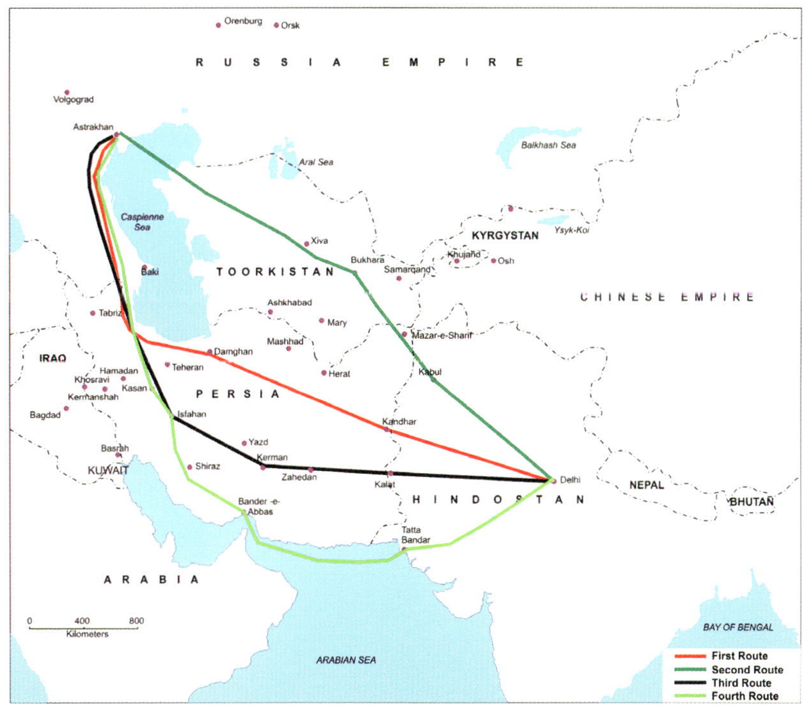

TOP: An 18th century illustration depicting vesper prayers in a *sarai* in Astrakhan. The sketch is by Y.M. Kernev, a companion of P.S. Pallas.

ABOVE: The trade routes between Delhi and Astrakhan, as described by Marwari Barayev, a prominent Indian merchant from Astrakhan.

A file photo of Bhakra Nangal Dam, which Prime Minister Jawaharlal Nehru called one of the temples of modern India. ACC Ltd's cement was used in the making of this historic project.

BUILDING INDIA

ACC LTD, India's most admired and pioneering name in cement has completed seventy-five years since it was incorporated.

ABOVE, *left*: One of the founding fathers of ACC Ltd, Dharamsey Khatau set high standards for the company as its chairman. *Right:* The company's first office.

Created out of a historic merger of 10 cement companies, ACC Ltd was initially christened The Associated Cement Companies Limited, till it adopted the simpler acronym of ACC. From the start, ACC has enjoyed a high level of equity in the Indian cement market, which, interestingly, is as competitive today as it was in the 1930s when four Indian business groups—Tata, Killick Nixon, Khatau, and F. E. Dinshaw—decided to merge their cement businesses into one entity.

The company's first board under N.B. Saklatvala as chairman was filled with business and legal luminaries like J.R.D. Tata, Ambalal Sarabhai, Walchand Hirachand, Sir Homy Mody, Sir Akbar Hydari, and Nawab Salar Jung. Among its founding fathers, Dharamsey Khatau was a notable chairman who set high standards in corporate governance. He was followed by Nani Palkhivala, India's most distinguished lawyer, whose legendary oratory skills ensured that the company's annual general meetings always drew a full house.

Attending ACC's first board meeting, chaired by N.B. Saktalvala, were such luminaries as J.R.D. Tata, Ambalal Sarabhai, Walchand Hirachand, Sir Homy Mody, Sir Akbar Hydari, and Nawab Salar Jung.

A NATIONWIDE FOOTPRINT

When the company was formed, domestic cement companies were finding it difficult to compete against imported cement in a skewed tax regime which seemed to discriminate against local products. Since then, a lot has changed: India's cement industry has grown to become the world's second-largest, recognized for its technical excellence. The company's operations are spread countrywide with 16 cement plants, 21 sales offices, and a vast network of dealers. Through a wholly-owned subsidiary, it has 55 ready-mix concrete plants across India. In 2005, ACC joined the worldwide Holcim group, and is the largest company within the group.

PIONEER AND INNOVATOR

Recognized as a pioneer in India's cement and concrete industry, ACC built the country's first indigenous cement plant at Chaibasa in Jharkhand. It introduced bulk cement distribution and environment-

ABOVE: ACC's Katni brand advertised in *The Indian Concrete Journal*, manufactured at its Madukkarai works. MIDDLE: in sharp contrast to its new plant at Wadi. TOP: The ACC brand continues to signify industry best practices.

friendly blended cements based on industrial waste by-products. Ready-mix concrete was another of its innovations first started in Mumbai in the early 1990s. In its platinum jubilee year, the company proudly commissioned its latest plant, Wadi II, in Karnataka, said to be the world's largest.

COMMITTED TO THE PLANET

ACC has been a trendsetter in sustainable development. The company inducted the use of pollution control equipment as early as 1966. Today, each plant has sophisticated environment management systems with state-of-the art pollution control equipment.

ACC plants, mines, and townships visibly demonstrate successful endeavours in quarry rehabilitation, water management techniques, and greening activities. Better and cleaner mining techniques have helped safeguard and conserve mineral resources.

ACC has achieved spectacular results in the utilization of two industrial wastes—slag from steel plants and fly ash from thermal power stations—to make blended cements that offer unique advantages to concrete. ACC actively promotes the use of alternative fuel and raw materials, and offers total solutions for waste management including testing, suggestions for reuse, recycling, and co-processing.

CHAMPION OF SUSTAINABLE CONSTRUCTION

ACC's headquarters, the 70-year-old Cement House in Mumbai, was built following an all-India competition in 1938 which invited designs from leading architects for building an iconic structure. Won by Ballardie Thompson & Mathews and ready by 1943, the building was requisitioned for use by the Royal Air Force during the war period. Today, Cement House has the distinction of being the first renovated building in India to win the coveted green building LEED gold certification. The company has three other green buildings, each one a showpiece of its planet-friendly agenda.

A GOOD CORPORATE CITIZEN

The company's earliest initiatives in community development date back to the 1940s in a village on the outskirts of Bombay, while the first formal Village Welfare Scheme was launched in 1952.

The company's articles of association were amended in 1971 to add an article highlighting its 'social and moral responsibilities to consumers, employees, shareholders, society and the local community'. ACC was the first recipient of India's first ever award for rural welfare and agricultural development activities instituted by the Associated Chambers of Commerce and Industry of India (Assocham) in 1976.

Each of the company's plants has a healthcare centre; mobile medical services are provided in the vicinity and regular medical camps are held to eradicate diseases, offer medical help, treatment, and preventive care. It provided timely financial relief and invaluable training in the construction of earthquake-proof structures for the benefit of the victims of earthquake-hit Gujarat in 2001.

In 2006, ACC adopted a workplace policy aimed at protecting the fundamental rights of any employee afflicted with HIV/AIDS. In 2007, it set up a standalone anti-retroviral treatment centre for treatment of HIV/AIDS in Wadi, Karnataka. The ACC CMC Centre for Infectious Diseases was set up in 2008 in partnership with the reputed Christian Medical College at Vellore for the treatment of patients with infectious diseases in Tamil Nadu, which has the country's highest incidence of HIV/AIDS. Between them, the two centres have treated over 10,000 affected persons who are not employees of the company. The Sumant Moolgaokar Technical Institute at Kymore in Madhya Pradesh trains young ITI graduates in specialized technical trades of electrical, instrumentation, diesel, and fitting to serve as supervisors in cement plants. The ACC Cement Technology Institute located near the company's Jamul plant in the Durg district of Chhattisgarh offers an advanced programme in cement technology to train fresh engineers as frontline managers in the company's cement plants. ACC is working with government and industry associations to upgrade as many as seven ITIs located near its cement plants and transform them into centres of excellence by improving the quality of training and facilities.

A classroom for community children at its cement facility—right from the start, ACC ensured the wellbeing of the local community.

A SUPERBRAND

ACC is listed among the consumer Superbrands of India, the first cement company to be accorded this status. The brand is recognized for cement that has been used to build some of India's finest masterpieces—from the enduring Bhakra Nangal Dam and Mumbai's iconic Marine Drive and J.J. Flyover to new-age structures like the Metro Rail projects in Kolkata and Delhi. While it takes pride as the supplier to the nation's most admired projects, ACC is essentially still a people's brand of cement. With more than four-fifth of sales made through its countrywide dealer network that covers every state in India, ACC's customer base truly represents the masses of India—individual home builders in small towns, rural, and semi-urban India.

An anti-retroviral treatment centre at an ACC facility. The company has ensured there is no discrimination in the workplace and provided treatment of workers and their families.

A view of Bhakra Nangal dam, one of Jawahar Lal Nehru's 'temples of modern India'.

LITOSTROJ
20
5

Indian Enterprise since Independence
FROM TRADE TO INDUSTRY

2

ASHOK V. DESAI

LEFT: The Perambul Coach Factory, near Madras, 1955. One of the key railway coach factories in India, it was typical of Nehruvian vision in which the state was responsible for taking charge of the industries—of their character and of everything that would be made in India.

RIGHT: Jawaharlal Nehru addressing the midnight session of the Constituent Assembly of India, 14–15 August 1947. As one of the first Crown colonies to become independent, India's democratic birth was watched with a lot of interest, and initial goodwill, around the world.

Indian enterprise has been through tumultuous times since Independence. The change from colonial to democratic government was supportive of Indian entrepreneurs, but it had strong views about which industries, enterprises, and ownership structures it liked; its prejudices distorted competition. It changed its ideological orientation a number of times; with each change came a new set of policies. Particularly important among them were changes in the exposure of Indian enterprise to the external world—to trade, technology, and finance. The world changes in ways no one controls: consumers alter their preferences, innovations create and destroy businesses, and capital moves in search of profits; industries adapt themselves to the changes or disappear. Indian enterprise had to adapt itself to these external forces as they unfolded.

In its early years, the government was intent on occupying 'the commanding heights of the economy', and monopolized those industries that it regarded as commanding heights. Although it eventually abandoned this discrimination in favour of itself, the era of government activism has left its imprint on the industrial structure. Government enterprises are strewn across the industrial landscape.

When they get into trouble, the government often bails them out, but rarely gives any assistance to their private competitors. This discrimination has sometimes distorted competition, for instance, in the oil and the airline industries.

The changes in environment and policy have taken their toll. Today's leaders, managers, and entrepreneurs have not descended from their predecessors in an orderly manner. Almost no business house from those times has survived till today, and the few that have survived have diversified into different industries.

This essay outlines briefly the history of these cataclysmic changes, starting from the state of enterprise in 1947, which owed much to the British rule of the previous 150 years, while summarizing the impact on industry of the changes in policy following Independence. The ambitious policies of post-1947 State-led industrialization led to a prolonged economic crisis in the 1960s, which was aggravated by the oil crisis of the 1970s. Finally, in the late 1980s, the economy suffered one crisis too many against which none of the government's traditional instruments worked. They were abandoned, to be replaced by liberal policies which gave enterprise more freedom than before, but also exposed it to global changes as the Indian economy grew faster in the past decade than ever before. However, fresh challenges have emerged that confront Indian enterprise today, as it faces the world with all its strengths and weaknesses.

LEFT: Maharashtra State Power Generation Company's Khaperkheda power station, 1950. An electrification programme was launched soon after Independence, and though capacity has continued to grow steadily, parts of India still remain in the dark.

FACING PAGE: Bokaro Thermal Station. Government enterprises laid the foundations for development and industrialization in India, which, today, has given rise to discussion on the merits of public versus private sector development at a critical point in the country's history.

THE OLD INDUSTRIES

The British took Madras in 1639, Bombay in 1668, and Calcutta in 1757; their empire spread inland from these ports. Delhi was taken after the 1857 revolt. The industrial revolution began in England with James Watt's invention of the steam engine in 1775; the inventions that followed were brought to India, which was progressively colonized from 1818 when the British finally defeated the Marathas.

In the years that followed, railways were built to connect these four cities. The railways became the arteries along which India's exports and imports moved, and later, the first modern industries came up along them. Industry has grown since Independence. Its output has increased more than 40-fold, and industrial output per head of population has risen eight-fold since 1947. It has also diversified, and spread across the country. Many products that we take for granted today were unknown then. Though, for instance, synthetic fibres had been invented, they were not products of mass consumption, and had not yet arrived in India. Plastic footwear did not exist, and leather was expensive; consequently, a large proportion of the population went unshod. Computers had been invented, but there were fewer than a dozen in the world; they were as big as a room, took years to build, and were confined to elite laboratories. Industry was far more localized than it is today. There were fewer industrial centres, separated by vast stretches where the neighbourhood flour miller was the closest one came to industry. Industry was mostly concentrated near the three major ports and along roads connecting them to the hinterland. Local power stations supplied electricity to the elite in a few cities; the rest lit kerosene lamps.

FAR LEFT: Locomotive and workshop logos. The British government launched a rigorous programme for the development of India's railway network.

BELOW, *left*: A lithograph depicting an urban skyline. British establishments in Madras and Bombay in the 17th century, and Calcutta in the 18th century, developed around ports that helped the spread of Empire.

BELOW, *right*: The Jubilee railway bridge over the Hooghly river built by Sir Bradford Leslie. The first modern industries in India came up close to railway facilities. India is currently in the process of developing its first dedicated freight corridor, and associated infrastructure and townships, between New Delhi and Mumbai.

ABOVE: India's first supercomputer, PARAM, Pune. Though denied computing technology by the West for a long time, India is now at the forefront of computer-related technology, software, and services.

JUTE, an industry that grew during colonial times, was a familiar product in Bengal for many centuries, used for making ropes. Flax, a similar fibre, was grown in Russia, whence it was exported to Dundee in Scotland and made into a thick fabric. Although not as warm as wool, it was cheaper, and was used for canvas and coarse clothing. In 1791, the East India Company took a shipment of jute to be tried out in the flax mills. The fibre was too hard. Although a way of softening it with oil and water was worked out, jute did not immediately find favour in Dundee.

In 1838, the Dutch government specified jute bags for packing coffee exported from Java. In 1854, the Crimean war broke out between Russia and Britain, and flax supplies from Russia ceased. That is when the flax mills of Dundee looked seriously at jute as a substitute. Jute proved to be a cheap packing material; jute mills sprang up across Europe, all of them dependent on jute from Bengal.

The spinning and weaving of fibres could not be mechanized without steam power (there was no electric power at that time; the steam turbine, which made it possible to convert steam power into electricity, was invented only in 1884). Steam engines became common in the British jute as in the textile industry from the 1830s; but they could not be used in India because cheap coal was unavailable. The first **COAL MINE** was opened in Raniganj in 1854; once local coal became available, the use of steam engines also became possible. In 1855, the first Indian jute mill was built in Rishra on the banks of the river Hooghly in Bengal. George Aukland, its pioneer, failed, but the next mill that opened in 1859, succeeded, beginning an investment boom. By 1880, there were 22 mills in Bengal employing 22,000 workers; by 1939 there were 110 mills employing 2,99,000 workers. A large proportion of jute mills was managed by firms of managing agents, of whom Thomas

FACING PAGE: Though they might have faced initial discrimination, Indians entered the jute business only to find it languishing when Partition separated the jute fields in East Pakistan from the mills in east India.

RIGHT: Following the first coal mine in Raniganj in 1854, coal mining has been critical for the development of India's manufacturing and coal industry, though its allocation, in recent years, has come in for unsavoury controversy and demands for greater transparency.

Duff, Macneills, Bird & Heilger, and Andrew Yule & Co. were the foremost. Thomas Duff and Macneills survive in Calcutta as names, though they have nothing to do with their initial incarnations. The goverment nationalized the Bird group in 1980.

The old British managing agents who could no longer manage the companies they controlled in the interests of their British shareholders after Independence because the new government imposed heavy taxes on profits and made it difficult to repatriate them to England or pay dividends, sold off their businesses to Indian managing agents. Many of the jute mills were bought by the Indian traders they had employed. In the 1970s, the jute industry faced a crisis because of competition from plastics. In 1979, Andrew Yule & Co. came close to bankruptcy and was nationalized by the Indian government. It went bankrupt in 2001 and was referred to the Bureau of Industrial Finance and Reconstruction (BIFR); it is expected to come out of BIFR supervision shortly. The companies belonging to the Bird group were nationalized by the Indian government in 1980 following their inability to pay wages. Another six companies were also taken over and placed under the National Jute Manufacturing Corporation. It went bankrupt and was referred to BIFR in 1992. BIFR recommended its liquidation, which was opposed by employees and the issue remains stuck in courts. The jute industry in the last decade witnessed a revival with global environmental consciousness and continued statutory packing of foodgrains in jute bags. Amongst the good mills in India are Cheviot, of the H.V. Kanoria group, Gloster, of the G.D. Bangur group and Ludlow, of the S.S. Kanoria group. India has an output exceeding 1.5 million tonnes. Bangladesh is the only other significant producer producing about 6,00,000 tonnes a year. Out of 8,00,000 tonnes, 70 per cent of exports are from Bangladesh and about a quarter from India.

Though **TEA** would hardly qualify as an industry any longer, but in its use of industrial processes and supply of a product of mass consumption, the industry is similar to that of 65 years ago. Tea is the oldest industrial product in India, excluding textiles, of which India was the world's leading producer before the advent of industry. It has been drunk in China for many centuries, and made its first entry into Europe when it was shipped by the Dutch from Java to Amsterdam in 1606. It was first advertised by a coffee house in London in 1658. Some was presented to King Charles II in 1664. Catherine of Braganza, whom he married, and who brought with her Bombay to the British Crown as dowry in 1668, was very fond of tea; she made tea fashionable in England.

FACING PAGE and *left*: The foundations for the tea industry were laid by the British, and it is still organized in much the same manner in Munnar, Kerala. The slopes of the Himalayan foothills in West Bengal and the terai of Assam were particularly conducive to the cultivation of tea, and the region still produces the equivalent of the champagne of teas in, particularly, the Darjeeling region.

By the 18th century, tea had become a staple commodity of import. The East India Company, established in 1600, had a monopoly of trade with China, and made huge profits from tea it imported from there. This monopoly was abolished in 1834. Lord Bentinck, governor-general of India, spotted an opportunity and sent a memorandum to the council of directors of East India Company proposing the cultivation of tea in India, which had been tried out in the Company's gardens in Assam. A sample of local tea was sent to London in 1837. In 1839, Cockerell, Larpet and Co. floated Assam Company in London with 10,000 shares of £50 each. They appointed as their Calcutta agents Carr, Tagore & Co., which Dwarkanath Tagore, Rabindranath Tagore's grandfather, had formed with William Carr in 1834. But Chinese tea dominated the British market till 1868, when its market share was 93 per cent. The opening of the Suez Canal in 1869 greatly reduced the cost of transportation between India and Britain. But the crucial obstacle in developing tea gardens in Assam was land transport. Railway lines were being laid in many corners of India from 1851 onwards; but they took years to reach Assam because the many rivers on the way required bridges. These bridges were built slowly over the decades; meanwhile, the coming of steamboats reduced the cost of river transport in Assam and Bengal. Over the 1870s and 1880s, a large number of companies were floated in London to grow tea in Assam. The British companies appointed managing agents in Calcutta to manage the tea gardens; as the railways were extended into Assam, tea began to flow to Calcutta and Chittagong and onward to England. These companies continued to exist till the 1950s, post which almost all British Indian tea companies were sold to Indians as the government made their ownership by foreigners unattractive.

The story of Williamson Magor is typical. In 1869, Captain J.H. Williamson, who had managed tea gardens in Assam, got into partnership with R.B. Magor; by the turn of the century, they had 44 tea gardens under management. They also had another firm, McleodRussel, which managed another 27 gardens. The business remained with the family, but had close connections with tea marketers in Calcutta. In 1954, B. Bajoria made a bid to take over Bishnauth Estates, one of Williamson Magor's most important tea estates; the bid was defeated with funds from Brij Mohan Khaitan, who was a supplier of tea chests and fertilizers to the business. He thus became a major shareholder; in 1987, he bought out the Williamson and Magor families from Williamson Magor as well as McLeod Russel. The Williamson family continued to hold 17 tea estates under Borelli Tea Holdings till 2005, when they too were sold to the Khaitans. Today, McLeodRussel owns tea estates in Vietnam and Uganda apart from India, and manages a tea estate for the government in Rwanda; it employs 90,000 workers, mostly women.

ABOVE: Curzon Ganges Bridge, Allahabad. The railways developed rapidly after 1851, but Assam remained inaccessible for much longer because of the number of bridges that were required to be built over its numerous rivers and their tributaries.

FACING PAGE, *Far left:* Lord Bentinck, governor-general of India, was the first to suggest the commercial cultivation of tea in the Company's gardens in Assam.
Middle: Dwarkanath Tagore, 'Dewan of the Board of Customs, Salt and Tea', laid the foundations of modern enterprise that included tea estates among its portfolio. He formed Carr, Tagore & Co. with William Carr in 1834. Dwarkanath Tagore was Rabindranath Tagore's grandfather.
Right: B.M. Khaitan, a major shareholder in Williamson Magor, brought out the holdings from both companies to become a tea magnate.

The story of Tata Global Beverages started with Tata's joint venture with James Finlay. James Finlay was a cotton goods seller in Glasgow in the late 18th century. His son Kirkman was more successful; he bought three spinning mills, which he supplied with the cotton imported from the US. In 1816, he sent three ships to India and opened offices in Bombay and Calcutta; but the business soon ceased. John Muir joined the Finlay firm in 1849, became a junior partner in 1861, and took over the firm in 1883. He moved to India in 1871, set up a jute mill in 1873, and started managing two gardens. He bought up a number of tea gardens over the years that followed. He developed tea gardens and rubber plantations in the Nilgiris too. His son Kay sent Indian planters and set up tea plantations in Kenya. After the Second World War, the group's textile mills got into difficulties together with the rest of the British textile industry. In 1976, it sold its tea gardens to the Tatas who had been partners for some years.

Bombay Burmah Trading Company was the first company floated in Bombay, in 1863; it was originally into import of teak from Burma. It started planting tea in the Nilgiris from 1913 onwards.

FACING PAGE: Tata Global Beverages got into the tea business when the Tata group bought out the company it had started as a joint venture with James Finlay in the late 18th century.

FAR LEFT: Nusli Wadia's Burmah Trading Company started by importing tea from Burma in 1863. Though it is better known for its Bombay Dyeing range of home furnishings, the company first planted tea in the Nilgiris in 1913.

LEFT: B.K Birla's Jay Shree Tea and Industries owns 22 tea gardens, and is reputedly one of the largest tea producers in India.

Today, it is a Nusli Wadia company and is also into laminates, springs, weighing machines, auto-electricals, and dental, ophthalmic, and orthopaedic products. After Independence, the share of tea exports declined, and that of home consumption increased. As the home market grew in importance, most of the tea came to be auctioned in India; the government encouraged the shift. And as auctions developed, production and marketing of tea were divorced.

Today, there are major tea marketers who buy most of their requirements from the market; conversely, there are many tea gardens with no marketing. Among the former, Unilever is the largest marketer of tea in the world; its Indian subsidiary is also a major marketer. Its brand, Lipton, is perhaps the best known tea brand in the world. Tata Global Beverages bought Tetley, the British tea company, in a landmark acquisition in 2000. Today, Tata Global Beverages has evolved from its heritage in tea plantations to become a marketing and brand-focused organization with a portfolio of dynamic brands. It is the second-largest tea company in the world. Jay Shree Tea and Industries, which owns 22 tea gardens, is reputed to be the largest tea producer in India; it belongs to the B.K. Birla group.

In **TEXTILES**, India was a leader even prior to the industrial revolution. The mechanization of textiles gave Britain a competitive advantage which led to some decline in Indian production. However, the first mechanized textile mill was set up in Bombay in 1854 by C.N. Davar. In the American civil war in 1861–5, the north intercepted cotton being exported from the south to Britain. The British textile industry experienced a severe cotton shortage and began importing it from India. The cotton exporters in Bombay saw yarn being imported from Britain, sensed an opportunity, and began to import machinery for setting up spinning mills. There were 10 mills by 1865, 58 by 1880, and 271, employing 2,60,000 people, by 1914. By then, a pattern of trade had developed. Indian mills specialized in coarse yarn; finer counts were imported from Britain. Handweavers, spread all over the country, retained a high share of the fabric market

RIGHT: Mural, Ajanta, showing the sophistication of Indian textiles in the ancient period.

FACING PAGE, *left*: An agreement was signed in 1854 between the shareholders of Bombay Spinning and Weaving Company, and Cowasjee Dawar (inset). *Right, top*: Women spinning yarn on wooden charkhas, Rajasthan. In spite of industrialization, India still produces a large quantity of handwoven textiles. *Right, bottom*: Power looms have made inroads into the handloom industry in even the interior, textile producing areas.

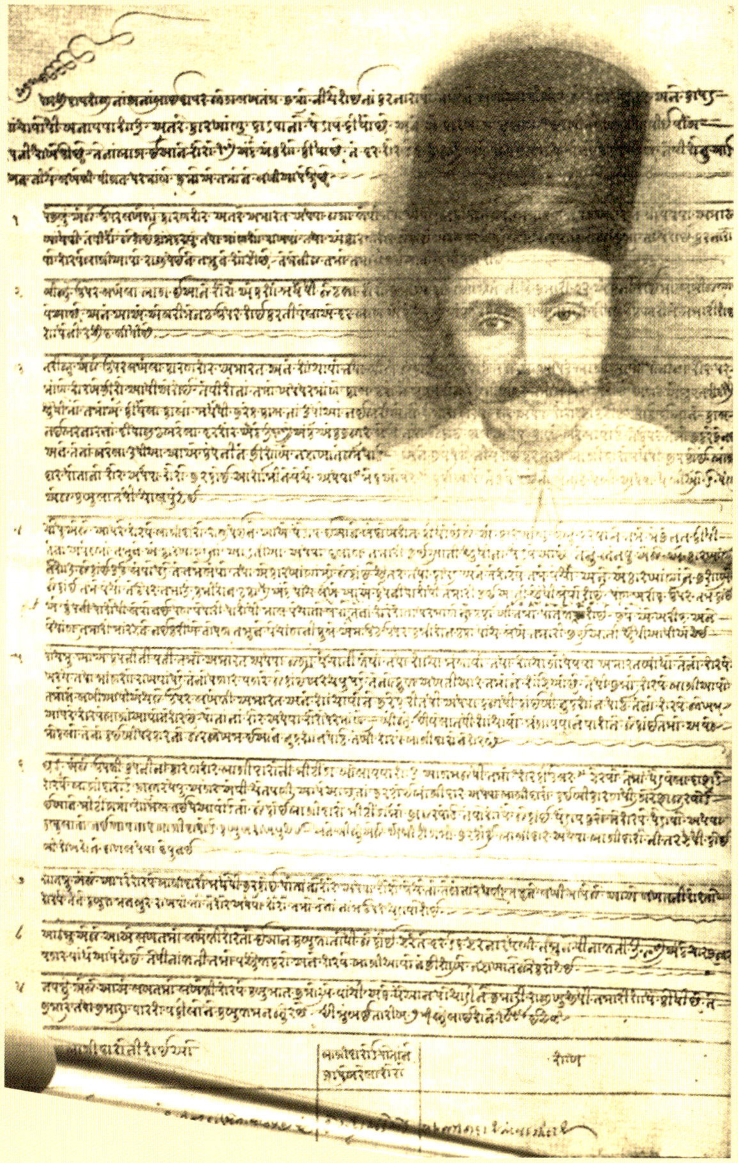

After Independence, the government prevented the mills from expanding their capacity to create employment in small labour-intensive units. Slowly, the spread of electricity led to the installation of mechanical looms in smaller cities. Because of their lower wages, these looms gained market share, and a large number of weaving and composite mills closed down. In 2010, the ministry of textiles counted 1,249 SSI and 1,657 non-SSI spinning mills, 184 weaving mills, and 177 composite mills (it is strange that it found more non-SSI than SSI mills; it suggests that the distinction was an officially made one, and had nothing to do with size). There were 4.99 lakh power loom firms which had 22.24 lakh looms; the organized sector had only 57,000 looms. There were 38.31 lakh handlooms, whose output per unit would, of course, be much lower than that of power looms. Weaving has largely passed to small units, and weaving mills are a dying breed. Spinning mills continue to hold their own, but are largely localized to centres such as Coimbatore and Dindigul in Tamil Nadu, and Ludhiana in Punjab. These, in turn, meet the yarn requirements of power loom weavers in Malegaon, Ichalkaranji, Erode, and Salem, or knitting clusters such as Tirupur. The industry as a whole is highly fragmented today.

GARMENT production was entirely a cottage industry in the 1940s; everyone got their clothes stitched either at home or from the neighbourhood tailor. Industrialization began in the 1970s as industrial countries began to source standardized garments from developing countries. China, Korea, and Taiwan rapidly took the lead. Industrial countries favoured their ex-colonies through tariffs and quotas; India was excluded. India eventually developed sizeable exports of garments. But the industry remained small-scale, and exports were mostly in the hands of multi-product export firms that handled garments as one of the products. However, a few large companies have emerged out of this mélange in recent years. Alok Industries, which belongs to the Jiwrajka group, is an example. It covers a product range across yarn, fabric, garments, linen, towels, and handbags.

ABOVE, *left and right*: The Lalbhai Group's flagship Arvind Mills set up in 1931 today supplies textiles, including denim, to leading companies and designers around the world.

FACING PAGE, *top*: Mechanical looms changed the fortunes of smaller cities where they provided employment and created wealth for a rising middle class. Conventional loom (*left*) and earnest yarn (*right*) at a mill of the Lalbhai group.
Below: An advertisement of New Egerton Mills, later Dhariwal Mills, in the Punjab, from *The Times of India* annual, 1921. Punjab remains a leading centre for quality woollen apparel.

Lithograph depicting a tailor, Malabar, 19th century. Till recently, most people had their clothes stitched by a tailor, but the recent advent of readymade garments has changed that and a tailor now provides bespoke rather than neighbourhood services.

INTEGRITY IN DIVERSITY

Integrity is the cornerstone upon which MW Corp has been built as a truly global company with an Indian soul

In 1948, history was created when two brothers, Shambhukumar Kasliwal and Abhayakumar Kasliwal founded S.Kumars with a view to create a national textile brand at a time when the concept of branded textiles did not exist. From those humble beginnings, S.Kumars grew into one of India's most well-known and well-loved brands. Popularly known for its catchy jingle and for being a pioneer in producing quality fabrics, S.Kumars went on to pave the path for several popular Indian textile brands that were to follow suit.

Six decades down the line, the S.Kumars Group was restructured four ways to make way for a new beginning, led by the Kasliwal scions. Therein emerged MW Corp, founded by Mukul and Warij, sons of Shambhukumar Kasliwal and Abhayakumar Kasliwal respectively.

MW Corp is a generation-next, dynamic business conglomerate that has business interests in diverse fields ranging from textiles to renewable energy to infrastructure development, with operations spread across three continents: Asia, Europe, and Africa. In essence, MW Corp is a truly global company with an Indian soul. Its two verticals consist of MW Unitexx, its textile arm, and MW Infra Developers, the energy and infrastructure arm.

IN THE TEXTILE BUSINESS

MW Unitexx: The textile arm of MW Corp is a consolidation of the 64-year-old textile business, S.Kumars Limited, the market-leader in uniforms, and the number one European high-performance textile company Klopman International and S.Kumars Unitexx, its Ready-to-Wear uniforms division. The formation of MW Unitexx brought about a marriage of the world's leading textile brands, S.Kumars and Klopman. MW Unitexx has consolidated annual revenues of over Rs 1,000 crore, and a consolidated production capacity of 70 million metres per annum, making it the world's largest uniform textile manufacturer.

S.Kumars: A fully integrated, composite manufacturer of textiles with a wide range of fabrics to suit the entire gamut of industries/

LEFT: S.Kumars range of school uniform fabrics.

FAR LEFT: Klopman's state-of-the-art manufacturing facility at Frosinone, Italy.

BELOW: S.Kumars original textile manufacturing plant at Dewas, Madhya Pradesh.

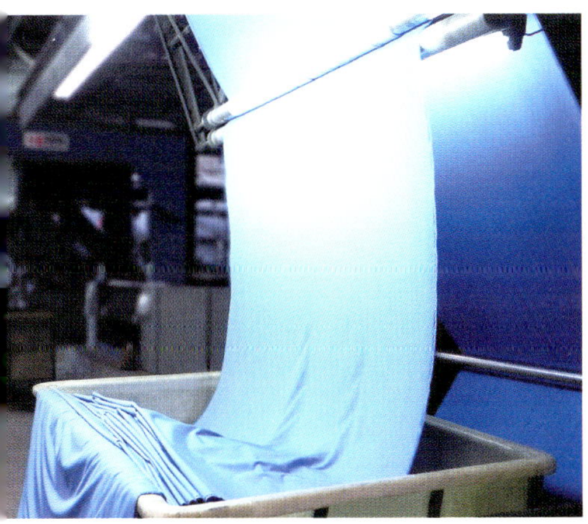

sectors—that is, school uniforms, workday wear, and corporate wear fabrics, S.Kumars' original textile business was established in Bombay and the first manufacturing unit was set up in Dewas, Madhya Pradesh. The old plant at Dewas now boasts of a state-of-the-art manufacturing unit with modern modern Sulzer looms in keeping with the advancement in technology. Thanks to these high-end machines, the plant also produces high quality finishes like Teflon, water-repellent, sweat-absorbent, and stain-resistant fabrics.

The company recently celebrated the addition of a new fibre-dyed spinning unit in Pithampur that produces over 50 shades in fibre dyed across various qualities. These two plants manage to successfully produce about 20 million metres of fabric per annum. With a market share of over 30 per cent in the uniform fabrics segment, S.Kumars has evolved from being just a fabric supplier to a one-stop-shop for all uniform requirements.

S.Kumars Unitexx: Upon being firmly entrenched in the textile business and after becoming a household name in the uniforms segment in India, moving on to the ready-to-wear uniforms business was but a natural progression. S.Kumars Unitexx launched two uniform brands in 2004, WorkStarr for ready-to-wear corporate uniforms, and Medallion for ready-to-wear school uniforms.

Klopman: Having established a leading position in uniforms in India, MW Corp acquired Klopman International, Europe's No.1 brand in work wear and protective wear. Klopman has modern manufacturing and distribution facilities in Italy. It is the largest pan-European manufacturer (50 million metre capacity per annum) and marketer of poly-cotton, polyester, and cotton fabrics for work wear and protective wear.

The manufacturing units in Frosinone, Italy, rank among the most advanced in the world, and adhere to the highest and most stringent European Quality Management standards while being fully accredited to ISO 9001:2000. A leader in Europe, Klopman is expanding its market base to India and the Middle East. Klopman has also consolidated its position in two new markets, Australia and New Zealand, and has ventured into the US market via Israel.

The metamorphosis of the original textile brand into such a diverse business group has not been without its challenges. What is most inspiring is that the 81-year-old co-founder of S.Kumars, Shambhukumar Kasliwal remains as dedicated and continues to drive the business he originally founded.

ENERGY AND INFRASTRUCTURE BUSINESSES

MW Infra Developers: MW Infra, the company's renewable energy and infrastructure arm comprises of Entegra Limited, the renewable energy business of the group and Dasna Developers, the infrastructure business. Back in the 1990s, with the textile business flourishing, the Founder Chairman of MW Corp, Mukul Kasliwal had a vision for creating a cleaner, greener nation by tapping sources of renewable energy. This was long before the effects of climate change began to impact Indian businesses.

Solar Photovoltaic Panels.

LEFT: Protective wear. RIGHT: Work wear by Klopman.

Entegra: Entegra is MW Corp's commitment to energize the future with green, sustainable, cost-effective, renewable energy solutions through cutting-edge technology and reputable collaborations. Entegra is spearheading India's efforts to harness energy sources like hydro, solar, and wind energy.

Shree Maheshwar Hydel Power Corporation Limited: Entegra's pioneering venture, the 400 MW Maheshwar Hydro Power Project on the river Narmada, has set it apart from other projects by taking the road less travelled. It is a part of the Narmada Valley Development plan, located at Mandleshwar, in the district of Khargone, 108 km south-west of Indore in Madhya Pradesh, India. With an investment of Rs 40 billion, it is on the verge of generating electricity with three turbines ready for commissioning. The remaining seven turbines will be commissioned in a phased manner by the end of 2012.

The Maheshwar Hydro Electric Project (MHEP) is the first private-sector hydro project in Madhya Pradesh. It is a run-of-the-river project which does not disturb the natural flow of the river. Being a renewable, eco-friendly, and hydro-based project, it has zero carbon emissions. It will effectively reduce the peaking power shortage in Madhya Pradesh by over 25 per cent and provide much needed water to Indore and adjoining areas. More importantly, it will effectively impact the lives of the people of the region, most of whom hail from the weaker sections of society.

The Maheshwar project has the least submergence area per megawatt among all the upcoming hydro projects in the state. It has one of the most liberal, gender-neutral Rehabilitation and Resettlement (R&R) plans set up for the families impacted by the project, more than 70 per cent of whom hail from the backward sections of society. The Maheshwar project has used the R&R policy to transform the lives of hundreds of people, bearing in mind their needs and aspirations.

In addition to the R&R programme, the Maheshwar Project has also engaged in several community development programmes to bring about awareness among the people on common issues like health, education, and sanitation, as also to make the new sites self-sustainable in an endeavour to help raise the standard of living of the lower sections of society in the region.

The Maheshwar Project will bring about an increase in tourism and allied industries in Madhya Pradesh. Maheshwar is the first project in the state where the fishing rights for the reservoir have been awarded to the local fishermen. The project truly reflects Entegra's motto of 'Energising the Future' while endeavouring to leave behind a legacy that will benefit future generations to come.

The company partnered with Pandit Jasraj for a Public Service Film in order to spread awareness about the alarming rise in the pollution levels of the rivers of our country. The Indian classical maestro especially visited the project site and sang a glorious raga dedicated to the Narmada, by the banks of the river. This Public Service Film is featured on YouTube as under 'Narmada Public Service Film'.

Entegra's other projects: Entegra has bagged several prestigious renewable energy projects including the supply and installation of Wind-Solar-Hybrid systems for the President's Estate at the Rashtrapati Bhavan, New Delhi. The company has successfully completed the supply and installation of solar water heaters of a capacity of 3,900 LPD (litres per day) at the Raj Bhavan, Dehra Dun and Nainital.

Pandit Jasraj performing at the Maheshwar Project site.

Rehabilitation and Resettlement of the Maheshwar Project.

TOP: (*from left*) Kari Granger, Michael Jensen, Gonneke Spits, Werner Erhard, and Mukul Kasliwal at the Concluding Dinner of the leadership seminar, Panchgani.

ABOVE, *left*: Solar wind hybrid systems at Rajiv Gandhi Proudyogiki Vishwavidyalaya (RGPV), Madhya Pradesh.
Right: Solar Water Heating System at Manikchand Hospital, Shirur (Pune).

Entegra has successfully established four energy parks in Madhya Pradesh as well. Entegra has been approved as an empanelled consultant by the Uttar Pradesh Power Corporation Limited (UPPCL) and has submitted a detailed project report for the Decentralized Distributed Generation (DDG) scheme of the Rajiv Gandhi Grameen Vidyutikaran Yojana (RGGVY) of the Ministry of Power covering 327 villages.

Dasna Developers: Dasna Developers, the infrastructure company of MW Corp, is valued at Rs 15 billion. Dasna owns the development rights of 82 acres of land in Ghaziabad and it proposes to develop this land bank in phases over the next five years. This project will consist of mass housing, commercial spaces, and educational institutions. The development site is centrally located and well connected to National Highway 24 and New Delhi's Indira Gandhi International Airport.

Apart from interests in textiles and renewable energy, MW Corp has forayed into the business of water purification and education. It has a strategic alliance with United Waters India (UWI), a wholly owned subsidiary of United Waters International AG, a company that specializes in the purification of groundwater. UWI has chosen to avoid chemical treatment technologies, and instead focuses on technologies that are environment-friendly and have long-term, sustainable solutions—a motto that is well in line with the MW Corp's strategy of building businesses that are eco-friendly and sustainable.

AN ONTOLOGICAL TALE UNFOLDS

In 2010, MW Corp partnered with renowned Harvard professor Michael Jensen, Werner Erhard and their team to organize a leadership seminar based on the 'Ontological' model for the first time in India. Over 250 participants from various flourishing businesses in India and around the world attended the seminar, which was organized in Panchgani.

The company's single-minded focus has been to create brands that are representative of its philosophy, and businesses that bring some meaning to people's lives. The textiles, renewable energy, and infrastructure businesses of the company pulsate with that very sense of purpose with which the founding Kasliwal brothers incorporated S.Kumars, and are a standing testimony to those ideals and values responsible for making MW Corp the success story that it is—a legacy of values and ideals that scions Mukul and Warij Kasliwal have imbibed.

Such has been the journey of this diverse, multifaceted company, with several accomplishments, challenges, and historic moments, making MW Corp a well-known name in India.

MSD
Be well
Catch a case of the giggles.
HOW?
By providing people all across the globe, with innovative prescription medicines, vaccines, consumer care and animal health products. We also provide healthcare solutions that make a difference. And we do it by listening to patients, physicians and our other partners- and anticipating their needs.
At MSD, we work hard to keep the world well.
See all we're doing for you at msd.in
Copyright ©2011 Merck Sharp & Dohme Corp., a subsidary of Merck & Co., Inc. Whitehouse Station, NJ, USA. All Rights Reserved.

Mechanical harvester at India's largest sugar producer, Renuka Sugars. Because of government regulation, the sugar industry has not developed freely, yet it remains the second-largest in the world after Brazil.

SUGAR has been a mass consumption product for centuries; growing demand for it in Europe was a factor behind the colonization of the West Indies, where sugar plantations were developed with slave labour from Africa. In India, there was a widespread cottage industry producing *gur* and *khandsari*, an unrefined sweetener and a semi-refined sugar respectively. The present technology of vacuum pan refining was patented in the US by Norbert Rilieux in 1843. It rapidly spread across plantations. Although slavery was abolished in British colonies in 1833, and in the US in 1863, sugar continued to be produced and exported from the West Indies, whose large plantations remained highly competitive. In India, the first sugar mill was set up in the 1920s; by 1932, there were 29 sugar mills. The mill-owners asked for and got tariff protection in 1932; after that, sugar production increased rapidly; from 1,70,000 tonnes in 1932-3 it rose to 9,50,000 tonnes in 1934–5, and 1.28 million tonnes in 1938–9.

The sugar industry has been subject to considerable government regulation. Its land ownership regulations prevent the mills from owning land, and they must buy their sugarcane from farmers. It regulates the cane price to be paid to farmers, and buys up a certain proportion of sugar output for its public distribution system at lower-than-market prices. Its import duties are so high as to prevent imports most of the time, but at times of shortage it imports sugar or allows its import at low duties. It also arbitrarily allows or bans exports. Maharashtra has financed a large number of mills set up

Sugar warehouse. Inconsistent and unstable policies have not let sugar mills grow in size to offer competition to those in other major sugar producing countries, which could easily become the case provided the goverment does not insist on manufacturers buying all sugarcane produce at subsidized prices.

by farmers' cooperatives; the cooperative mills have given no return on the government loans, and so offer unfair competition to private sugar mills. As a result of these unstable, unpredictable, and intrusive policies, sugar mills have remained much smaller and less efficient in India than mills in major sugar producing countries. Because of the large Indian market and the protection, India today is the world's second-largest sugar producer after Brazil, but its share of world trade is close to zero. Its output is extremely unstable. Government-ordered minimum statutory prices are usually so high that they lead to periodic overproduction of sugarcane. The government forces sugar mills to buy it. That leads sugar mills to produce too much sugar, and stocks build up. High stocks make sugar mills reluctant to produce more, and to cut down cane purchases; that leads to a decline in cane output. So the sugar industry suffers from a strong cycle of about four years' duration. It has tried to reduce its dependence on sugar by diversifying into ethanol and power co-generation using byproducts like molasses and bagasse. Alcohol is mostly sold to the potable liquor and chemical industries; but in the last few years, mills have also been marketing anhydrous sprit or ethanol to oil marketing companies for blending up to 5 per cent in petrol.

Sri Renuka Sugar is India's largest sugar producer, which apart from having mills and refining capacities within the country, also owns sugar units in Brazil. Bajaj Hindustan comes next, followed by the likes of Balrampur Chini, Triveni Engineering, and Sakthi Sugars.

The **STEEL** industry is a creation of the industrial revolution. There was a large cottage industry producing pig iron for swords, shields, spears, and ornaments in small furnaces before the industrial revolution; it was as widespread in India as in the West. The industry was revolutionized by the invention of the Bessemer converter in 1858 and the open hearth in 1866. John Erskine first made pig iron in open top furnaces in 1870 in Bengal Iron Works in Kulti, Bengal. It was taken over by Sir R.N. Mookerjee and Sir Acquin Martin in the 1890s. They produced steel in open hearth furnaces, but it was not competitive. The Tata Iron and Steel Company (TISCO) was set up in 1907. G.H. Fairhurst set up a steel plant for Burn and Co. in 1918 in Burnpur; its first blast furnace produced steel in 1922. Sir R.N. Mookerjee was one of his associates. Indian Iron and Steel Co. (IISCO), which owned this plant, was merged with Bengal Iron Works in 1936. TISCO and IISCO were the only steel producers in India before the Second World War. IISCO went bankrupt and was taken over by the government in 1972. It slowly went to rust. After the War, the government prevented the expansion of private steel plants and set up its own plants in Bhilai, Rourkela, Durgapur, and Bokaro. Prevented from expanding, TISCO concentrated on efficiency and emerged as one of the lowest-cost steel producers in the world by the early 1990s. After liberalization in 1991, it was highly profitable and spread outside India, buying plants in Singapore and Thailand. In 2007, it bought Corus, which was created in 1999 with the merger of British Steel and Koninklijke Hoogovens of Holland.

CEMENT, in the sense of calcinated building material, goes back millennia, but the patent for Portland cement was taken by John Aspdin in 1824. If we exclude a number of failed enterprises, the history of cement in India starts with the Porbandar plant of Indian Cement Company inaugurated in 1914. In the 1920s, cement manufacturers complained to the government about imports and got protection. In 1927, they formed Indian Cement Manufacturers' Association, which turned into a marketing cartel. F.E. Dinshaw brought together four cement manufacturers in

FACING PAGE: Tata Iron and Steel Company's new and old mills in Jamshedpur. Set up in 1907, but prevented from expanding because of steel nationalization, its emphasis on efficiency made it one of the lowest-cost steel producers in the 1990s. Post liberalization, TISCO has expanded rapidly all over the world, and bought British-owned steel major Corus in 2007.

LEFT: The Aditya Birla promoted Grasim's cement venture and acquistion of a majority stake in L&T Cement Ltd in 2004 resulted in the new UltraTech Cement brand.

1936—the Tatas, the Khataus, Killick Nixon, and himself—to form Associated Cement Companies, which survives till today as ACC. In 1939, the industry came under price and distribution controls, which lasted till 1989. In the absence of competition, many small plants came up; in 1989–90, 91 plants produced 43 million tonnes of cement. Output in 2010–11 was 251 million tonnes—next only to China's.

The industry continues to have a large number of small plants; but at the enterprise level, there has been considerable consolidation in recent years. Grasim, which is an Aditya Birla Group company today, diversified into cement in the mid-1980s, setting up its first cement plant at Jawad in Madhya Pradesh. Around the same time, Larsen & Toubro went into the manufacture of cement plants, and some years later, set up cement plants itself. Grasim acquired a stake in L&T Cement Ltd. The stake was further increased to a majority stake in 2003, thereby giving Grasim a pan-India presence and an increased market share. In 2004, the demerger of L&T's cement business was completed, and Grasim acquired a controlling stake in L&T Cement Ltd. The name was subsequently changed to UltraTech Cement. In September 2010, UltraTech Cement Middle East Investments Limited, a wholly owned subsidiary of UltraTech Cement acquired management control of ETA Star Cement Company, along with its operations in the UAE, Bahrain, and Bangladesh, thereby putting UltraTech on the global map. Today UltraTech Cement is the tenth largest producer of cement globally.

Narottam Seksaria and Suresh Neotia set up Gujarat Ambuja Cement in 1986, and soon made it an extremely efficient producer; it claims to produce cement at the lowest cost in the world. It has its own port and ships, and distributes its cement to various points on the west coast. Holcim took a controlling 46 per cent stake in it in 2006, and renamed it Ambuja Cement. At the same time it made an open offer for ACC, in which Gujarat Ambuja had a 13.8 per cent holding. At the end of the offer, Holcim held a 34.69 per cent share in ACC and took control of it. Lafarge entered India with the purchase of the Tata Steel cement plant in 1999, and bought the Raymond plant in 2001 and Larsen & Toubro's ready-mix concrete plant in 2008.

Despite these mergers and acquisitions, the industry continues to have a large number of producers. When the industry's capacity was controlled, a large number of mini-cement plants came up to evade industrial licensing, mostly in the 1970s and 1980s.

SOUTHERN STAR RISING

INDIA CEMENTS LTD is consolidating its pan-Indian presence through the cement economy—HELPED ALSO BY ITS Chennai Super Kings franchise

RIGHT: Co-founder S.N.N. Sankaralinga Iyer showed rare courage when, way back in 1946, with T.S. Narayanaswami, he launched one of Tamil Nadu's earliest public limited companies.

FAR RIGHT: Promoter N. Srinivasan has guided the diversification plans of India Cements into the generation of non-conventional power, as a major player in the sugar industry, and also deals in trade and finance.

India Cements began in 1946 with the establishment of a cement factory in an almost unmapped hamlet in India's southernmost district in Talaiyuthu, Tamil Nadu.

From modest beginnings in 1949, when Sankar Cement made its first appearance in the market, it has grown hugely in size and reputation into a multifaceted organization with activities that span cement, power, sugar, trading, and finance.

FOUNDERS AND PROMOTERS

India Cements Limited was jointly founded and promoted by S.N.N. Sankaralinga Iyer and T.S.Narayanaswami in 1946 as a public limited company. The decision to start a capital-intensive industry was an act of foresight and courage when it launched its maiden public issue of Rs 1 crore, which was over-subscribed. The industrial progress of the state in the Sixties owed much to Narayanaswami who looked beyond cement to aluminium production, chemicals and plastics, sugar, and shipping, after stabilizing India Cement's potential for expansion. The promoters today are represented by N.Srinivasan, who is vice chairman and managing director of India Cements Limited. A postgraduate of the Illinos Institute of Technology, USA, and a well-known industrialist, opinion maker, and sports administrator, he is joined by Chitra Srinivasan, director, and Rupa Gurunath, whole time director. Together, they have made India Cements with its 15.5 million tonnes capacity, the fourth-largest cement group in the country and the largest player in the south with a 16 per cent market share and eight composite cement plants spread over Tamil Nadu, Andhra Pradesh, and Rajasthan, and two cement grinding units, one each in Tamil Nadu and Maharashtra. The company's gross turnover in 2010–11 was Rs 4,011 crore while the net profit was Rs 68 crore.

ASSUMING LEADERSHIP

Since 1990, the production capacity of the company has increased from 1.6 million tonnes to 15.5 million tonnes in 2011–12. This has been due to the aggressive moves initiated to expand capacity both through the greenfield as well as the acquisition route. Beginning with the takeover in Chilamkur in 1990, the company has expanded capacity through the greenfield Dalavoi Cement plant in Tamil Nadu, followed by a spate of acquisitions in Visaka, Yerraguntla, and Raasi in Andhra Pradesh in 1997–8, and in Banswara in Rajasthan in 2009. Some of these projects were part-financed by funds raised from international markets. The turnover of the company vaulted from Rs 149 crore in 1990 to Rs 4,011 crore in 2011.

The type of cement manufactured by the company is mainly Portland Pozzolana (or blended) cement and ordinary Portland cement. Over the years, the production of blended cement has gradually increased to 70 per cent of its total production. This is marketed under brands such as Sankar Cement, Coromandel King, and Raasi Cement.

DIVERSIFICATIONS

Power: The company entered non-conventional electric power generation in 1996 with the harnessing of wind energy at Palladam in Coimbatore and Tirunelveli to produce 17 MW of clean energy. This was augmented in 2004 with the commissioning of a 25 MW gas-based power plant in Ramanathapuram, Madurai. The power generated from these sources is utilized fully by the company's cement plants in Tamil Nadu. In 2004, the company installed a waste heat recovery plant, an Indo-Japanese collaboration, at its cement plant in Vishnupuram.

Trading and Finance: In 1997, the company took over Aruna Sugars Finance Limited with a diversified business portfolio covering truck financing, leasing, money changing, forex, and stock broking—the India Cements Capital Limited.

Sugar plant: In 1999, the company ventured into the field of sugar production with the commissioning a 2,500 TCD sugar plant with a co-generation plant at Mandya in Karnataka. The capacity was expanded to 3,500 TCD in 2011.

A STRATEGY FOR THE FUTURE

The company is in the process of setting up two 50 MW power projects, one each in Tamil Nadu and Andhra Pradesh. With the proposed addition of 100 MW, the company will have 200 MW of captive power.

India Cements has plans for expansion both within India and overseas, and has captured popular imagination as owner of IPL cricket team Chennai Super Kings.

It has also obtained coal mining rights in Indonesia to meet the requirement for power generation as well as for cement manufacture. Two ships are to be inducted by the company to transport the coal from Indonesia, thereby combating freight costs.

The company's plans include the setting up of cement plants in Himachal Pradesh, Madhya Pradesh, and Chhattisgarh, and it is taking necessary steps to obtain mining leases and acquire land for the purpose. Its expansion foray in the northern region, and its initiatives in acquiring and developing the cricket Indian Premier League team Chennai Super Kings, as well as its brand value, have gone a long way in establishing and strengthening its presence all over the country.

ABOVE and TOP: The 13th-century Neemrana Fort, before and after renovation, on the Delhi–Jaipur highway, is the flagship property of the eponymously named Neemrana Group of Non-Hotels famously created out of heritage buildings.

ABOVE, *right*: A vintage photograph of India's first luxury hotel, the Taj Mahal Palace, Bombay, 1903, built by Jamsetji Tata is an architectural marvel. This landmark on Bombay's sea-face, has been reopened recently, after a painstaking restoration.

FACING PAGE: The historic Shiv Niwas and Fateh Prakash wings of City Palace, Udaipur, have recently been taken over for management by the Tata-owned Taj Hotels.

The concept of **HOTELS** was brought to India by the British. Before they came, the rich travelled with their own portable hotels: they carried tents, carpets, furniture, cooking vessels, and whatever they needed on elephants and camels. The less fortunate took shelter in free facilities such as *serais* or *dharamshalas*. Early European travellers had to adjust themselves; those of them who could afford it set up their own households, with wives, servants, cooks, torchbearers, horses, and all other amenities. However, their growing numbers eventually led to the setting up of hotels. Though it is probably not the oldest hotel, Watson's Hotel in Bombay was opened in 1867; the building, known now as Esplanade Mansion, was leased to Diler Jung, an official of the Nizam of Hyderabad, for 999 years at 92.12 annas a year. Connemara in Madras was opened in 1854, Grand Hotel in Calcutta in 1890, and the Taj Mahal Palace, Bombay, 1903. Metropolitan Hotel, opened in 1894 in old Delhi by the Maidens brothers, closed down, but their Maidens Hotel, opened in 1902, is still functioning as an Oberoi hotel. Hotels were also built in the hills, often with Gothic or half-timbered buildings reminiscent of England: Elgin Hotel and West End in Darjeeling were opened in 1887, Clarkes in Simla, where Mohan Singh Oberoi began his career as a clerk, dates back to 1898, and Savoy in Mussoorie was opened in 1902. After Independence, the number of hotels has multiplied everywhere. Three major hotel chains have emerged run by the Oberois, the Tatas, and ITC, but there are also smaller ones. Aman Nath and Francis Wacziarg teamed up to turn the ruins of the 16th-century Neemrana Fort on a hill near Delhi into a hotel in 1987; since then, they have converted many old palaces, forts and mansions, and warehouses into heritage hotels.

With the Taj group taking over The Pierre in New York, the Tata-owned chain has signalled its intention of globalizing its hospitality business.

FACING PAGE: ITC's hotels in Mumbai include its Grand Maratha (pictured) and Grand Central, both in the suburbs, which have catered to a new breed of, chiefly, business travellers to the city's spreading businesses.

Founder Velegapudi Ramakrishna laid the foundations for the KCP Group seven decades ago.

MACHINED FOR SUCCESS

The KCP GROUP's industrial machinery has fuelled the growth of industry in the south

Inspired by the leadership and technological foresight of Velagapudi Ramakrishna, it has been 70 years since the foundation of the KCP Group was laid in 1941. His vision has transformed KCP into a Rs 700 crore company that has contributed to the growth of industrial technology. As a premier producer of cement and industrial machinery, KCP has diversified into a $140 million group with interests in heavy engineering, sugar, hydel power, information technology, and biotechnology.

EXCELLENCE THROUGH INNOVATION

Currently under the leadership of chairman and managing director Dr V.L. Dutt, joint MD Smt. V.L. Indira Dutt, and executive director Smt. Kavitha Dutt Chitturi, KCP has evolved into a multi-crore company with an uninterrupted dividend record. The KCP Group continues to march in the direction that its founder envisioned of 'Excellence through Innovation'

KCP was established with a single co-operative sugar factory in Andhra Pradesh. It set up an establishment for heavy engineering in Tiruvottriyur, Tamil Nadu, in 1955 to cater to core industries like sugar, cement, steel, and power. The KCP cement division was started in 1958, at Macherla, Andhra Pradesh. Its hydel power division came up in 1999 at Nekkarikallu on the Guntur Canal of the river Krishna. KCP Biotech, launched in 2004, specializes in producing natural colours. KCP also promotes three associate companies: Fives Cail-KCP Limited to develop and design machinery for the sugar industry; KCP Technologies Limited to provide software solutions and products; and KCP Vietnam Industries Limited to manufacture and refine sugar at its factory in Vietnam.

FOOTHOLDS OF GROWTH

The Heavy Engineering Unit in Tiruvottiyur is one of the largest and most highly integrated centres in India with casting, fabrication, and machining facilities required for the manufacture of large infrastructure machinery for sugar, cement, steel, alumina, hydro, thermal, and wind power plants, fertilizer, chemical, refinery, petrochemical, mineral processing and mining, and for space and defence industries. The organization employs expertise in technology and infrastructural advancements to create machines that are precise and provide futuristic, adaptive, and cost-effective engineering solutions. The organization's uncompromising approach to quality has earned it ISO 9001 and other prestigious certifications.

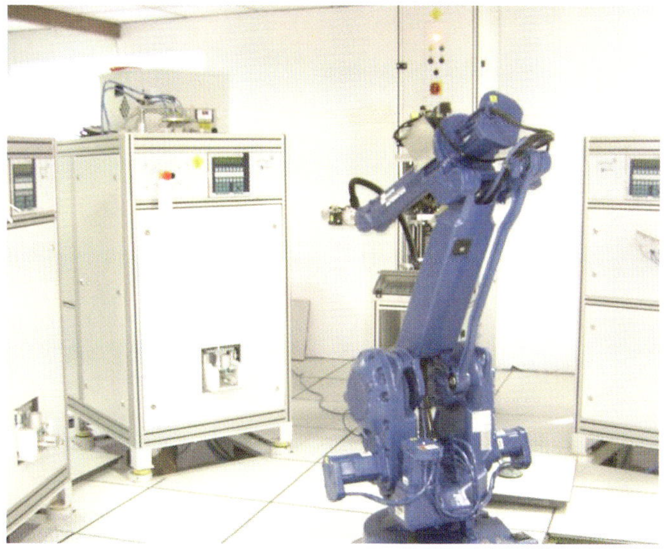

KCP's initial foray into cement manufacturing in southern India proved a success. Its recently launched plant in Muktyala (*left*), with its advanced robotics from Denmark (*middle*), is possibly the most advanced facility of its kind in the country. (*Right*) Its hydel power project at Nagarjunasagar Dam banks excess generation and sells it to the power grid.

The cement division of KCP began in 1958 as a half-million tonne capacity, state-of-the-art cement manufacturing facility in Macherla, Andhra Pradesh. With a strong emphasis on new technology characterizing all operations at the Macherla plant, it facilitated India's first dry process kiln of 400 TDP by Humboldt, Germany, in 1958. In 1962, it surpassed this by installing a 600 TDP wet process kiln in collaboration with Fives Lille Cail France. The Nagarjuna Sagar Dam is the cement division's outstanding achievement. The company's 100 per cent modernized cement plant has a World Bank funded outlay of Rs 36.7 crore. The plant at Macherla incorporates a sophisticated centralized process control system using hardware and software from Siemens, Germany.

CEMENTING THE FUTURE

With its strong presence in the south Indian cement market, KCP chose Ramakrishnapuram as the next site for a cement plant. Located in the Krishna district of Andhra Pradesh, the area promised access to large limestone reserves which would enable easy access to key markets in Andhra Pradesh, Tamil Nadu, Karnataka, and Orissa. KHD Humboldt, Germany, was enlisted to design an energy-efficient and state-of-the-art plant that could deliver an annual capacity of 1.52 million tonnes of cement. The resulting plant, commissioned in 2011, was one of the most modern in India with the best in technological advancements provided by FL Smidth, an engineering company from Denmark which facilitated the use of a fully automated robot lab capable of preparation and analysis of sampling and sample transactions.

GENERATING POWER

When the state government of Andhra Pradesh first permitted private enterprises to generate their own renewable power, KCP established mini hydel projects on the Guntur branch canal of the Nagarjuna Sagar Dam. Utilizing innovative technology and cost-effective methods, KCP built a small hydro-electric dam on an irrigation canal at five different points. These canal drops have been in function since 1999, with a collective output of 8 MW of power annually.

Incorporating 'Semi Kaplan Variant' turbines, the first of their kind in India, any excess generation is banked on a monthly basis and used in cycles, while unused electricity is sold to the grid. With improved production techniques and technological innovation, the KCP hydel division has witnessed a constant, significant increase in power generation with an average of 3.5 crore kWh per year since 2005–6.

FRENCH COLLABORATION

A profitable joint venture with the French Fives Cail Group has exhibited the seamless combination of KCP's experience in the industry with the cutting-edge expertise of the Fives Cail Group. Since 1995, the collaboration has enabled increased efficiency in the production of new equipment, development of processes, automation of plans, and modernization and expansion of existing factories. This joint venture heralds the dawn of a new age for the Indian sugar industry.

To enable the manufacture of critical components, KCP's ISO 9001 and ASME certified heavy engineering division, one of the largest and professionally integrated workshops anywhere in the world, is available for casting, fabricating, and machining heavy and large steel machinery.

BIOTECH — BY SPECIFICATION

KCP's biotech division is situated in Alexandria Knowledge Park, Genome Valley, Hyderabad. KCP Biotech uses raw materials cultivated with the highest standards and specifications, adequate processes to ensure the safety of the workforce, and a system of effluent treatment to safeguard the environment. The natural colours produced have a diverse range of applications in the food, cosmetics, and pharmaceutical industries. KCP Biotech has its sights on the future, and the company's interests in frontier areas of biotechnology include enzymes, proteins, diagnostics, et cetera.

SWEET SUCCESS IN VIETNAM

In 1990, the company took on the challenge of setting up and developing the sugar industry in Vietnam. The government of Vietnam approved the setting up of a sugar factory in the Son Hua district of Phuyen province in Vietnam. The plant and the machinery was designed by Fives Cail KCP. Commercial production and manufacture of export quality refined sugar and white sugar successfully started from January 2002.

The management systems are certified to the Quality Management System Standards ISO 9001. Another factory with a crushing capacity of 1,250 TCD of sugarcane opened with commercial production being operated from the year 2010 at Dongxon.

ROOM FOR HOSPITALITY

KCP proposed to improve its corporate visibility by setting up a four-star business hotel in Somajiguda, Hyderabad. The decision was in keeping with the extent of land available, its strategic location in a commercial area, and the wide gap in this distinct segment of the hospitality industry. When ready in April 2013, the hotel will have ground-plus 11 floors, a 24-hour coffee shop, multicuisine and speciality restaurants, a terrace swimming pool, gym and health-spa, besides meeting halls for conferences and social functions. It will offer 130 standard and deluxe rooms and suites with such mod-cons as electronic connectivity, convenience of plug-ins, wi-fi, et cetera.

CORPORATE SOCIAL RESPONSIBILITY

***Kids Patasala, Andhra Pradesh*:** The Kids Patasala E.M. School is a branch of the Kids Academy of General and Technical Education established in 2002 by the promoters. Catering to the needs of children of KCP employees as well as those from the surrounding villages of Palanadu, the main goal of this institution is a child-centred education system with equal importance given to physical, intellectual, and spiritual development of children. The current strength of the English medium school is 750 students who follow the SCERT syllabus.

***V. Ramakrishna Polytechnic, Tiruvottiyur*:** Established in 1982, Sri V. Ramakrishna Polytechnic College is managed by the V. Ramakrishna Charitable Trust to perpetuate the memory of the founder-chairman of the KCP Group. Situated close to the industrial belt of Chennai, the college on a 72,500 sq. ft campus has a staff strength of 110.

A sleepy looking village by the coast of the Arabian Sea is waking up travellers from around the world to its battle-scarred, history-laden forts. Thrashed unceasingly by the stubborn waves, the magnificent Bekal Fort, a 17th century edifice, stands nonchalantly stoic amidst legends of sea battles, invaders and empires. Last captured by the English from Tipu Sultan before India gained independence, Bekal is definitely the most well-preserved fort in the State. Besides history, the sea winds, swaying palms and the magical views all together make Bekal an enchanting experience.
To check out Bekal fort and a whole range of experiences that make Malabar a unique, exotic part of God's Own Country, log on to www.keralatourism.org. You'll wake up to a new world.
Wake up to Malabar
Experience Malabar | Tropical forests | Tree houses | Drive-in beach | Historic forts
Spice trails | Theme village | Temple art forms | Malabari cuisine and more
To Mangalore
Kasaragod
Chandragiri Fort
Kappil Beach
Bekal Fort
Bekal Beach
Aqua Park
Pallikere
Railway Station
Arabian Sea
Kannur
To Calicut
Not to scale
kerala
God's Own Country
www.keralatourism.org
Call 1-800-425-4747 Kerala Tourism Park View Thiruvananthapuram 695 033 Kerala India
Fax: +91 471 2322279 Email: info@keralatourism.org

ABOVE, *left*: Still as well as film photography had an early start in India, which kept up with inventions and technological advancements around the rest of the world. *Right:* A still from Richard Attenborough's film *Gandhi* with Hollywood actor Ben Kingsley playing the title role.

FOLLOWING PAGES: The hundred years of the Indian film industry, starting in 1913, has mapped an exciting course. Like cricket, cinema is considered a religion in the country. Both the cinematic content as well as viewing experience has changed considerably post-liberalization.

The **FILM** industry began in colonial times, was stifled after Independence, but has blossomed in more recent times. The history of photography begins with the creation of a picture by a recognizably modern chemical process by Joseph Niépce in 1826. A series of improvements followed in France in the next few years until Louis Daguerre, who worked with Niépce, invented the Daguerrotype in 1839, which produced black-and-white photographs. In 1847, Count Sergei Levitsky invented the bellows camera, which was essential for focusing. In 1884, George Eastman replaced the glass plate in the camera with a film, and created the portable camera. Once film was invented, showing a series of films rapidly to create an illusion of movement was an obvious step; the first movie picture was shown at a music hall in New York in 1896. The next step too was obvious: making actors mime speech, recording the speech separately, and running the soundtrack with the film. That had become common by the 1920s.

In India, the first silent film was shown in Bombay in 1896. Harishchandra Bhatavdekar made two films in 1899, one of a wrestling match in Hanging Gardens, and another one of monkeys. The first commercially released film was *Raja Harishchandra* by Dadasaheb Phalke in 1913. The first talkie, *Alam Ara* of Imperial Film Company, was released in 1931. By the time of Independence, films were the only form of mass entertainment for most Indians. The expansion of the film industry was restricted in the days of controls. Import licences for getting equipment from abroad were denied. The industry was not given bank credit; nor was it allowed to raise equity capital. But controls also generated funds that could not be easily invested in conventional businesses, since tax rates were high. Rumours suggested the industry was funded by profits from smuggling and black money though these, for obvious reasons, were never confirmed. Investment inflows limited the growth of the industry which had an enormous potential market in the country.

The reforms of the early 1990s changed the prospects of the industry. Liberalization of import controls made it easy to import technology, equipment, and to shoot abroad, while the advent of multiplexes in shopping malls changed the viewing experience, making it a more pleasurable one. Liberalization of the import of foreign films brought some competition, especially from Hollywood, but Hollywood itself had declined considerably by then because of competition from television, and was no threat to the Indian industry. The industry is inhabited by producers, directors, actors, and distributors and the boundaries between them are hazy. Many well-known stars have become producers with their own production companies

TELEVISION PROGRAMMING, closely linked to the film and entertainment industry, was a monopoly of the central government. It was opened up to private investors in 1994. It brought competition for viewers. Television channels also emerged which depended a good deal on films and dances from them. But they were not profitable enough to support financing of new films; they only brought a supplementary source of profits for films already made. In the last few years, content has become niche, with news, soaps, serials, and reality shows commanding their own niche, repeated in several languages and regions. Hollywood underwent the same process much earlier, since television became common in the US in the 1950s. The film industry there became an adjunct of the television industry; films were debuted in theatres, but made most of their money from repeated shows on television. Television drove the content and form of films: films became short, and serial films came into being. Thus, the US and other Western countries developed a new industry which primarily supplied television with shorter, cheaper films. That process is still incomplete in India. Going to see films in theatres continues to be popular, and multiplexes are coming up all over the country.

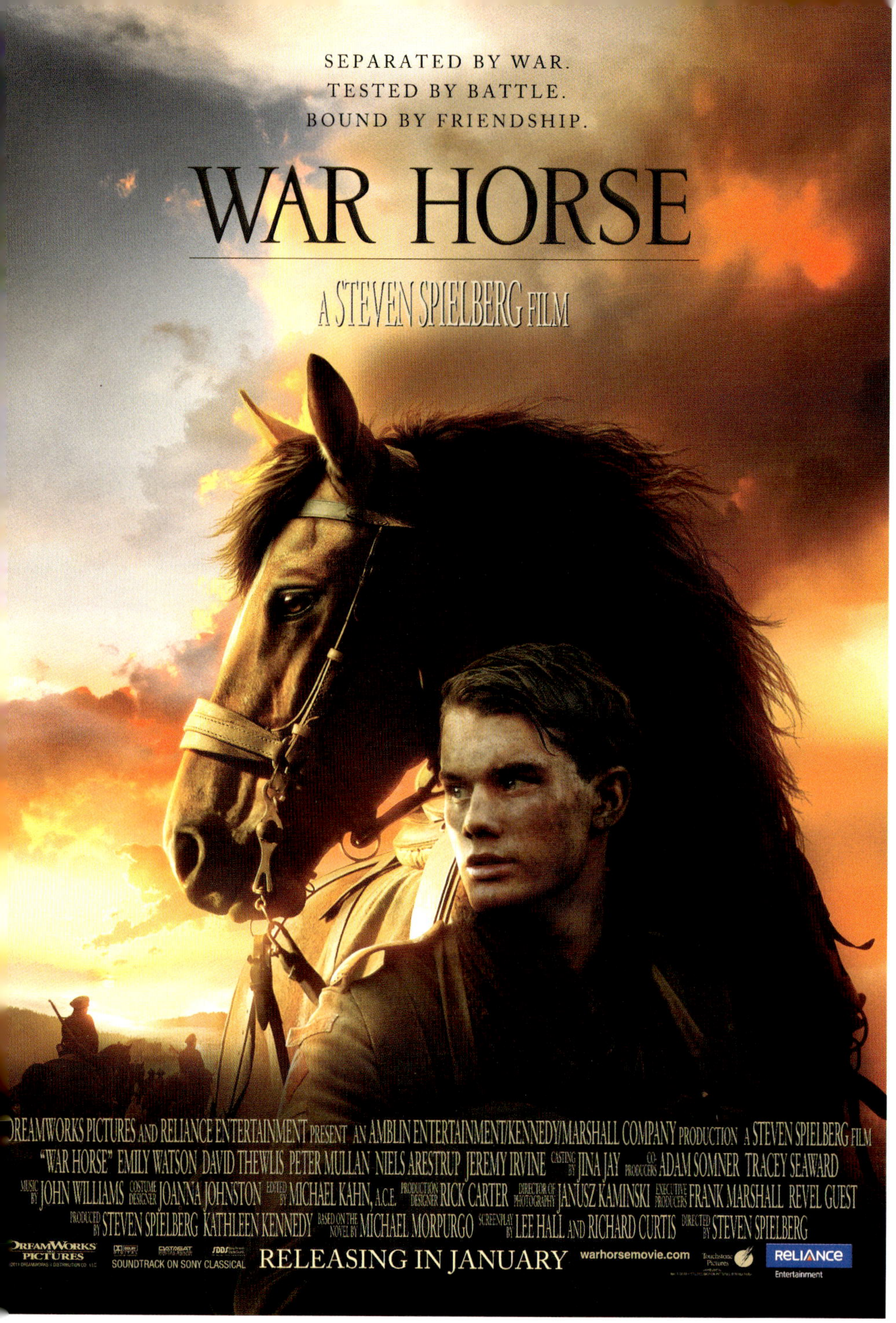
SEPARATED BY WAR.
TESTED BY BATTLE.
BOUND BY FRIENDSHIP.
WAR HORSE
A STEVEN SPIELBERG FILM
DREAMWORKS PICTURES AND RELIANCE ENTERTAINMENT PRESENT AN AMBLIN ENTERTAINMENT/KENNEDY/MARSHALL COMPANY PRODUCTION A STEVEN SPIELBERG FILM
"WAR HORSE" EMILY WATSON DAVID THEWLIS PETER MULLAN NIELS ARESTRUP JEREMY IRVINE CASTING BY JINA JAY CO-PRODUCERS ADAM SOMNER TRACEY SEAWARD
MUSIC BY JOHN WILLIAMS COSTUME DESIGNER JOANNA JOHNSTON EDITED BY MICHAEL KAHN, A.C.E. PRODUCTION DESIGNER RICK CARTER DIRECTOR OF PHOTOGRAPHY JANUSZ KAMINSKI EXECUTIVE PRODUCERS FRANK MARSHALL REVEL GUEST
PRODUCED BY STEVEN SPIELBERG KATHLEEN KENNEDY BASED ON THE NOVEL BY MICHAEL MORPURGO SCREENPLAY BY LEE HALL AND RICHARD CURTIS DIRECTED BY STEVEN SPIELBERG
DREAMWORKS PICTURES
SOUNDTRACK ON SONY CLASSICAL
RELEASING IN JANUARY
warhorsemovie.com
Touchstone Pictures
RELIANCE Entertainment

PVR

RELIANCE
Entertainment
RELIANCE ENTERTAINMENT presents
a REEL LIFE PRODUCTION PVT. LTD. production
BODYGUARD
written & directed by SIDDIQUE produced by ALVIRA AGNIHOTRI ATUL AGNIHOTRI & RELIANCE ENTERTAINMENT
executive producer NIKHIL NAMIT music HIMESH RESHAMMIYA & PRITAM cinematography SEJAL SHAH editor SANJAY SANKLA
www.bodyguardthefilm.com www.facebook.com/relianceentertainment
IN CINEMAS THIS EID
ਬੌਡੀਗਾਰਡ
बॉडीगार्ड
باڈی گارڈ

RAMOJI
MOVIE MAGIC

Most of the multiplexes are local and single, but BIG CINEMA, owned by Anil Ambani's Reliance MediaWorks, has 253 screens and accounts for 10–15 per cent of the industry's revenue. DLF has its own chain, DT Cinemas. Cinepolis, a Mexican chain, has multiplexes in Bangalore, Amritsar, and Thane.

After the reforms, the Indian film industry exploded, and soon overtook other countries in terms of the number of films produced. In 2009, it produced 1,288 feature films and 1,673 other films. However, the industry remains fragmented between producers, directors, stars, and languages; although a number of producers have incorporated themselves, there are no outstanding leaders in the industry.

The **TELEVISION SET** industry followed the trajectory of the programming industry. Industrial and import licensing policies were unfriendly to the industry, and restricted its growth. But after the small liberalization of 1977, small-scale enterprises sprang up, especially in the north and the south, to make cheap and not very reliable television sets. Licensing restrictions were lifted in 1993 following which production exploded. Delicensing also brought in foreign producers. Today, Sony and Samsung are the leading foreign producers; Videocon and Samtel are the leading Indian ones.

FACING PAGE: Anil Ambani's MediaWorks has invested in Steven Spielberg's Dreamworks Studios (in picture, from left, Spielberg, Stacey Snider, Ambani, and David Geffen), marking the emergence of India as a major player in the entertainment industry.
Above, right: MediaWorks involves itself with the creation end of the company's business which (*below*) also has a retail end in its BIG CINEMA multiplexes.

RIGHT: Satish Kaura, managing director, Samtel Group, a pioneer in the development of tube parts for television sets.
The television industry's first taste of changing times came when colour broadcast—and television sets—were promoted in 1982 for the Asian Games.

Post-liberalization, the television content and delivery industry has exploded, leading to production on an unprecedented scale and global names such as Samsung becoming familiar. Flat panel TV ES7000 *(above)* is one of the highest selling product category for Samsung. it is known as the Samsung Smart Television with voice control, motion control, and face recognition features

JEWELLERY has existed for thousands of years—at least since Harappa and Mohenjodaro, whose ruins yielded necklaces and bracelets. As a handicraft that requires skilled workers, until recently it was dominated by small enterprises. The import of gold was banned at the beginning of the Second World War to conserve foreign exchange. The ban was moderately effective till the 1970s. Then the oil boom of the 1970s led thousands of Indian workers to go and work in the Middle East; they earned dinars which they wanted to send to their families in India, principally in Kerala. Indian banks were owned by the government and incapable of developing money transmittal services. So, informal *hawala* operators emerged who bought the dinars from the workers and promised to deliver the money to their families. They bought gold in Switzerland, brought it to Dubai, loaded it in fast boats, unloaded it on India's west coast, and distributed it all over India in exchange for rupees, which they delivered to the workers' families. It was an extremely smooth and efficient operation. In the mid-1990s, around some 500 tonnes of gold a year was being smuggled into India.

TOP and FACING PAGE: A 17th century Mughal sarpech or turban ornament, and a recently made necklace, both handcrafted in the *kundankari* technique in which 22-carat gold and enamelling are used for the setting of rough cut diamonds and precious gemstones using a technique that has remained unchanged over the centuries.

RIGHT: An old photograph showing gold craftsmen at work. Little has changed in the way goldsmiths work on at least traditional jewellery, which remains the preserve, still, of family jewellers.

TOP: Zoya, Tata's luxury jewellery brand, has considerably enhanced the retail experience. While India is among the largest jewellery buying markets in the world—60 per cent of all gold is crafted into jewellery—there are few brands and the market is made up of mostly the unorganized sector.

RIGHT: Tata-owned Titan watches and Tanishq jewellery are among the players that have changed the face of the accessories business in the country. India has traditionally been the largest importer of gold in the world, most of which is a hedge for future security.

FACING PAGE: An heirloom 19th century gold necklace worn by the bride in a mercantile Chettier family.

In 1998, finance minister P. Chidambaram gave permission to eight banks to import gold. Soon, all gold began to come through legal channels. It also legitimized the jewellery business. Today, India is the largest consumer of gold in the world. In the year ending in September 2011, it consumed 1,059 tonnes of gold (when total world consumption was 3,500 tonnes), 958 tonnes of which was imported. Roughly 60 per cent of the gold is crafted into jewellery; the rest is hoarded in the form of ingots and coins. A number of large jewellers have emerged in the past 20 years; some of them are incorporated. Tata-owned Titan Industries sells watches under the Titan brand and jewellery under the Tanishq brand in the metros and tier 1 and tier 2 cities, and Goldplus sells jewellery in tier 3 and tier 4 towns. Its exclusive Zoya by Tanishq boutiques deal in only high-end jewellery. Tribhovandas Bhimji Zaveri has a chain of shops; so does Gitanjali Gems. D'damas and Swaroski are foreign companies that have opened a number of retail outlets. But a major part of the industry continues to be small-scale; there are estimated to be 2.25 million small jewellers in the country.

The related **GEM-CUTTING** industry is almost entirely export-oriented. Mines in South Africa and Australia yield raw gems which must be cut and polished before they can be set in jewellery. Gems have been mined in Golconda for centuries, and have been cut by skilled craftsmen mostly in Jaipur, while diamonds are polished and cut in Surat. Among the leading export-oriented gem-cutters are Gitanjali, Sanghavi, Navinchandra, Suresh, Ramakrishna, and Venus Jewels.

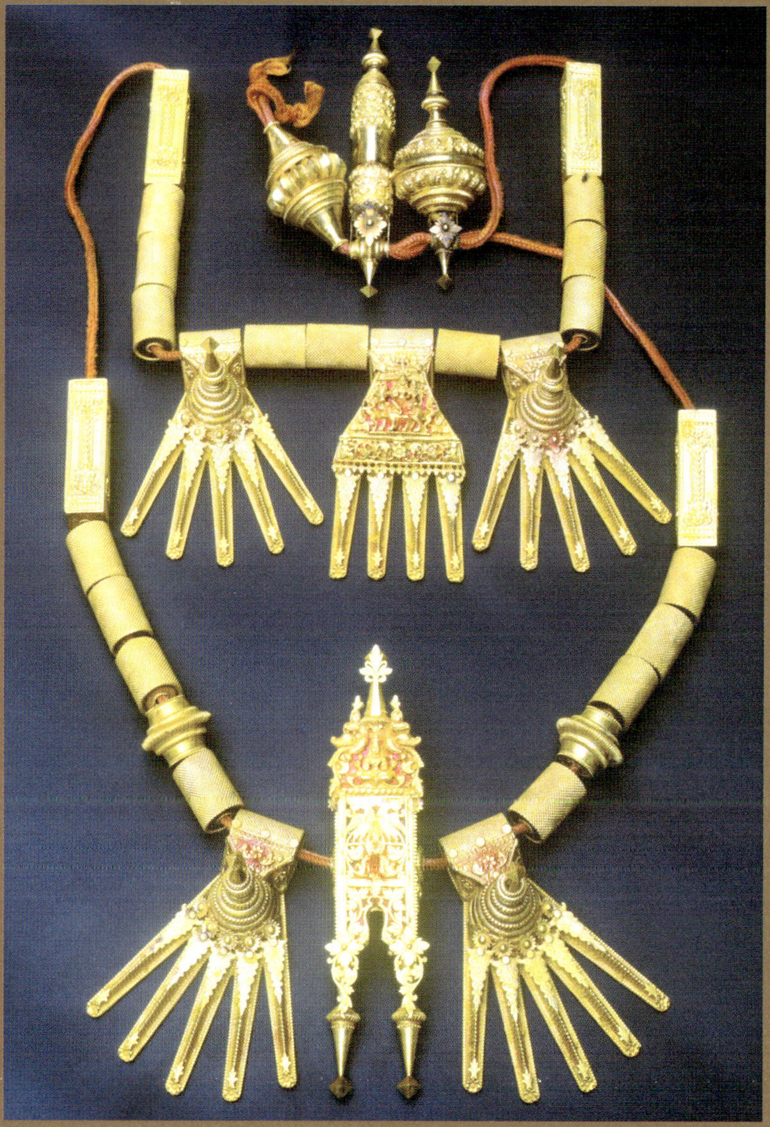

ABOVE and FACING PAGE: Earrings and necklace crafted by Zoya using emeralds and diamonds. Jaipur, in Rajasthan, is the world's largest centre for the handcutting and polishing of precious gemstones, while diamonds are cut and polished in Surat, whose traders now control a large chunk of the diamond trade in Antwerp, Belgium.

THE NEW INDUSTRIES

The **MINERAL OIL** industry was the first major one to come up in the years after Independence. Today, it is a sophisticated process industry which extracts a variety of specialized products from crude oil. Crude oil used to be collected for medication and fuel; most reserves were underground, and there was no way to extract it. Then a number of events coincided. By the mid-19th century, the number of steam engines and machines driven by them had created demand for lubricants. There were many oil seeps, but they did not yield enough oil. In the 1850s, a process was developed in Poland and Romania in which crude oil was heated in a container, and the vapour from it collected and cooled to make a product like kerosene which could be used in lamps. In 1859, a young man named Edwin L. Drake drilled into the ground and oil gushed out in Pennsylvania. In the succeeding years, several oil wells were drilled, and the oil obtained from them was refined into kerosene, which replaced whale oil, the common illuminant in the United States then. Still, kerosene was only a small part of the components of crude oil; it was some time before markets were developed for other components. The most important ones in the long run were petrol and diesel oil. The internal combustion engine was invented in 1807, but had made no headway because no existing fuels worked well in it. In 1885, Karl Benz designed a car with a petrol engine. In 1892, Rudolf Diesel patented his diesel engine. The first assembly line for cars was set up by Ransom Olds for his Oldsmobile model in 1902. These developments together created the automobile industry that has since driven the oil industry.

Oil seeps have been known in Assam since 1825 at least. In 1880, Assam Railways and Trading Company signed a contract with the secretary of state for India to build a railway line between Dibrugarh and Sadiya. While constructing the railway line, it struck oil, and Assam Oil Company was set up in 1889 to exploit it. To refine the oil, it built a refinery in Digboi in 1901. The refinery survives to this day, and has a capacity of 3,00,000 tonnes.

ABOVE: The state-owned behemoth Indian Oil Corporation Limited was set up with the merger of Indian Refineries Limited with Indian Oil Company Limited.

FACING PAGE: An Indian Oil filling station in remote Ladakh when it first opened (*below*) and a new contemporary outlet in the plains in New Delhi after recent renovation and enhancement of facilities (*above*).

The new government of independent India was extremely concerned about the balance of payments. There were a few oil wells in Assam, and a 1,50,000-tonne refinery in Dibrugarh, but for most of its oil product requirements India depended on imports, mainly from the Abadan refinery of Anglo-Iranian Oil Company. It was nationalized by Prime Minister Mohammed Mossadeq of Iran in in 1951; after that, the Indian government felt the need for more stable sources of oil products. It negotiated the construction of three refineries by Burmah Shell, Standard Vacuum (Stanvac), and Caltex in the early 1950s. Soon thereafter, there were tensions between the three companies and the government. The government set up Oil and Natural Gas Directorate (converted into a commission and, in 1993, to the present Oil and Natural Gas Corporation) for exploration and production in 1956, Indian Refineries in 1958 for oil refining, and Indian Oil Corporation in 1959 for distribution, and assumed control over oil product pricing and distribution; in 1964, Indian Refineries was merged into Indian Oil Corporation. The three refineries of Shell, Stanvac, and Caltex were nationalized in 1974–6. The government had a monopoly of the oil industry for the next 20 years. Then, in 1994, it licensed new refineries to be built by Reliance and Essar. Today, the 62-million-tonne Reliance refinery in Jamnagar is the largest in the world, and also one of the most versatile and efficient. Close by, in Vadinar, also in Gujarat, Essar has built a 14-million-tonne refinery which it is expanding to 20 million tonnes. The government subsidizes kerosene and diesel oil sold through Indian Oil Corporation but does not give the same subsidy to the two private refiners. So, Reliance has set up subsidiaries in the Middle East, Africa, and Australia, and export much of its output. Essar sells most of its output through Indian Oil Corporation. The government refineries are owned by four companies: Indian Oil Corporation, which owns 10 refineries with a combined capacity of about 45 million tonnes; Bharat Petroleum, which has three refineries with a capacity of 22.5 million tonnes; Hindustan Petroleum, which has two refineries with a capacity of 13 million tonnes; and ONGC, which has two refineries with a capacity of 9.77 million tonnes.

Reliance India Limited's petrochemicals refinery in Jamnagar, Gujarat. The private sector player's heady growth has been fuelled by its petrochemicals ambitions in India and, increasingly, overseas.

LEADING BY EXAMPLE

KANORIA CHEMICALS & INDUSTRIES has banked on technology and 'Waste to Wealth' practices as part of its strategy

Kanoria Chemicals & Industries Limited (KCI) is a leading manufacturer of chemical intermediates in India. Established in the 1960s, KCI started with a chlor alkali plant in Renukoot in the state of Uttar Pradesh. Spread over nearly 350 acres, the integrated chemical plant was developed over the years to include a staff housing complex, hospital, club, and entertainment facilities. It was to the credit of the visionary approach of the promoters to set up the plant that was not only at a remote location, but also lacked basic infrastructure. The decision, however, was guided by the fact that a major aluminium manufacturing unit was located nearby, and the caustic soda that KCI would manufacture was a key input for alumina processing.

ORGANIC GROWTH

Beginning with a single product, KCI soon added other chlorine-based chemicals to its product portfolio. Chlorine is a co-product in the manufacture of caustic soda. Being hazardous in nature, utilizing it for making forward integrated products was a strategic decision that helped the company to chart a sustained growth momentum. Another important expansion was by way of two 25 MW state-of-the-art thermal power plants that provided relatively low-cost electricity, a key input for the energy intensive caustic soda manufacturing process.

Set up in 1986 in Ankleshwar to manufacture alcohol-based intermediaries, this plant gave the company exposure to organic chemicals.

Distillery effluent is recycled at Ankleshwar to extract water, and its 'waste to wealth' programme converts biogas to electricity.

The company's growth is also characterized by its social responsibility. Not only did it contribute to enhancing infrastructure in and around Renukoot, but it also carried out community outreach programmes that sought to improve the quality of life of the people in the vicinity, largely constituted of economically backward villages with a significant tribal population. A noteworthy programme was water harvesting through small check dams to improve the availability of potable water and irrigation.

The company set up a second plant in the 1980s in Ankleshwar, Gujarat for manufacturing alcohol-based intermediates. This manufacturing facility also included an ethanol distillery. It manufactured pentaerythritol, a product largely used by the paints industry, and other products like formaldehyde and hexamine. Over the years, KCI's Ankleshwar plant developed a process of recycling distillery effluent. The company's highly successful 'Waste to Wealth' programme at Ankleshwar, which includes extraction of water from distillery effluent, generation of power directly from biogas, and manufacture of bio-compost, is a case in point to the proactive approach of the company in waste management.

Kanoria Chemicals & Industries launched a greenfield project in Vishakhapatnam in 2011 to ensure its leadership position in formaldehydes, which it now proposes to develop as upstream products.

In 2011, KCI commissioned a greenfield formaldehyde and hexamine project at Vishakhapatnam, Andhra Pradesh. This increased the company's total formaldehyde manufacturing capacity to 1,80,000 TPA. The company now proposes to go upstream with formaldehyde-based products. While KCI divested its chlor alkali business in 2011, the company continues to enjoy a position of leadership in India for pentaerythritol, formaldehyde, and hexamine.

FUTURE STRATEGY

After nearly five decades of manufacturing different chemicals, KCI looks to expand its product portfolio to include value added fine and speciality chemicals. An R&D centre has been set up at Ankleshwar to develop new products and processes, and the company expects to realize incremental gains over the next few years. In line with the driving force of sustainable development, it has made a foray into renewable energy sector by setting up a grid interactive solar energy project near Jodhpur, Rajasthan, with an initial generation capacity of 5 MW.

An important component of the company's diversification plans is a focus on knowledge-based, high-value sectors. The company recently acquired APAG Holding AG, Switzerland, engaged in the development and sale of electronic and mechatronic modules and control devices for the automotive, consumer goods, power tool electronics, and building automation industries. APAG Holding's designing and engineering facility is located in Switzerland, while the manufacturing facility is in the Czech Republic. The company is in the process of setting up a greenfield textile manufacturing unit in Ethiopia. It believes that future economic growth would be driven by Africa and intends to create a foothold for future expansions.

A focus on sustainable business processes of the company is reflected in its record of profitability since its inception. It has concentrated on manufacturing technology and of finetuning to achieve low costs of production through effective integration of products and processes.

The company has strong corporate governance and social responsibility practices that have been widely recognized and have won it several awards, including the TERI award for corporate excellence in environment management.

The oil refining industry supplies feedstock to a complex **PETROCHEMICAL** industry. Most of them are made from naphtha or related lighter fractions. Heavy fractions are also cracked to provide lighter fractions. They yield intermediates such as ethylene, benzene, zylene, and propylene. These are then processed into more specialized inputs such as MEG, PAN, and LAB. From these emerge several streams of products—fibres and yarns such as nylon and polyester, polymers such as PVC and PET, and nitrogenous fertilizers such as urea and synthetic rubber. The number of manufacturers of these products is very large; their major feedstock suppliers are Indian Petrochemicals and Gas Authority of India in the public sector, and Reliance and NOCIL in the private sector. NOCIL is also the leading manufacturer of synthetic rubber.

Colouring agents and dyes (used as printing inks) are being promoted by both Indian and international companies and have usage that ranges across various industries.

TOP, *left*: ICI Dulux paints.

TOP, *right*: A printing press that uses micro inks for printing.

MIDDLE: The magazine industry is a beneficiary, and user, of micro ink printing.

BOTTOM: An expert checks the colour and ink resolutions in a printing press.

Colouring agents can be divided into **DYES, PAINTS, AND PRINTING INKS**. The leading dye manufacturers are Clarian, IDI, Mardia, and ColourChem, a subsidiary of Hoechst. Among paint manufacturers, Goodlass Nerolac, Asian Paints, ICI, Courtaulds, Jensen & Nicolson, and Berger Paints are important. Micro Inks, DIC, and Sakata are the leading printing Ink manufacturers. MicroInks, part of the hubergroup, Germany, is acknowledged as one of the leading printing ink manufacturers and is equipped with the know-how to manufacture and market printing varnishes, dampening solutions, additives, and printing auxiliaries. Its plant is located in Vapi, Gujarat.

BELOW: Set up in 1968, Lupin Industries is among the better-known and successful Indian pharma companies that has made acquisitions in overseas markets. It has been promoted by Desh Bandhu Gupta (*left in the picture below*); a formulations manufacturing facility at Lupin Research Park, Pune (*right*).

BOTTOM, *left*: Dr Reddy's Laboratories in Hyderabad is among pharma companies that have an excellent track record in formulations and manufacturing.
Right: President Barack Obama met Ajay Piramal of Piramal Healthcare during his Indian trip in 2010. The company has since divested its domestic formulation business to Abbott for $3.2 billion.

FACING PAGE: Dr K. Anji Reddy of Reddy's Laboratories, which is the second-largest pharma company in the country.

The **PHARMACEUTICALS** industry has experienced rapid and eventful development after 1970. The standard pattern in pharmaceuticals is that firms invent new drugs, patent them, and then enjoy a monopoly for the life of the patent. During its life, they try to make the maximum profits. Patent descriptions are public documents; although patentors try to make them obscure and unspecific, others can follow the documents and produce copies of the patented drugs. That would be illegal while the patent lasts. But once it expires, anyone can produce the drug. Countries legislate monopoly of use to patentors during the patent's life.

At the time of Independence, most drugs were imported, chiefly by multinational firms that held their patents. Hence, drugs were expensive. When the Indian government was trying in the 1960s to promote import substitution, some Indian firms were prepared to produce import substitutes. But they faced the threat of litigation from foreign companies holding patents for the imported products. Some were sued by foreign companies in Indian courts, which generally followed the patent law and mostly ruled in favour of the patentors.

Keen to replace imports of patented drugs with cheaper domestic substitutes, the government abolished product patents in the food and chemical industries in 1970. That led to the proliferation of product breaking in the next two decades; thousands of small firms emerged which read foreign patents and followed them to produce pharmaceuticals, which they sold. Their costs were low, and were driven down further by competition among them. The abolition of patents protected them only in India; if they tried to export their products, the patent holders could sue them abroad. But once they got into the process of following patent descriptions, they could also produce generics, that is, drugs whose patents had expired. In this way, a highly competitive pharmaceutical industry took root; it also built up sizeable exports of generics, and of patented drugs, to developing countries with weak patent protection. After all pressure failed, industrial countries which were home to drug multinationals offered India a bargain in the course of the Uruguay round of trade negotiations. They offered to dismantle import restrictions on textile imports from developing countries, and to extend the offer to India if it reintroduced product patents in food and pharmaceuticals. Threatened with the loss of textile markets to other developing countries, India accepted the offer, and tardily reintroduced product patents in 2005. The patent office received thousands of patent applications from foreign firms, and has been processing them extremely slowly. Meanwhile, the reintroduction continues to have reverberations in the industry; it will be some years before the transformation works out.

But a number of trends are discernible. Some Indian firms sold majority or minority stakes to multinationals. Some started to do contract research for them. Some confined themselves to formulations. Some turned to generics. All became more aware of the need to own intellectual property; 35 per cent of drug master files and 25 per cent of abbreviated new drug applications filed globally come from Indian firms. As of 2007–8, Ranbaxy was the largest pharmaceutical producer in India; it exported 80 per cent of its output, and had subsidiaries in 13 countries and plants in eight. It lost a number of cases in the US; that proved expensive, and the Singh family sold the company to Daiichi Sankyo. Dr Reddy's was the second-largest pharma company by revenues after Ranbaxy. Cipla, the third-biggest, exported a large proportion of its output, but avoided buying plants, setting up subsidiaries or building up sales networks abroad. Ranbaxy, Cadila, Piramal, and Sun were the largest firms in formulations. The market share of foreign firms was 20 per cent; the leading ones were GlaxoSmithKline, Pfizer, Abbott, Sanofi-Aventis, and Novartis. Ranbaxy, Dr Reddy's Laboratories (over 80 per cent), and Cipla were the largest exporters with export ratios well over 50 per cent. The R&D-to-sales ratio was over 25 per cent for Suven Lifesciences; for most of the large firms, it was over 8 per cent. For Dr Reddy's the R&D was 6 per cent of sales in Fiscal Year 2012. The high profits of the industry and its investments in future inventions and markets are good signs for its future.

A VISION FOR EXCELLENCE

THE APEEJAY STYA GROUP has played a pioneering role in building businesses, but is focused on creating wealth through knowledge

A young Stya Paul (*right*) examining a part of steel making machine.

Tu shaheen hai parwaz hai kaam tera,
tere saamne aasman aur bhi hain
(You are a falcon. Soaring high is your nature.
There are skies yet for you to conquer.)
—Iqbal

The soaring falcon of poet-philosopher Iqbal aptly captures the life and work of Dr Stya Paul, eminent industrialist, educationist, philanthropist, and freedom fighter, who provided the foundation and inspiration for the emergence of the Apeejay Group and Apeejay Education Society as symbols of excellence in India's industrial and educational landscape. A pioneering entrepreneur with a deep commitment to nation-building and self-reliance, Dr Paul was a leading architect of the country's rise as an industrial superpower.

'Mighty oaks from little acorns grow'—a statement so true of the Group that started in 1923 as a small manufacturing factory in Jalandhar (run by Stya Paul's father Payare Lal). In spite of being struck with polio in early childhood, but fired by the zeal to contribute to India's freedom struggle, young Stya was imprisoned by the British during the Quit India Movement. A university gold-medalist, he had to cope with the early loss of his parents, shouldering the twin responsibilities of bringing up his six siblings and consolidating the family business. The post-Independence era saw a massive demand for steel to expand India's railway network. Capitalizing on this opportunity, Dr Paul began to import steel to meet this demand.

In 1951–2, land was acquired from the Calcutta Port Trust for a warehouse, and steel rolling mills were set up in Jalandhar, Calcutta, Bombay, and Vizag. Apeejay's steel-making units in Calcutta and Jalandhar were technical pioneers in steel casting. Before long, Apeejay had a number of divisions engaged in steel-making and related products such as valves and water-fittings.

In 1958, Rolling Mills of Hindustan was established for the import of mining and allied machinery for collieries and other mines. A grey iron foundry and steel foundry were added, and steel units set up at Durgapur and Calcutta in 1961. In 1962, Steelcrete, a company that manufactured tetrapods, was purchased, and in 1967, the manufacture of centrifugal pumps started. Apeejay Structurals, set up at Rajbandh, manufactured heavy structural and gas cylinders and tubes for export. As the business grew, Dr Paul ventured into newer business verticals such as pharmaceuticals, shipping, real-estate, and hospitality, in addition to entering into alliances and collaborations around the world.

Dr Stya Paul set goals to support and strengthen his only child, his daughter Sushma Berlia, and ventured into new businesses. Production of pharmaceuticals began through Martin & Harris (a flagship company in the pharmaceutical sector), and marketing through Walter Bushnell, which introduced several unique research products in India. State-of-the-art factories were established along with R&D units dedicated to the development of new products and formulations. In 2004, the Group acquired and expanded a world-class bulk-drugs facility in Kolkata to pursue backward integration of API and intermediates in the steroids and hormones segments.

Dr Stya Paul was among the foremost industrialists to integrate corporate social responsibility in the running of an enterprise. He wanted to set up educational institutions to promote a system of integral and inclusive education, and so set up the first Apeejay school in Jalandhar in 1968. In order to preserve, promote, and inculcate an appreciation of Indian culture, arts, and heritage, he set up the Rajeshwari Kala Sangam and the Apeejay College of Fine Arts in Jalandhar in 1974. Today, the Apeejay Education Society provides quality education from the pre-primary to the doctorate level through 29 not-for-profit institutions and the Apeejay Stya University, India's first liberal arts and meta university.

A true *karmayogi*, Dr Stya Paul retained his zeal for hard work right up to his passing away in June 2010. Sushma Berlia—renowned entrepreneur, educationist, and the first-ever woman to head a multi-state apex chamber of commerce in India—who had

Dr and Mrs Stya Paul with their daughter Sushma Berlia, son-in-law Vijay Berlia, and grandchildren Nishant, Neha, and Aditya Berlia.

taken over the reins during his lifetime, carries forward his legacy at the Apeejay Stya Group, together with her husband, Vijay Berlia (a pioneering industrialist in the chemical industry and chairman of the Svran Group). They have now been joined by their sons Nishant Berlia and Aditya Berlia, and daughter Neha Berlia. Educated in the world's leading universities and steeped in the best Indian traditions and values, this next generation of business entrepreneurs has introduced innovative processes and systems based on the best international business practices.

Today, the Apeejay Stya Group is among the leading corporate houses of the country, with several global alliances and collaborations as part of the Svran Group. It is active in business verticals such as chemicals and plastics, pharmaceuticals and life sciences, real-estate development, international trading, logistics and retail, information technology, financial investments and services, and publishing, apart from its large social commitment in education. Dr Stya Paul's ideals remain a constant inspiring force as the Group continues to take new strides in adapting to the challenges of a globalized world and carries forth the vision of a strong and prosperous nation.

The **ELECTRIC POWER** industry in India goes back to 1895, when Indian Electric Company was floated in London. It built a 139 KW hydroelectric power station in Sindrapong in Darjeeling district. Calcutta Electric Supply Company was set up in 1903 to supply electricity to Calcutta. Tata Hydroelectric Power Supply Company built a dam in Khopoli in 1915 to supply electricity to Bombay and Poona. Both CESC and Tata Power continue to be in business. They set the pattern up to Independence, where private companies were set up to supply power to particular cities. With the exception of CESC and Tata Power, all others were nationalized in 1949, and the power industry was taken over by state governments.

As time went, four things happened. First, the state electricity boards started price discrimination in favour of farmers and domestic consumers, and raised industry tariffs. Second, they kept prices down, and began to make losses. Third, the loss-making boards could not invest enough to meet the demand for power, and instituted frequent and unpredictable power cuts. Finally, industry could no longer depend on the state electricity boards for power supply, and began to generate captive power after the 1970s. This has led to the growth of a number of industries to produce furnaces, generators, control instruments, et cetera.

ABOVE: The Tatas founded the Hydroelectric Power Supply Company in 1911 to supply electricity to Bombay. It continues to service the city's needs till date.

FACING PAGE, *above*: Captive power generation by industries was necessitated because of acute demand shortage and frequent power cuts. Tata transmission towers at its thermal power station. *Below*: Aerial view of Jindal Power Limited, Raigarh, promoted by Jindal Steel & Power Limited (JSPL).

Reliance Infra's thermal power station at Dahanu Power Plant is one of its five such facilities spread across Maharashtra, Andhra Pradesh, Kerala, Karnataka, and Goa.

BEYOND PROFIT

In the heart of Odisha, INDIAN METALS & FERRO ALLOYS LTD is making a difference to the community around it

Indian Metals & Ferro Alloys Ltd (IMFA) is the largest producer and exporter of value-added ferro chrome in India, and among the largest globally, with an installed furnace capacity of 187 MVA capable of producing 2,75,000 TPA. Founded in 1961 by Dr Bansidhar Panda, a technocrat who worked as a research scientist in the US, and late Mrs Ila Panda, IMFA today has evolved into a Rs 1,000 crore company. Its current managing director, Subhrakant Panda, is assisted by a team of professionals and an eminent board, managing a company that provides direct employment to 2,000 people.

GLOBAL PROGRESS, LOCAL TECHNOLOGY

IMFA is the first company in the Indian private sector to produce ferro silicon and silicon metal—that too using in-house technology. Today, the primary focus is on ferro chrome where it has attained formidable cost competitiveness through backward integration. Its own chrome ore mines, captive power plant, and, soon, captive thermal coal mean that the company straddles a significant portion of the value chain. Comprehensive multi-product and multi-location quality management certification along with environment management and occupational health and safety certification sets IMFA apart from its peers.

Three furnaces adding up to 82 MVA nestle in picturesque Therubali, in Odisha. Another three furnaces adding up to 105 MVA have been set up in Choudwar in the state, which also houses the captive power plant(s) of 138 MW with another 120 MW under construction. Choudwar is one of the largest ferro alloy complexes in India and is home to the 76:24 joint venture between IMFA and Korea's Posco to produce ferro chrome. The company operates captive chrome ore mines in Jajpur and Keonjhar districts of Odisha, most notably in Sukinda, which has the bulk of India's known reserves of chrome ore, and will soon start operating a captive coal block in Angul district.

Odisha's lush greenery is the setting for IMFA's ferro-alloy plants, such as this one at Therubali where it has three furnaces that, along with those at Choudwar, make it one of the largest centres for the production of ferro chrome.

The company's captive mines in Jajpur and Keonjhar districts are sophisticated and use the latest technologies for the safety of workers and the environment.

The company operates captive chrome ore mines in Jaipur and Keonjhar districts of Odisha. Its exports accounts for almost 80 per cent of its revenues. Amongst others, Posco, Nisshin Steel, and Jindal Stainless Steel are its main buyers.

Over the years, IMFA has emerged as a preferred supplier of ferro chrome to leading stainless steel producers like Posco, Nisshin Steel, and Jindal Stainless, besides large trading houses like Glencore and Marubeni. While exports currently account for 80 per cent of total revenues, the company is well placed to meet the projected increase in domestic demand for ferro chrome based on rising stainless steel consumption and production.

IN TOUCH WITH THE COMMUNITY

Education has been an area of focus with the IMFA-managed Chinmaya Vidyalaya in Therubali shaping the future of thousands of children in the tribal areas of south Odisha over the past 25 years. An Industrial Training Centre also provides vocational training, thereby empowering local youth in their quest for employment; another Industrial Training Centre along similar lines is now being planned at Sukinda. Health, livelihood, and water and sanitation projects are common to all sites.

In Angul district, where operations are about to commence under the aegis of Utkal Coal Ltd, various initiatives for the benefit of the local community have already been taken up in right earnest. The Ila Panda Gynaecology Ward in Angul District Hospital is synergistic with the group's intervention on child and maternal health and a successful public private partnership with National Rural Health Mission (NRHM) for the Janani Express programme (a transport service for pregnant women to the nearby community health centre) has seen the infant mortality rate and maternal mortality rates for the district come down significantly. IMFA has instituted the Sarala Award for Odia literature and Ekalabya Puraskar for budding Odia sportspeople—both of which are considered the highest awards in the state for these respective disciplines. Its Professor Ghanashyam Dash Scholarship for Higher Education has also been instituted to enable children of employees and those of economically weak families domiciled in Odisha to pursue education in engineering and medical streams. The Bansidhar and Ila Panda Foundation (BIPF) has been specially formed to take up sustainable initiatives in, particularly, healthcare and education.

The Chinmaya Vidyalaya in Therubali is representative of the access to education provided by IMFA's Bansidhar and Ila Panda Foundation to manage education and healthcare for the local community.

THIS PAGE and FACING PAGE:
(above) Hindalco's cost-efficient-aluminium and copper production processes (*left*) go into the making of a variety of products as well as usage in a range of associated industries, such as foil and glassware holders (*facing page*).

Another industry is the **NONFERROUS METALS** industry. Sixty years ago, power conductors and wires were mostly made of copper. Aluminium, which required electric power to make, was expensive. Over the next 30 years, power became cheaper, and the power efficiency of aluminium production increased. Consequently, the relative price of aluminium came down. Today, it is the primary raw material of conductors, and is produced on a much larger scale than copper.

The first **ALUMINIUM** smelter was set up in 1938 by Indian Aluminium Company with the help of Alcan; the next one to come up was the Hirakud smelter of Hindustan Aluminium in 1959. Then followed a period when the aluminium industry was reserved for the government. It set up a smelter through its Madras Aluminium Company near Mettur Dam in 1965. In the same year it set up Bharat Aluminium Company, which set up a smelter in Korba in 1974. In 1981, it created National Aluminium Company to set up a smelter in Angul, Orissa. It transferred controlling equity in MALCO and BALCO in 2001 to Vedanta Resources of London, which holds the equity through Sterlite Industries. Today, Hindustan Aluminium, the Aditya Birla metals' powerhouse, Hindalco, is among the world's most cost-efficent aluminium and copper producers; Hindalco-Novelis is the world's largest rolling company and the global leader in beverage can recycling. Hindalco is also one of the three biggest producers of primary aluminium in Asia. Hindalco has built a copper smelter in Dahej through its subsidiary, Birla Copper, which is the world's largest single location smelter.

Sterlite acquired a majority stake in the government's Hindustan Zinc in 2003; Hindalco has built a copper smelter in Dahej through its subsidiary, Birla Copper. Hindustan Copper, which has four copper smelters across Jharkhand, Madhya Pradesh, Rajasthan, and Maharashtra, is the only nonferrous metal producer owned by the government.

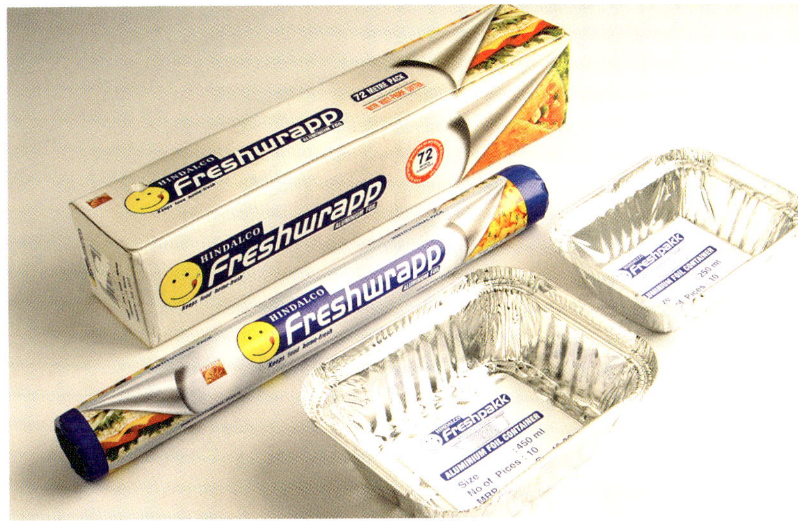

A vintage shot of Hindustan Motors' factory in Calcutta. Set up in technical collaboration with Morris Motors and Studebaker, the company's Ambassador car was, for decades, a symbol of Indian self-sufficiency as well as political power, but recent injections of technology have not been able to exorcise its heritage tag.

At the time of independence, the **AUTO INDUSTRY** was negligible. **MOTOR VEHICLES** were entirely imported. B.M. Birla registered Hindustan Motors in 1942, but it was 1957 before it began to assemble Morris Oxford under licence. Rechristened Hindustan, the car continues to be manufactured till now in small numbers, and even exported as a heritage car. HM's tractor and earthmover businesses were sold and are now absorbed into other companies. Premier Motors was set up by the Doshi family in 1939, and assembled some Dodge trucks and Plymouth cars under licence. After the War, it started making Fiat cars, starting with Fiat 500 and Fiat 1100. The venture was extremely successful till the 1990s, when new competition began to eat into Fiat's markets. Premier Motors started making Peugeot cars in 1999, but they were no more successful. Today, the company is defunct.

Tata Motors was registered in 1948 to make locomotives, but the government set up its own locomotive factory and gave no orders to Tata Engineering and Locomotive Company (TELCO). So it began to make Daimler trucks in 1954.

Maruti Suzuki vehicles ready for shipment at its factory in Gurgaon. The Indo-Japanese, public–private sector collaboration gave India its most popular car in 1983. Even though the market has since opened up to other, equally accepted automobile manufacturers, and the government has divested its share in the company, Maruti Suzuki retains 50 per cent of the country's auto market share.

In 1998, Tata Motors launched its first car, Indica. In 2004, it acquired Daewoo, the South Korean truck manufacturer. In 2006, it started making low-floor buses in a joint venture with Marcopolo of Brazil. In 2008, it acquired Jaguar Land Rover. But Tata Motors is now acknowledged around the world for its success in delivering on its promise of making the world's most affordable four-seater car, the Nano.

In 1955, Raghunandan Saran set up Ashok Motors to make Leyland buses under licence in Madras; soon, it had a virtual monopoly of the bus market. In 1987, it was taken over by the Hinduja group which acquired Land Rover Leyland International Holdings.

Maruti Udyog was set up by Sanjay Gandhi, the younger son of Prime Minister Indira Gandhi, in 1977. After he died in an air crash in 1980, the government took over the venture, formed a 50:50 joint venture with Suzuki Motors, and produced an extremely popular car, Maruti 800, in 1983. Along with current technology, Maruti Udyog empowered local industries to start making car parts, boosting the local industry which now supplies them to automobile manufacturers around the world. Suzuki took a controlling interest in the company in 2002, and bought the entire government equity in 2007. Being a government undertaking, Maruti Suzuki was overmanned; the management's efforts to reduce the workforce and labour costs have led to industrial unrest from time to time. There are other labour issues too that need sorting out. But Maruti continues to be India's largest car manufacturer. Ford started assembling and servicing cars in India in 1926, but closed down in 1954 after import restrictions stifled its business. It set up a joint venture with Mahindra & Mahindra in 1995; in 1998, it took majority control. It exports almost half of its output of 20,000 cars.

FACING PAGE: Tata Motors' Nano, manufactured in India and launched in 2009, captured popular world attention for being the world's most affordable car.

KL 05 X 7726

LEFT: Mahindra & Mahindra's Anand Mahindra has taken the automobile company to great heights with recent launches (pictured here with the earlier Classic Jeep); the company has a technical collaboration with Ford for its tractors, and has also set its sights on the manufacture of small aircraft.

BOTTOM: The first Willys Jeep model produced in India by Mahindra & Mahindra in 1949.

FACING PAGE, *above*: A line-up of Jeeps ready for delivery.
Below: Mahindra & Mahindra's recent SUV, Mahindra Bolero.

Mahindra & Mahindra was set up in 1945 by two brothers, initially to make steel; soon it began to make Willys jeeps under licence. Today it is the leading manufacturer of utility vehicles, and the world's largest manufacturer of tractors, in which it has been setting up production and sales facilities all over the world. It also has a small presence in motorcycles. Korean car maker Hyundai Motors started production in 1998. It has concentrated on small cars, and is the second-largest manufacturer of cars in India, and exports 40 per cent of its production of 6,00,000 cars.

Closely linked to the auto sector is the **MOTORCYCLE INDUSTRY,** a cheaper mode of transport than the automobile for many Indians. A vehicle that can be recognized today as a bicycle was first made in the 1860s in Paris by Pierre Michet, a blacksmith; its back wheel was much bigger than the front one. He tried to fit a steam engine to it. Many others tried it too in the succeeding years, but no one was commercially successful. It was only after Gottlieb Daimler fitted an oil engine in 1885 to a bicycle that the motorcycle became viable. The first motorcycle of the kind we know today was invented by brothers Heinrich and Wilhelm Hildebrand in 1894 in Munich. They made a few hundred, but were not successful, and closed their factory in 1919. Royal Enfield was set up in England to make bicycles and tricycles in 1898. It failed a number of times in fitting engines to a bicycle, but finally managed to make a motorcycle in 1910. India was an importer of motorcycles. After Independence, the government wanted motorcycles for the armed forces. So it allowed a joint venture in which Madras Motors produced Royal Enfield Bullet motorcycles on licence. When Royal Enfield closed down in England, the Indian company bought the rights and began to export the antique motorcycle all over the world.

The four Munjal brothers migrated from Kamalia (now in Pakistan) to Amritsar in 1944; they began to sell bicycle parts. In 1956, they started manufacturing bicycles in Ludhiana. In 1984, they set up a motorcycle factory in collaboration with Honda. They bought back Honda's equity in the company in 2010. Today, Hero Motors is the largest Indian motorcycle manufacturer, followed by Bajaj Auto.

Bajaj traces itself back to Bachhraj Trading Corporation, a firm set up by Jamnalal Bajaj in 1945. In the 1950s, it was importing Vespa scooters from Piaggio. But as import restrictions intensified, it obtained a manufacturing license and started making the scooters under technical tie up with Piaggio in 1961. The foreign technology tie up could not be renewed in 1971 owing to the government's socialistic policy at that time, and the relationship with Piaggio ended. Bajaj Auto continued to manufacture and sell the scooters; Bajaj's engineers developed even new models of scooters. It became the world's largest manufacturer of scooters and three-wheelers; its exports have made Bajaj famous to such an extent that three-wheelers in some countries are called Bajaj. Bajaj's Discover bike is part of its series popular with city commuters. Another successful model is its Pulsar bike.

The Royal Enfield has had a long run in the country and is still coveted by aficionados even in the face of sports bikes now available in India.

LEFT: Bajaj popular model, Pulsar.

FAR LEFT: Bajaj scooters ready for dispatch; the company that was set up in 1945 went on to become one of India's largest manufacturer of scooters.

FACING PAGE, *right*: Jamnalal Bajaj with Sardar Vallabhai Patel and Mahadev Desai at Wardha, Gujarat. Despite the early promise of a symbiotic relationship between the country's entrepreneurs and leaders, the government's orthodox socialistic concerns after Independence failed to capitalize on it. *Left*: Brijmohan Lall Munjal (Chairman), Hero Motors with his son, Pawan Munjal (MD & CEO) which is the largest Indian motorcycle manufacturer.

Turbine plant, Bharat Heavy Engineering Limited. The public sector company involved itself with core industries to build a strong foundation for industrial development.

Before Independence, there were workshops to service imported machines , vehicles, and do repairs; but **ENGINEERING AS A MANUFACTURING INDUSTRY** emerged after Independence. The two largest engineering firms today are Bharat Heavy Engineering Limited (BHEL) and Larsen & Toubro. BHEL was set up in 1964 to make equipment for the nationalized electric power industry; it is responsible for almost two-thirds of the existing power generation capacity. Another government company that came up in the same period is Engineers India Limited. It was set up in 1965 to provide engineering consulting services to government refineries. It then diversified and has tried its hand at a very broad range of projects. But being under the ministry of petroleum, it continues to give priority to oil-and-gas-related projects. Lately, it has been active in offshore oil and gas projects.

Larsen & Toubro goes back to Henning Holck-Larsen and SOren Christian Toubro, two young Danes who came to India in 1938 and formed a partnership, primarily to import engineering equipment from Europe. But when the Second World War choked trade routes, the enterprising partners got down to making some of what they imported earlier. It was the first line in what was to become one of the most remarkable success stories of Indian industry. At first they started repairing ships and installing and servicing machinery. After the War ended in 1945, they took up a number of import agencies. In 1948, they took 55 acres of jungle land north of Bombay to build an engineering plant. More importantly, they established a tradition of taking on technological challenges and excelling in whatever they did. Although Toubro stepped down from chairmanship in 1978, and Larsen retired in 1983, the company continues to be a technological leader.

Coal gasifier, Larsen & Toubro. The myth of China being a country you could import from but not export to, was countered by L&T's export of sophisticated coal gasifiers to the Middle Kingdom.

BELOW: Sanjay Kirloskar, who heads the Kirloskar Group started in 1890 by his grandfather Lakshmanrao Kirloskar, manages its agriculture, water supply, power, and air-conditioning business.

FACING PAGE: Built by Larsen & Toubro for the Konkan Railways, one of Asia's highest viaducts represents the company's engineering capabilities that have been tested all the way from Jordan to Malaysia.

Over the years, L&T has been associated with several enterprises of national significance—the green revolution, the nuclear power programme, space research, and defence. It has also been able to export coal gasifiers to China and other sophisticated engineering equipment to the US, the UK, France, and Australia. In a completion of a grand circle, L&T now markets software services to Denmark—the very land from which its founders had sailed to India 75 years ago.

The Kirloskar group owes its origin to Lakshmanrao Kirloskar who started repairing bicycles in Belgaum in 1890, and later diversified into agricultural implements. His son Shantanurao set up a diesel engine factory in Poona in 1946 in collaboration with British Oil Engine Export. That business has today diversified into a number of companies in the fields of agriculture, water supply, power, and airconditioning, which is now headed by Sanjay.

Crompton Greaves specializes in transformers, which the Indian power systems require by the thousands. Crompton Parkinson Works and Greaves Cotton were set up in 1937 in Bombay as the workshop and the sales organization respectively of Crompton Parkinson, a British electrical equipment manufacturer. B.M. Thapar took them over in 1947, and merged them into Crompton Greaves. In the 1960s, it diversified from motors and consumer products and found an especially lucrative market in transformers, which the state electricity boards bought in thousands.

BHEL, L&T, Kirloskar, and Crompton and Greaves belong to an age of engineering specialization. The government's stress on import substitution led to the birth of a host of firms, many of which ceased to exist in the recession of the late 1960s. The industry has since grown and has thousands of firms today. But the larger ones are often extremely diversified; although they may be known after their foremost products, they also make machinery for themselves and for sale. In the last 20 years, a genre of engineering companies has come up which implements large infrastructure projects and combines engineering with construction and property development. With the exception of Gammon India, they did not exist till the 1990s because the government monopolized infrastructure building; after the reforms, this area was opened up to private enterprise. Gammon India goes back to J.C. Gammon, who laid the reinforced concrete foundations of the Gateway of India in Bombay in 1919. It specializes in large construction projects such as highways, railways, bridges, tunnels, and dams.

TOP: The Sardar Sarovar Dam on the Narmada in Gujarat had a controversial history with regard to, especially, the dislocation of villagers, but now supplies 1450 MW of power to the state. ABOVE, *left*: The Jaypee Group's Bela cement plant in Madhya Pradesh. Begun modestly in the 1970s, the company is associated with realty, highway, and hydroelectric projects which it has crowned with bringing the Formula One car race to the country. ABOVE, *right*: The Jaypee resort in Greater Noida, with a Six Senses spa, is part of the group's infrastructure in the area that includes an F-1 racetrack, an expressway, and townships.

Punj Lloyd's Sabah Sarawak gas pipeline project is typical of its reach in creating large infrastructure projects for, especially, oil and power companies in Malaysia, UAE and Kazakhstan, besides India.

Jaypee is typical of the **PERIPATETIC GROUPS** being referred to. Started by a civil engineer who started his career in the public works department of Uttar Pradesh in the 1970s, it took on construction contracts in Saddam Hussein's Iraq, which was extremely hospitable towards Indian enterprises. It then built a couple of hotels in Delhi. Next, it built a cement plant, and turned to hydroelectric projects. Recently, it has ventured into building highways and residential townships.

Punj Lloyd began with an oil pipeline project. The pipeline brought it work for constructing oil tanks, refineries, and power plants. It found work in oil-rich Indonesia; when Indonesia got into a crisis, Punj Lloyd went to other oil-rich countries—Malaysia, UAE, and Kazakhstan. Pipelines require insulation, so it bought Simon Carves. Simon Carves was set up by Henry Simon, a young German who migrated to Manchester in 1860 and developed steam-driven flour mills. On an educational tour of France in 1878, Simon was impressed by the technology of coke ovens developed by Francois Carves, patented it, and created Simon Carves to sell it. The firm has been doing projects in oil, gas, fertilizers, and petrochemicals for over a century, and is a treasure house of technology.

The Jaypee Group's recently launched Yamuna Expressway connects New Delhi via its Greater Noida suburb in Uttar Pradesh with Agra over a 165 km toll highway that is characteristic of the nature of infrastructure development that is linking habitations and creating new opportunities for related real estate.

YAMUNA EXPRESSWAY
AGRA 185 Km

HOME-GROWN CONSTRUCTION FIRM

The second-largest construction company in India, PUNJ LLOYD is concentrating on its international projects and the home market for fuelling growth

ABOVE: Atul Punj in a family group photograph (*standing, second from right*) with his parents S.N.P. and Indu Punj and siblings.

RIGHT: Chairman, Atul Punj poses for a formal picture. Atul has steered the growth of one of India's largest construction companies that began as a construction firm in 1988.

TOP: A bulk liquid blending and storage facility on the Jurong Island, Singapore.
ABOVE: Hydrocracker and hydrogen project, Haldia refinery, India.

Punj Lloyd is the second-largest construction company in India. In over a decade, its climb has been steep in spite of a turbulent beginning. The company started oil and gas operations as Punj Lloyd Engineering Private Limited in 1988, but changed its name to Punj Lloyd Private Limited the following year. By 1992, it had become a public limited company, and in 2006 a listed entity.

In the early 1990s, when Atul Punj took charge of the firm from his father S.N.P. Punj, it was just a small part of a large family business selling airconditioners, industrial insulation, and project services. It was not easy to start afresh with the burden of a strong business heritage, but in over two decades, Atul Punj has proved his mettle.

THE RISE AND RISE OF PUNJ LLOYD

Today, Punj Lloyd is a highly reputed company with over 50 subsidiaries across 21 countries. What began with the first overseas pipeline contract in Indonesia on a working loan from ICICI Bank, is now a $2.13 billion enterprise spread over the Middle East, the Caspian, the Asia-Pacific, Europe, Africa, and South Asia. In fact, the business is so diversified geographically that about 50 per cent of its turnover comes from the Middle East and only 20 per cent from the home market.

With expertise in EPC (Engineering Procurement Construction) contracts across oil and gas, power, and civic infrastructure sectors, the company has constructed mega projects for renowned government-owned oil companies throughout the world and for global oil and gas majors, as well as built airports, jetties, mass rapid transit and light rail transit systems, and hotels and resorts. Today, the Gurgaon-based group employs 30,889 employees worldwide from 37 countries.

In order to better integrate its core business, Punj Lloyd acquired Singapore-based Sembawang Engineers & Constructors in 2006, and, through it, the 125-year-old engineering firm, Simon Carves of UK. In the same year, a joint venture with KAEFER Isoliertechnik was formed for thermal insulation, refractory lining, fire proofing, and scaffoldings.

With its business spread across the world in 21 countries, Punj Lloyd has grown into a global entity with a diversified portfolio in oil and gas infrastructure.

Fuel systems, New Doha International Airport, Qatar.

Punj Lloyd Aviation picked up a 33 per cent stake in aviation service support firm Air Works India in 2007.

In 2007, the company incorporated Punj Lloyd Upstream to address the opportunities in the integrated drilling services market. Soon after, the company bagged a prestigious order for deploying two onshore rigs in the Gialo oilfield of the prolific Sirte Basin for Waha Oil Company, Libya.

Focusing on international projects has helped Punj Lloyd de-risk its business from the economic vagaries of a single geographical region.

GROWING PROJECTS AND COMPANIES

The company's infrastructure development subsidiary, Punj Lloyd Infrastructure, recently developed and commissioned a 5 MW solar power plant in Bap, Rajasthan, under the Jawaharlal Nehru National Solar Mission. Diversifying further, the company forayed into the defence sector in 2008. It has built capabilities and set-up a world-class facility in Malanpur near Gwalior for manufacturing, integration, and testing of defence and non-defence productions.

To meet the global demand for renewable sources of energy, the group established Punj Lloyd Delta Renewables to provide turnkey solutions across multiple sectors. In a short span, the company has won projects in on and off grid power generation, water, waste to energy, buildings, and infrastructure.

Strengthening its design and engineering prowess, Punj Lloyd formed an independent design arm called PL Engineering. The company has grown manifold to execute design projects for the oil and gas, infrastructure, power, automotive, and aerospace.

COMING HOME WITH PUNJ LLOYD

Besides creating infrastructure, Punj Lloyd has pioneered several initiatives for better and enriched living. One such instance is of Bhadohi in eastern Uttar Pradesh, where Punj Lloyd has adopted three villages: Baripur, Narepar, and Bankat. Efforts made in the field of social development can be gauged in the holistic development of the district. Besides addressing education among village children, Punj Lloyd worked for the creation of village infrastructure comprising a state-of-the-art hospital, mobile clinics, free medicines, and free ration.

The company believes in training and employing the local community as a skilled workforce. They have been sensitised to working close to archaeological sites. Back home, the group has focused on facets of development ranging from education, awareness, and control of HIV/AIDS to support for the underprivileged. Life Enrichment, the Group's programme for welfare of construction workers, was supported by International Finance Corporation of Washington as a holistic programme for migrant labourers.

FINE SUITINGS FROM
DIGJAM
it's who you are
absolutely
impressive

We have hitherto covered manufacturing industries; but after Independence, Indian entrepreneurs have spread far beyond industry. Their most spectacular success has been in **INFORMATION TECHNOLOGY**. In the early post-War years, computers were few and expensive, and their owners employed captive groups of software engineers. This industrial structure broke up after the invention of the personal computer. Innovations followed rapidly after the invention of the microprocessor in 1971; the construction of Apple 1 by Steve Jobs and Steve Wozniak in 1976 was a milestone. IBM introduced its first personal computer in 1981. After that, technology improved rapidly, costs came down, and the market for personal computers grew exponentially.

TOP: IBM revolutionized the personal computer market with this chunky version in 1981, changing the way people worked.

ABOVE: The rudimentary Apple 1 computer, created by recently deceased Steve Jobs, and Steve Wozniak, in 1971, was a far cry from its sleek computing machines that are market leaders in innovation (*right*).

ABOVE, *left*: K V Kamath, who headed ICICI Bank, is the first non-promoter chairman of Infosys, which revolutionized the IT business model in India, and is currently one of the country's largest IT companies.
Right: Azim Premji, one of India's richest tycoons and philanthropists, heads software firm Wipro, having got into the computer business in the 1980s.

BELOW, *left and right*: Wipro's Learning Centre, Bangalore. Though it occupies a part of the personal care segment, Wipro is largely associated with the IT and software businesses and counts major Fortune 500 companies among its clients.

It created an enormous demand for software. American manufacturers and developers ran short of programmers; some of them came and lured away programmers from government laboratories in India. Programmers were much cheaper in India, but they could not be used unless their work could be transmitted quickly to the US. The department of telecommunications prevented this for long, but finally allowed satellite transmission in 1987. That led to the emergence of a horde of firms employing young programmers and working for American software firms—mostly those on the American west coast. The time difference between the west coast and India was 10-and-a-half hours; programmers in Bangalore could work while their colleagues in the US slept. Today, information technology is India's biggest export industry. It began with a host of small firms. Quite a few were weeded out when the US software industry turned down in 2000. There are still many firms in the industry, but they are led by large firms such as Cognizant, Wipro, and Infosys.

airtel

RELIANCE
3G Tab
7" Screen
32 GB Expandable Memory
Dual Camera
Gtalk
Twitter
Facebook
Docs to Go
GPS
Wi Fi with Hotspot
Bluetooth
Up to 9 Hours Talktime
Live TV
Voice Calling
YouTube
Android 2.3

The growth in the **TELECOMMUNICATIONS** industry is even more recent. Telecommunications had been a government monopoly since they were first invented in the 19th century right until the early 1990s. Even today, BSNL has an 11 per cent market share. But experiments to introduce competition from private firms in the US and Europe in the 1980s were moderately successful; they led to similar initiatives in India in the early 1990s. Telecommunications are a network industry; no firm in them can do business unless the calls it generates can pass seamlessly to customers of other firms. Although the first licences to private firms were given in 1994, the department of telecommunications set interconnection charges impossibly high; that made private firms unviable.

It was finally forced to reduce its interconnection charges in 2001. That led to a very rapid spread of cellphones. According to the Telecom Regulatory Authority of India (TRAI), there were 951.34 million telephone subscribers on 31 March 2012; teledensity was 78.66 per cent. Teledensity was 35.6 per cent in villages and 169.55 per cent in towns—that is, there were 1.6 telephones for every man, woman, and child in cities. This may be a gross overestimate of telephone ownership, but it is clear that cellphone penetration is high; it is well known that telecom charges in India are among the lowest in the world. This is the consequence of the competition unleashed by the reforms. Seven telecom service providers have over 500 million subscribers: Airtel, Reliance, Vodafone, BSNL, Tata, Idea, and Aircel. Idea Cellular Ltd., an Aditya Birla Group company, has emerged as the third largest telecom services provider with a customer base of over 120 million subscribers. Idea holds the, distinction of having the largest proportion of rural subscribers (53.68 per cent) of its total subscribers. Idea's ratio of VLR (active) subscribers to reported subscribers is over 93 per cent, the highest in the sector and significantly higher than the industry average of 74 per cent. But with allegations of bribes paid and received in the 2G spectrum, several companies are seeing a certain volatility that might well change the market situation in the near future.

FACING PAGE, *far left*: Idea Cellular Ltd, an Aditya Birla Group company, has emerged as the third largest telecom services provider in the country with the largest proportion of rural subscribers.
Top, left: The telecom revolution provided upward mobility to millions of Indians, and there are seven telecom service providers, of whom Bharti Airtel has a major market share in India and is present in 20 countries across Asia and Africa. Chairman and managing director Sunil Mittal of Airtel (left in the picture) with CEO Sanjay Kapoor at the launch of its new brand identity.
Bottom, left: Reliance Communications' pan-Indian telecom company is among the top four in the world and has a customer base of 124 million subscribers across India, USA, Europe, the Middle-East, and the Asia Pacific region.

In the **AIRLINE/AVIATION** industry, state carrier Air India has done worse following the entry of competitors in 1993. Jet Airways and its cheap sister airline Jetlite had a market share of 24.8 per cent in October 2011. IndiGo came next with 19.6 per cent; Air India, Kingfisher, and SpiceJet had market shares between 16 and 17 per cent. Air India has been able to maintain its market share by building up capacity without caring about profits and by making large losses. Government subsidies to Air India have distorted competition in the airline industry, and this trend is likely to continue. The glitzy, Vijay Mallaya-promoted Kingfisher Airlines has been in trouble over losses, though recent policy decisions permitting international airlines from buying a 51 per cent stake in the business might avert its shutdown. A few Indian airlines are even considering selling a part of their stake to foreign airlines.

(*clockwise, from top left*) Jeh Wadia of GoAir airline, Dayandhi Maran of SpiceJet airline, Naresh Goyal of Jet Airways airline, and Rahul Bhatia of IndiGo airline.

The boost to civil aviation in the last two decades saw stiff competition being offered to state-owned Air India and the (now merged) Indian Airlines by private carriers. A surge in passenger traffic saw infrastructure improvements in terms of new airports in all major gateway cities, record orders for new aircrafts (*facing page:* Air India's latest acquistion, the Boeing Dreamliner), and increased bilateral route agreements. Despite high traffic loads, airlines are bleeding in India because of high airport and aviation fuel costs. However, recent policy decisions allowing FDI in aviation has brought some hope to the sector.

go
GoAir.in

SpiceJet

JET AIRWAYS

IndiGo

CONCLUSION

Indian enterprise has spread so far and attempted so much, especially in the past quarter century, that it is impossible to describe its performance adequately. There is much energy in Indian entrepreneurs; they will continue to rush forward in the coming years. One trend that is evident is internationalization. Indian businesses are outgrowing the Indian market and are venturing abroad. Their export ratios have been going up for the past two decades. But now they are also buying companies and setting up production facilities abroad. This is not so straightforward a process as domestic expansion: foreign markets, governments, and societies are unfamiliar, and Indian companies have to find out by trial and error what works abroad.

Another direction in which they are going international is in tapping sources of finance. Indian financial markets are not as well organized: banks are mostly government-owned and unenterprising, the capital market is shallow, and there is a large, opaque non-market financial sector which is not easy to tap. The poor state of financial markets at home leads Indian companies to London, New York, and Singapore, which have much more transparent, professional markets. This trend is likely to intensify.

However, this is not as easy as it sounds. The global economy has been shaken by episodes of instability since 2008. This difficult period began with the failure of banks and mortgage institutions in the US; the federal government had to pour considerable amounts of stimulus finance to rescue the economy. A different kind of crisis has engulfed the European Union. First, banks in Iceland and Ireland were saddled with bad debts and had to be bailed out by the governments of Scandinavian countries and Ireland respectively. Next, a number of governments became over-indebted. The reunification of Western Europe created a single capital market in which governments could borrow at low rates of interest.

Greece over-borrowed, and has been rescued a number of times by its richer neighbours. Worse, it is possible that Italy, Portugal, and Spain, who also have incurred unsustainable debt, will follow in Greece's footsteps. If their debts need refinancing, Germany, France and their banks will become ever more reluctant to refinance them. The possibility also remains that their capacity to refinance may fall short of requirements. Germany appears in a better position than France. If neither do, the consequences are unimaginable. Debt problems would be more manageable if the economies were growing; unfortunately, growth in southern Europe has virtually ceased. The Indian economy is in a healthier state. But Indian enterprises today are closely involved in the global economy and cannot hope entirely to escape international developments. So they will face turbulence which has no recent precedents, and will have to steer their way through it.

Finally, I have been struck by the complexity of organization of Indian groups. They are opaque and difficult to comprehened. Fifty years ago, industrial economist R.K. Hazari deconstructed the structure of Indian enterprise in a fairly comprehensive way. That would be impossible today, not just because business has grown so much, but also because unquoted companies have increased in importance, and cross-holdings have become more convoluted. Businessmen would no doubt know their organizations better than an outsider could. But many of the structures are so large and complex that I wonder how well their masters themselves know them. The Indian tradition of concentrating on the essentials—cash flows, debt stocks, and margins—no doubt continues and is helpful. But without transparent structures, things can sometimes go wrong—or be made to go wrong, as they were in the case of Satyam, for example. India Inc. needs to strengthen corporate governance and improve disclosure standards. Meanwhile, however, its story promises to be as exciting and unpredictable as its history.

A. VELLAYAN
MURUGAPPA GROUP
A.M. NAIK
LARSEN & TOUBRO
ANALJIT SINGH
MAX INDIA
ANAND BURMAN
DABUR INDIA
ANIL AGARWAL
VEDANTA RESOURCES
DEEPAK PAREKH
HDFC
DILIP S. SHANGHVI
SUN PHARMACEUTICALS
G.M. RAO
GMR GROUP
GAUTAM THAPAR
AVANTHA GROUP
GAUTAM S. ADANI
ADANI GROUP
K.P. SINGH
DLF LIMITED
K.K. MODI
MODI ENTERPRISES
KIRAN MAZUMDAR SHAW
BIOCON LTD
KUMAR MANGALAM BIRLA
THE ADITYA BIRLA GROUP
M.G. GEORGE MUTHOOT
THE MUTHOOT GROUP
P.R.S. OBEROI
THE OBEROI GROUP
PRATHAP C. REDDY
APOLLO HOSPITALS GROUP
RAMESH CHANDRA AGARWAL
DAINIK BHASKAR GROUP
RANA KAPOOR
YES BANK
RATAN TATA
TATA SONS
SUBHASH CHANDRA
ZEE GROUP
SURESH NEOTIA
AMBUJA CEMENT LTD
UDAY KOTAK
KOTAK MAHINDRA BANK
V.L. DUTT
THE KCP LTD
VENU SRINIVASAN
SUNDARAM CLYTON, TVS MOTOR COMPANY

GAME CHANGERS

SOME KEY PLAYERS WHO HAVE CHANGED THE WAY INDIA, INDIAN COMPANIES, AND FINANCIAL INSTITUTIONS DO BUSINESS, AND ARE PART OF INDIA'S EMERGING GLOBAL ECONOMIC PROFILE. MOST OTHERS CAN BE FOUND ELSEWHERE IN THE PAGES OF THIS VOLUME.

GREAT EASTERN ENERGY CORPORATION LIMITED

Coal Bed Methane: A viable solution to India's energy needs

The environmental, technical, and economic advantages of coal bed methane (CBM) have made it a global fuel of choice. India has the world's fourth-largest proven coal reserves and estimates suggest that there will be a 10 per cent increase per year in natural gas demand for the next five years. The opportunity remains for India to exploit unconventional energy sources, and particularly CBM, given its current reserves.

Great Eastern Energy Corporation Ltd (GEECL), listed on the London Stock Exchange, is the Indian pioneer in exploration, production, and distribution of CBM, holding two licences: the gas-producing Raniganj (South) block in West Bengal, with 2.35 TCF of original-gas-in-place (the result of upgrades of 466 per cent for 3P reserves since 2009 to 2012); and the Mannargudi Block. Five years ago GEECL announced that the company had commercialized CBM from its Raniganj (South) block. It was a giant step forward in harnessing a source of clean energy that was hitherto untapped in India. The Indian market is characterized by strong demand, driven by a large population and energy intensive industries. This demand, coupled with a limited local energy supply, has created a significant and growing market for natural gas. Given the absence of new domestic conventional oil and gas sources, CBM is now considered an alternative source for augmenting the country's energy resources.

Methane is the main energy source in natural gas, and CBM is simply methane found in coal beds. Many countries have been using it for years to meet their energy needs. The Raniganj (South) block find promised to drive several more such discoveries across India, and ultimately ease the country's energy burden. According to India's Directorate General of Hydrocarbons, the country is estimated to have around 4.6 trillion cu. m (162 trillion cu. ft) of CBM reserves. One trillion cubic feet of natural gas is enough to generate about 100 billion kWh of electricity or fuel 12 million natural-gas-fired vehicles for one year.

Great Eastern Energy sells its gas directly to various local industries such as steel and glass companies. It has invested in and built its own pipeline, a dedicated network of approximately 100 km which connects the area around the block through the industrialized belt to cater directly to the various industries it supplies. The main pipeline from Great Eastern's gas gathering station to its central gathering station in Asansol was completed in January 2009, with further pipeline completions from Asansol to Kulti and Asansol to Durgapur completed in April 2009 and October 2009 respectively. Metering systems have been installed at the plant and at customer premises to adjust for the pressure, and measure the quantity of gas being used. It is controlled by Great Eastern until the point of consumption, and there are no intermediaries involved.

The company has an aggressive drilling campaign, aiming to reach 300 wells by 2016–17, with which it expects to fully develop its producing block. The supply–demand dynamics in the Indian gas market are extremely attractive and are likely to remain so for the next 20 years. In a recent McKinsey report, Powering India: The Road to 2017, a statement concerning Indian power demand stipulates that in the next 10 years, this is likely to surpass 300 GW, and that meeting this demand will require a five- to ten-fold increase in capacity. As India will also need to reduce its dependence on imported fuels, the opportunity for CBM is clear and unlimited.

The entry of the middle class in the stock markets in the 1980's added to the stature of Mumbai as the country's financial capital. The unprecedented boom was nurtured by the Bombay Stock Exchange and saw the spread of incomes and wealth in India.

North Block and South Block, New Delhi, with the dome of Rashtrapati Bhawan in the background. The seat of policy and decision making, it is here that the heart of India's democratically-elected government beats loudest.

India Inc.
POLICY IMPACT ON BUSINESS (1947–2012)

3

T.C.A. SRINIVASA-RAGHAVAN

Leading industrialists gather at Kamla Retreat, 1955, in the Singhanias' family home in Kanpur, for a FICCI committee meeting. Those in the photograph include Shantilal Mangaldas, Padampat Singhania, B.M. Birla, Lakhimpat Singhania, Rai Bahadur G.M. Modi, and Tulsidass Kilachand.

In 1989, at a gathering of several of India's major industrialists, one of the leading lights, then in his early fifties, was asked whether he would be able to build a completely new company which could compete with the world's best companies.He thought for a while and then, very reluctantly, said no. 'My grandfather wouldn't have had any difficulty,' he said, 'and even my father would probably have pulled it off. But I am not so sure about myself.' Why, asked the listeners, who were obviously surprised by this candid admission of inadequacy. 'For the same reason that India doesn't win gold medals at the Olympics,' explained the industrialist plainly, 'It isn't that I don't know how. It's just that I don't have enough match practice.'

He could have been right. By the end of the 1980s, few Indian companies had the management capabilities, capital, and technology required to build a world-class company which could hold its own in the 1990s in the international marketplace. But in the two decades since then there has been a sea-change. The Indian private sector has come into its own. It has become the engine of India's extraordinary rise to global eminence.

TOP, *right*: On 1 January 1877, the day Queen Victoria was proclaimed Empress of India, Jamsetji Tata's Central India Spinning, Weaving and Manufacturing Company Limited was inaugurated. It was promptly dubbed 'Empress'.

RIGHT: A cement plant belonging to ACC Limited (formerly The Associated Cement Companies Limited) formed out of a unique merger of 10 companies in 1936. Known for many innovations, the company erected the country's first wholly indigenous cement plant in 1947.

FACING PAGE: G.D. Birla and Mahatma Gandhi enjoy a walk and a tête-à-tête. Indian industrialists could support the country's freedom struggle only covertly if they were not to be denied British support before Independence.

So what went wrong in the half century between 1950 and 2000? How did a country which could boast of a Ghanshyam Das Birla, a J.R.D. Tata, a Jamnalal Bajaj, and others, stop its entrepreneurs dead in their tracks? What happened to the famous 'animal spirits'?. To understand what happened during 1947 and 1991, it is necessary first to understand what happened in 1937 and 1944. Very briefly, in 1937, the socialist elements gained the upper hand in the Congress party. Mahatma Gandhi had serious doubts over the wisdom of this but gave in eventually in order to win other, more pressing battles. Then, in 1944 came the ill-advised Bombay Plan in which the leading industrialsts of the day endorsed the need for central planning. The reasons and the pressures under which they did so have never been satisfactorily explained. But ask for direct government participation they did. Little did they realize that this would eventually mean a near-total emasculation of private enterprise and a ghettoization of corporate India. Indeed, the private sector itself was said to have thrown in the towel. But there is no contemporaneous and convincing evidence of this, only vague impressions. Equally, it is easy to say with hindsight that it was wrong of the public sector to take the leading role. But the context was completely different. The more important question was whether the private sector did indeed express its inability to undertake the massive investments required. The state wanted to be the arbiter of national resources. This was not conducive to private investment. The private sector was virtually locked out by the industrial policy resolutions (IPRs) of 1948 and 1956, by when the private sector had well and truly been locked out. Just how effective this exclusion was comes out strongly in the experience of the three of the largest companies of the period, TISCO, Century Mills, and ACC.

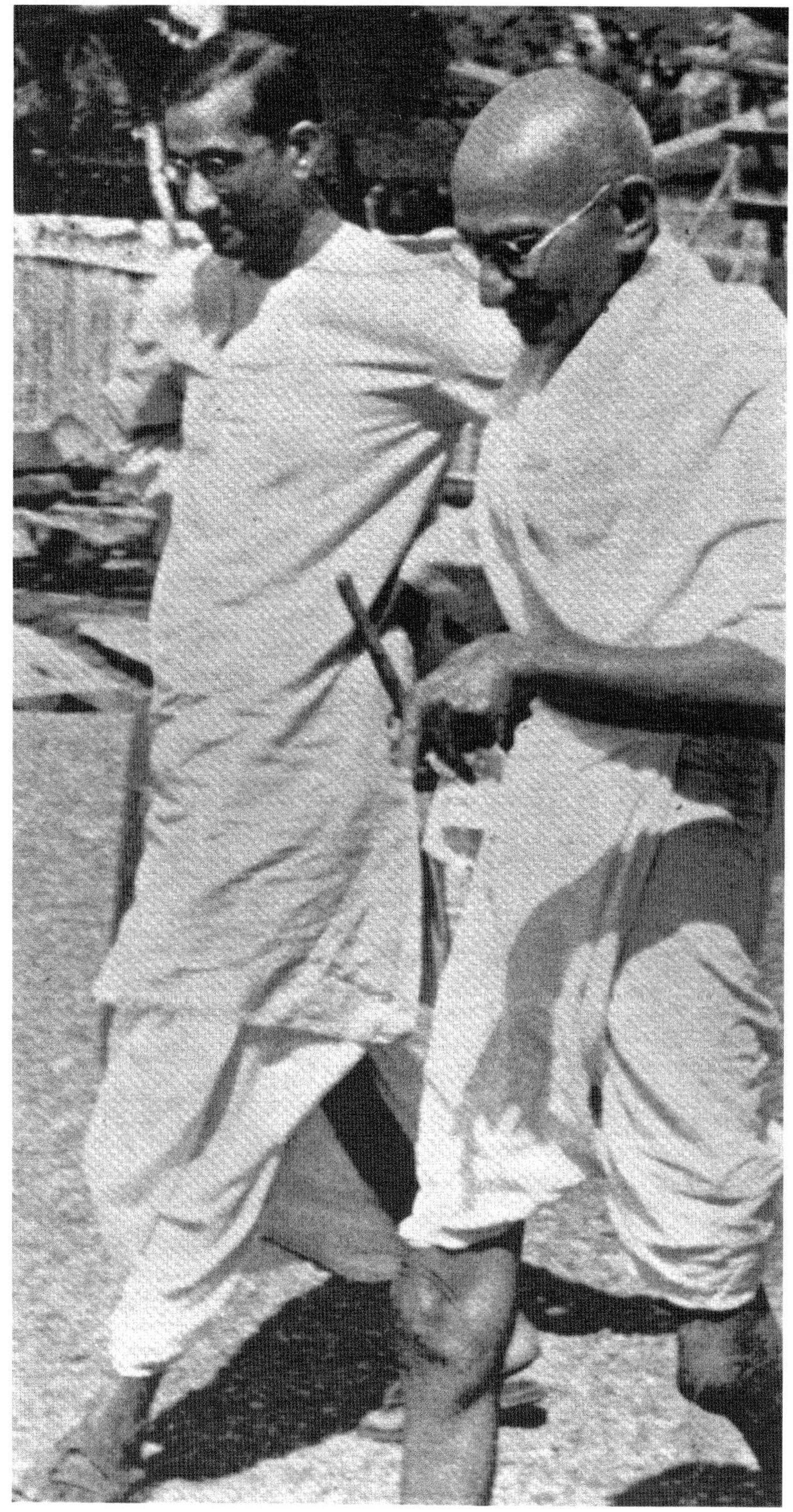

BELOW: J.R.D. Tata with Prime Minister Jawaharlal Nehru, with whom he enjoyed good relations even though he found himself unable to influence the latter's 'rigid' ideas regarding socialism; Nehru 'would freeze completely ... turn around and look outside the window' whenever Tata broached the subject of business.

FACING PAGE: Jawaharlal Nehru inspecting the Hirakud switchyard in 1957. The prime minister remained fascinated by and a great supporter of large infrastructure and development projects but wanted these to be retained in the public sector.

THE SCENT OF SOCIALISM

When the 1950s began, none of these companies took the IPR of 1948 seriously, which placed the onus of industrial investment on the state, and none would have believed that something like the IPR of 1956, which would further skew the investment climate in favour of the state, was only half a dozen years away. J.R.D. Tata and Prime Minister Jawaharlal Nehru were on friendly terms and Nehru would listen to Tata with attention. Likewise, G.D. Birla's views were taken seriously.

The evidence shows that the private sector was brimming with confidence and raring to go. Indeed, there was a massive increase in industrial output 'due largely' wrote George Rosen, the American economist who was active in India in that period, 'to the efforts of the private sector'. And, private sector investment accounted for just under 50 per cent of the total investment in the period, the highest level it has reached in independent India. And yet, things went wrong because, according to the eminent economist, Dr S.R. Sen, who was actively engaged in policymaking in those days, many of the private sector chieftains misued the trust the government reposed in them. 'Those of us who had to deal with economic policy matters had no experience of our own to fall back upon. Prior to independence higher economic policy was not dealt with in Delhi but

in London. Therefore [we] ... were virtually novices. We were only too conscious of our lack of practical experience. Some of us thought that since the business community had more intimate knowledge of economic affairs, we would profit by consulting them. But there were quite a few who would give us advice, get our reaction and then go out and speculate in the market. As a result many of us lost faith ... in these people and a rather adverse relationship developed between the senior government officers and some of the leading business people ... [that] took quite some time to get rectified.'

U.S.M.1576
N.R.

By 1954, it would seem that the initial trust between government and private industry had worn thin and when P.C. Mahalanobis, the chief planner, unveiled his grand strategy of capturing the 'commanding heights', the die was cast. If Mahalanobis' vision was to be realized, industrial licensing and price controls had to follow. It was inherent in the logic of the second five year plan, whose substance was announced by the Congress party at Avadi in 1956. The leading industrialists publically congratulated the government but privately they were dispirited.

If the IPR of 1956 defined the outer limits for the private sector, the policy of licensing and price controls provided the instruments of state control. It was an extraordinary regime which, because it conferred such overwhelming political legitimacy on the public sector, thought it only logical to deny any legitimacy at all to the private. Industrialization, to the politico-bureaucratic class, came to be seen as a zero-sum game. Despite the rhetoric about a mixed economy, it was generally accepted that the private sector could only grow at the expense of the public and, therefore, had to be curbed. The profit motive was seen as being incompatible with national priorities. Investment would have to come out of non-profit heads, like taxation or foreign aid, and these were available only to the government.

The national priorities were steel, power, and capital goods. All three were capital- and technology-intensive. And it was assumed, not entirely without reason perhaps, that the private sector would not invest in any of these. But no one wondered if its unwillingness to invest could be due to the regime of price and exchange controls and industrial licensing. Resources had not only to be found by the state, they also had to be directed. In practical terms, that meant pre-emption by the government and denial to the private sector. Whether it was equity or debt, government permission was needed. The denial was achieved not only by saying no to the private sector but also, more subtly, by introducing rigid price controls. No large company could raise prices without the permission of the government and permission was almost never given. The price of steel was not changed for nearly two decades.

FACING PAGE, far *left*: Accompanied by C.B. Gupta, chief minister of Uttar Pradesh, and industrialist Ghanshyam Das Birla, Jawaharlal Nehru surveys the Rihand hydro-electric power station after inaugurating it.
Left: The Durgapur steel plant of the Steel Authority of India Limited in Bengal was among the first to produce steel ingots when it became functional (*top, during the first phase of inception*) and is the only steel plant to make wheels for passenger trains at its well integrated modern facility (*oxygen plant, bottom*).

But there is also the widely-held view that there was no deliberate design to squeeze the private sector for the simple reason that the public sector's internal dynamics had not yet turned into vested economic and political interests, as they would later on. Public investment was still not very large in the 1960s and the trade unions were tiny. The political leadership had not yet seized control and the bureaucrats were all still idealistic in outlook. It was in many ways, romanticism, not realism and common sense, which drove policy.

Another set of factors was the extraordinary turbulence of the 1960s. Three wars, two major droughts, and one protracted political struggle brought on by Nehru's death, were all packed into an eventful seven years. The late D.P. Mishra, an important political player in the Congress, recalls in his memoirs that the political leadership was so preoccupied with just keeping things together that it did not have any time for economic policy. That, he suggests, was left to the bureaucracy with the broad direction to keep things under control. In some ways this culminated in the McCarthy-like atmosphere that painted some entrepreneurs/industrialists as licence-preempting, output-restricting, socially irresponsible organizations. The accusation against them was they had applied for, and obtained through political influence, scores of industrial licenses which they had no intention of implementing. The reason: to deny competitiors the chance to produce. The outcome: the Monopolies and Restrictive Trade Practices legislation which sought to prevent the emergence of giant business houses in the private sector.

By the end of the 1960s, the noose was drawn, and the sudden death of President Zakir Hussain in May 1969 pitchforked the power struggle within the Congress out into the open.

The ruling faction of the Congress party adopted an anti-private sector platform even though the private sector had done nothing to earn this wrath. Indeed, it had not been allowed to do anything. But so strong was the pull of the Congress socialists that the private sector became the convenient whipping boy. The result was statism in every form—from policy to direct participation. There was nothing the private sector could do without asking the government, not even raise the price of soap. The growth of companies became a major casualty because of production controls. Companies started investing in areas about which they knew nothing. Then everyone realized that it was a great thing to have the public sector entering an industry. Profits were guaranteed after that. The government followed cost-plus pricing, which meant a permanent advantage for the private sector which simply rode piggyback on the public sector's costs and made higher profits because it was more efficient.

But those instances were rare. Mostly, the private sector was simply excluded. By 1976, the public sector was even producing bread. And bicycles. Even condoms. It was six years of economic blitzkrieg by the state. The result, by 1976, was the creation of a system of complicated but wholly perverse signals and incentives. Ironically, instead of leading to a strong public sector and a weak private sector, it had exactly the opposite outcome.

A 765 sub-station of the National Thermal Power Corporation in Sipat, Chhattisgarh, has brought prosperity and literacy to the region with the commissioning of its super critical unit advanced technology.

The Ambani-promoted Reliance India refinery in Gujarat represents the private sector's ability to adapt and exhibit entrepreneurship that matches, if not exceeds, similar attempts around the globe. It is the largest refinery in the world.

BREAKING FREE

When a definitive corporate history of India's last quarter of the 20th century is written, one name will crop up with monotonic regularity—Reliance. Indeed, there are many who would even today claim that Reliance Industries Limited (RIL, or simply Reliance) represents a complete microcosm of India's private sector in the post-1975 period.

Reliance embodies three of the most important qualities which the Indian private sector possesses in abundance: entrepreneurship, the ability to adapt to the environment, and a never-say-die spirit. By 1976, a complex system of controls had come into existence. To navigate it, a firm needed not just patience but also contacts. During the Emergency and afterwards, it became the only way of doing business. After the defeat of Indira Gandhi in the general election of 1977, India started a very slow process of liberalization. The new government appointed the Dagli Committee as a first step towards dismantling controls on the one hand, but ejected Coke and IBM on the other.

How did corporate India react to the uncertainties of the period? Now that the word had gone out that the ancient regime would be dismantled, later if not sooner, what did it decide to do? Growth in the 1980s was possible only through diversification, so that is what it did. Thus began the process that would lead to firms moving away from their core businesses, a process that got reversed only with the dismantling of industrial licensing in 1991 and the subsequent opening up of India to foreign competition. Just as after 1991 there was a flurry of firms returning to their core competencies, in those days there was a flurry of them going away from it.

For the whole of the following decade, from 1980 to 1990, the political resistance had all but gone, and even though licensing controls remained, price controls had all but vanished. And even the licensing controls now worked in favour of the private sector. From about 1982 onwards, the government began to slowly give the private sector its head. The rigours of licensing were softened, ceilings on production removed, and the insistence on producing only what a firm had been licensed to produce dropped via the policy of broadbanding. Price controls, already under attack, began to be disamantled. The policies in respect of the capital market were also eased so that it became easier for firms to raise money directly from the public as equity rather than as debt from the development finance institutions.

FACING PAGE, *left:* Industrialist Bharat Ram of the DCM Group, a former president of FICCI, was the first Indian to be elected as head of the International Chambers of Commerce, Paris.
Right: Dhirubhai Ambani, promoter of the Reliance group, dared to dream big and created good shareholder value for people who invested in his project.

LEFT: H.P. Nanda, founder, Escorts, at the wheel of one of the company's tractors. The group was a pioneer in farm mechanization.

BELOW: Swraj Paul, chairman of the UK-based Caparo Group, seen here with his sons Ambar, Akash, and Angad, made a bid to acquire two Indian companies, Escorts and DCM, in the 1980s, a move that was swiftly thwarted by the government.

But change was slow. One thing which did not change was the obsession with size. This was partly because, by this time, the public sector had acquired its own dynamics and vested interests in the form of labour unions, ministerial corruption, and market dominance. It was also partly because there was still suspicion in the minds of the intellectual elite that the private sector was somehow irresponsible and venal.

The Monopolies and Restrictive Trade Practices (MRTP) Act thus remained on the books, which meant that it became impossible for firms to grow in their own areas of expertise. It would be another decade before the Act was dismantled. Hence came the huge wave of diversification, either via greenfield investments or through takeovers. ITC, which only knew how to make cigarettes, went into hotels and paper. The Mahindras toyed with the idea of going into aluminium and oil drilling. Decisions, which in other countries would have sent the stock plunging, were received with ovation by investors. This was also the time when a number of foreign firms were pulling out because of the insistence that foreigners hold only 40 per cent of the equity. That made for easy pickings in the market, without rancour or recrimination. Indeed, throughout the 1980s there was only one instance of an attempt at hostile takeover when a non-resident Indian businessman, Swraj Paul, launched a raid on two firms—DCM and Escorts. The raid would have succeeded but for the intervention of Prime Minister Rajiv Gandhi who announced on the floor of the House that there should be a ceiling of 5 per cent on the equity that a foreign investor could own in an Indian firm.

That virtually stopped the flow of foreign funds into the corporate sector. But it did result in increased confidence among Indian 'promoters'. The consequence was an unprecedented boom that began around the middle of 1984 and carried on, with some hitches, until 1995.

That was also the period when the wonders of marketing were brought home to the Indian corporates. The advent of colour television after the Asian Games in 1982 opened up the advertising market. Companies which until then had been content to sell without making the effort to market their produce, were now forced to build brand loyalties. At first, they piggy-backed on well-known foreign brands with whose proprietors they had collaborations. Then came purely Indian brands with deep market strengths. Many were owned MNCs like Hindustan Lever, but Indian brands like Godrej and Bajaj also ruled the roost.

FACING PAGE, *top*: Hindustan Unilever Limited's office in Andheri, Mumbai. The multinational which has been completely Indianized, is one of the strongest players in the country's FMCG market.
Below: A young Rahul Bajaj poses at a pavilion with his group's motorcycles. Prominently associated with two-wheelers, this group is a dominant global player in the segment.

RIGHT: Hindustan Lever's brands that are successful have been innovated in the Indian idiom for its domestic market.

BELOW: Adi Godrej with his company's array of fast-moving consumer goods. The company's business includes furniture, retail, and realty.

BELOW, *right*: Harsh Mariwala, CMD of Marico Ltd, has introduced a number of popular brands in the consumer space.

A variety of some of the top selling brands selling in the Indian market— Amul, Britannia Industries (Wadia Group), Dabur, Godrej, Hindustan UniLever (HUL), India Tobacco Company (ITC), Jubliant Bhartia Group, Marico, Nestle, and Procter and Gamble (P&G).

NEY
EED PURE
Meri Masala
Maggi
2-Minute noodles
100 Inspiring Years
AASHIRVAAD
WHOLE WHEAT ATTA
0% MAIDA 100% ATTA
Saffola
Arise
For a Healthy and Active Family
Basmati Gold
Surf excel
quickwash
100 Inspiring Years
Sunfeast
Dark Fantasy
Choco Fills
gentee
DEO-ACTI
POND'S
age miracle™
Cell ReGEN™ Day Cream
SPF 15
with Intelligent Pro-Cell Complex™
Dabur
gulabari
premium
OLAY
total effects
Amul
PASTEURISED
BUTTER
utterly butterly delicious
Gillette
SERIES
after shave
BRYLCREEM
PROTEINPLU
NutriChoice
Ragi
BRITANNIA
NutriChoice
Oats
Hajmola
Nimbu
kare khana complete

One other factor helped, namely, the policy of allowing imports of completely knocked down consumer durables. Together, these led to a huge boom for the private sector. Many new entrepreneurs emerged, such as the Dhoots, the Lohias, the Ruias, the Mittals, and so on.It also became easier for the private sector to enter commodity production such as cement, steel, polyester yarn, petrochemicals, and so on. Until the early mid-1980s, investment was usually financed by debt because it was cheap. But as the government's programme of fostering growth through deficit financing proceeded apace, it began to preempt an increasing portion of the available funds. This was done partly to finance its own needs and partly to offset the effect of excessive monetization on the price level.

Together, these factors ensured that interest rates would continue to rise throughout the 1980s. And as debt became expensive, firms increasingly turned to equity finance. They were helped by the fact that the government was keen on getting the small investor directly into the capital market—for which reason it kept equity prices artifically low via the office of the Controller of Capital Issues, abolished eventually only in 1993.

This, along with the fact that there were huge capital gains to be made during a bull phase, led the small investors to flock to the market in search for new issues.

Some of the newer entrepreneurs also decided to approach the public directly and thus the equity cult grew.The number of listed companies on the Bombay stock market more than doubled from under 2,000 in 1985 to over 4,500 in 1990. Today, there are over 30,000 listed companies. But all these Indian firms were working inside a system that pegged its maximum efficiency to the public sector norm and behind a high and thick wall of tariff protection. So, on the one hand, if a firm did only slightly better than a public sector competitior, it stood out; and on the other, because import duties started at 150 per cent—apart, that is, from the plethora of banned items—the average tariff was a shade over 250 per cent. There was thus no real compulsion towards cost efficiency. But in the 1990s when tariffs came down and competion started in real earnest, it all changed and raised some very serious questions about the future of Indian corporates.

FACING PAGE, *left:* Sunil Mittal has been able to capitalize the gains from India's economic liberalization to create the world's fourth-largest mobile telephone network (Airtel), and is poised for a breakthrough in the agriculture sector.
Middle: Shashi Ruia (*seated, right*) of Essar Group with his brother Ravi (*seated*), and sons Prashant and Anhsuman (*standing*). Essar Group, is an Indian MNC with presence in sectors such as steel, energy, power, shipping, ports, logistics, and construction.
Right: Promoter Venugopal Dhoot, with his son Saurabh, laid the foundations of the Videocon group, and is on Forbes' list of India's top twenty billionaires.

BELOW: Bombay Stock Exchange, Mumbai, is now woven into the fabric of global fortunes and trading.

The 1990s began inauspiciously. A minority government was in power. The prime minister was a realist but hamstrung by his political weaknessses. The finance minister was a socialist. And the fiscal was bust. Between January and June 1991, the fiscal excesses of the 1980s boiled over into a full-blown balance of payments crisis. By mid-June, India had only $1.1 billion dollars of reserves left and had to approach the IMF for support. It received a loan sanction of $5.6 billion—but on the condition that it would reform the economy. The government had no choice but to comply and thus, with the gun at its head, India reluctantly decided to cut the fiscal deficit, roll back tariffs, privatize the public sector, encourage foreign direct investment, dismantle industrial licencing, abolish price controls, and throw out the MRTP Act. Of this menu, the last three were designed to give the private sector the lead role in the industrializing and modernizing of India. Finally acknowledged as useful and necessary, the private sector was vindicated at long last.

The immediate consequence was a rush of investment, joint ventures, and strategic alliances. Throughout 1993, while Indian businessmen roamed the world looking for partners, foreign firms wandered about in India looking for Indian partners. The Indians were looking for capital and technology; the foreigners for established firms which would give them an entrée. The result was a spate of joint ventures and strategic alliances during 1994 and 1995. India had finally arrived on Wall Street's radar.

But there can be no pleasure without pain. The progressive lowering of tariffs and the entry of huge MNCs meant not just competition from cheaper imports but also competition from India-based production. Local producers were no match for the deep pockets of the MNCs. The harsh truth dawned on India Inc., especially the family-owned part of it: that freedom comes at a cost and that only the best would survive. The rest, under pressure to perform in a highly competitive arena, sold their stakes.

THE REFORMS AGENDA

The man who took over from Manmohan Singh after the Congress party was defeated was Palaniappan Chidambaram. A committed reformer, he had to work with 12 other parties, including the Communists. As such, he had even less elbow room than his predecessor. He brought down the maximum rate of income tax to 30 per cent, cut the corporation tax to 40 per cent, and reduced the average level of tariffs to just a shade over 25 per cent. The economy bounced up but the fiscal deficit remained stubbornly high at 8 per cent.

For a time it looked as if a new golden age was about to begin as businessmen stepped up their investment plans. But political uncertaintly soon reared up and by October 1999, India had seen three prime ministers, a war with Pakistan, and a nuclear test that put it in the international dog-house for a few years.

At the same time, the DotCom bubble was about to blow out in the West, which it did in 2000. The global growth rate shrank. Then came the 9/11 attacks and the global recession became worse. To get out of it, the developed countries began to cut their domestic interest rates. India held out for a while but soon it became clear that it could not be the odd one out. So, in 2002, the Reserve Bank of India also followed suit. Money became progressively cheaper over the next few years—and investment, which had pretty nearly dried up since 1998, revived. The combined effect of the 1997 tax cuts and the steady decline in interest rates on total investment was dramatic. From 30 per cent of GDP in 2002, it went up to almost 37 per cent in 2008. Of this, the private sector accounted for the lion's share, almost 70 per cent. The broadest objective of reforms—to let the private sector have its head—had been achived. Although still very difficult by international standards, doing business in India had become much easier. The industries that benefitted most were

ABOVE: A colllage of old currency notes consisting of the following: Rs 10,000 (first issued in 1938), Rs 5000 (issued in 1954), Rs 1000(1938), Rs100 (1944), Rs 10(1949), and Rs 2 (1943). While none of these series is currently in circulation, the highest denomination note issued by the Reserve Bank is for Rs 1000.

FACING PAGE: Entrance, Reserve Bank of India, New Delhi. The national bank monitors functions of the banking system minutely and steers the fine line between growth and inflation.

TOP: Founded by Dr M.A. Chidambaram, Southern Petrochemicals Industries Corporation (SPIC) Ltd, Chennai, has operations in fertilizers, oil, natural gas, power, pharmaceuticals, and agriculture. Today, SPIC is a fertilizer major with a dominating presence in South India.

BOTTOM: Infosys's offices in Bangalore and Mysore represent a global platform for its information technology businesses that have seen a chain of succession at the helm that mark it as a truly professional and best-practices company.

FACING PAGE: A view of one of the most modern Heavy Enginineering Manufacturing Facilities at Walchandnagar Industries. Pune-based Walchand Group began with sugar, but its diversified business portfoilio now includes defence, aerospace, nuclear and renewable power, and cement.

Hindustan Construction Company's Bandra–Worli sea link in Mumbai could well become the city's most photographed feature. The company, promoted by Ajit Gulabchand, is an infrastructure major that is developing a fully integrated township called Lavasa outside Pune, India.

ADVENTZ creates a group identity for a slew of companies engaged in transforming India

Few companies have had as diverse a history as the Adventz Group which had its genesis in 1939 when Texmaco was established. Begun from scratch by pioneering industrialist K.K. Birla, G.D. Birla's second son, to manufacture spinning machinery—a fact almost forgotten, since it (Texmaco Rail & Engineering Limited) is now better known as a manufacturer of one-fourth of all railway freight cars produced in India, manufactured on the outskirts of Kolkata. Soon enough, the company was making huge sluice gates for dams—some of the first made for the Bhakra Nangal project, and among the largest for other dams in the country.

HISTORY IN THE MAKING

Zuari, the Group's foray into chemical fertilizers was registered as a separate company in 1967 when the first Chief Minister of independent Goa, Dayanand Bandodkar, invited K.K. Birla to establish an industry in Goa. On a barren landscape of rocks, Zuari Agro Chemicals began production as Goa's largest industrial undertaking at the time. It has notched up several records along the way, achieving over 140 per cent capacity utilization at its ammonia plant in 1996, zero-effluent discharge—the first such in India's fertilizer industry in 1997–8 and its highest ever sales well over two million tonnes of fertilizers in 2011–12.

Zuari has also had several other firsts to its credit. For instance, US Steel Corporation, Pittsburg, became a joint-technical

TOP: An ecstatic farmer with his crop—a fertilized bounty. Zuari Agro Chemical Limited (which later became part of the Adventz group) has been manufacturing quality chemical fertilizers for well over four decades.

ABOVE: Soil Testing in progress at Zuari's state-of-the-art agronomic services laboratory at Tirupati in Andhra Pradesh.

FACING PAGE: A view of the Ammonia plant at Zuari Agro Chemicals Limited, Goa.

collaborator from inception, and construction was handled by Toyo Corporation, Japan, ushering in a multicultural environment from the start. One of the largest private sector fertilizer conglomerates in the Indian fertilizer sector, its products were initially marketed primarily in Maharashtra, Goa, and Karnataka, before expanding into most of peninsular India. Over time, Zuari grew into other agricultural-related business inputs, such as seeds, pesticides, and specialty fertilizers. From the 1990s, Zuari began to re-position itself to the next level, diversifying from a vanilla fertilizer producer to specialty fertilizers, sophisticated seeds, BT cotton, even financial services, engineering services, oil tanking, and emerging lifestyles.

Today, Zuari which launched Chambal Fertilizers and Chemicals Limited, India's largest private sector manufacturer of urea in the 1990s, has commissioned India's first joint venture collaboration with Israel in the manufacture of speciality fertilizers. In 2002, Zuari Industries collaborated with OCP Morocco to take over, Paradeep Phosphates Limited, a Government of India enterprise,the first such fertilizer venture to be privatized.

THE STORY OF ADVENTZ

Saroj Kumar Poddar, Chairman, Adventz Group.

The group was reorganized in 2011 by Chairman Saroj Kumar Poddar, who created the Adventz umbrella brand, under which each of the 23 group companies belonging to Zuari, Texmaco, and several other groups and including subsidiaries and joint ventures operating in key sectors of the Indian economy, maintain their independent identities, but in coherence with the parent entity.

In an interview to a financial daily, Saroj Poddar pointed out, 'All companies in my group have been working independently. I want them to work collectively, with a common logo, values, and finance. We would like to see that all key resources are integrated; hence, we will have integrated management, financial services, and human resources. This will certainly make the companies grow faster.'

As part of that scenario, Poddar outlined his plans as well as his vision—$2 billion to be invested over five years, in fertilizers to meet the capacity deficit through new installations as well as raw materials and finished fertilizer imports; in rail transportation through Texmaco to meet the demand for specialized wagons from the aluminium, steel, and automobile industries, and for the dedicated freight corridor; and in lifestyle areas, for real estate projects as well as the expanded manufacture of furniture and fittings. The benefits of being a single group were underlined by Saroj Poddar. 'By bringing the companies under a brand, we are not only creating a brand value, we are telling our associates and customers that we are here with certain commitment in terms of quality, business dealings, and ethics. We are going to produce products which meet certain quality parameters that the group is known for.' This, he explained, was necessary given the nature of investment—Rs200–300 crore in the last 20 years against $2 billion over the next five. 'We are willing to take a bigger step forward, and risk, to accelerate growth'.

A NATIONAL PORTFOLIO

With the responsibility, simultaneously, of nation-building as well as caring for its family of professionals, the Adventz group works closely with the community. 'We develop specifically formulated products and closely work with farmers educating them in scientific techniques for optimal results,' reads one report. 'Our commitment to the integrity and safety of our products is based on robust agricultural research and enriching partnerships with academia.' Pointing to its potential, Suresh Krishnan, managing director of Zuari Agro Chemicals Limited, says: 'Agriculture is poised to be the cornerstone for economic growth and social development in India. More than 30 per cent of Asia's irrigated land is in India. We have the highest proportion of arable land as compared to USA and China. However, this land is underutilized. Israel produces $5.8 million in agriculture output per sq. km of arable land, while India'—hold your breath—'just $88,000'. No wonder that 'with corporate involvement and the implementation of technology and modern methods of farming, farmers will be able to reap rewards'.

Besides fertilizers, seeds, and pesticides, Zuari has launched some path-breaking programmes such as *Jai Kisaan Sangam* for providing value-added services for farmers, Hello *Jai Kisaan* toll-free service to assist them, state-of-the-art soil testing and other agronomic services, an orchid project, as well as vermicomposting—thus delivering total farming solutions. Texmaco Rail and Engineering (as it it known post-Texmaco Limited's demerger), as India's largest private sector freight wagon builder and largest supplier of new-generation wagons, is also engaged in the manufacture of heavy steel structurals, hydro-mechanical equipment, and process equipment. It has a joint venture with UGL Rail Services, Australia, and a consortium and joint bidding agreement with Bombardier Inc.'s Indian company. Simon India Limited, a wholly-owned subsidiary of Zuari Global Limited, offers technical consultancy, project management, and contracting services to chemical, fertilizer, oil and gas, petrochemical, power, and other infrastructure projects, and has handled developments in the Middle East, specifically Saudi Arabia, besides India.

CHANGING LIFESTYLES

In keeping with emerging trends, the group now is addressing the needs of emerging lifestyles in specific categories. Adventz Infraworld concerns itself with developing world-class homes and office spaces, for which a 73.5 acre residential-cum-commercial project in Mysore is currently underway, the first of many others to come up all over the country. Indian Furniture Products Limited has the distinction of being the largest RTA furniture manufacturer in India and manufactures well over 2,00,000 units annually at its ready-to-assemble plant near Chennai. A part of this production is also exported to France, Germany, UK, and Belgium. The Adventz furniture group also includes two brands: Hettich India, a joint venture with the Hettich Group, Germany, and Style Spa Furniture Limited, with its own chain of 105 furniture stores in 65 cities constituting India's largest furniture retail chain.

A lesser-known but no less significant part of the Adventz group is its investment and financial services, insurance brokerage, trading house services in Dubai, and management services.

LOOKING AHEAD

'We will seek to leverage the power of the group's diversity in terms of knowledge, best practices, and technological excellence to effect genuine and exponential progress in the sectors that we operate in,' Chairman Saroj Poddar said in his message to shareholders

TOP: Hettich fittings on display—a kitchen rhapsody.

ABOVE: StyleSpa bedroom furniture.

RIGHT: Hettich fittings in the kitchen.

FACING PAGE, *left*: The ultra-modern Kunkel-Wagner Line at Texmaco's Foundry in Kolkata.
Right: A view of the 'Zuari Garden City' in Mysore.

Acid storage tanks at the Paradeep Phosphates plant (PPL), Orissa.

in 2011, 'not only to positively impact India's development and progress but also to emerge as a vibrant, global brand.' Brand Adventz, he emphasized, was based on four fundamental principles: collaboration, sustainability, inclusiveness, and being global. 'Not only does it represent the carrying together of many well-respected companies under a unified banner, but also seeks to harness and harmonize their vast reservoir of human talent, technological know-how, and other resources in a collaborative, inclusive, and sustainable manner, so as to drive India's development and progress.'

As the group represents the fundamental drivers of the Indian economy—fertilizers, heavy industry, lifestyle products, real estate, and financial services—it is expected to positively impact growth sectors. But a company is only as good as the larger community in which it operates. Recognizing this, the Adventz Group has reached out to local communities with its welfare activities that create long lasting solutions through livelihood, education, and training projects. Farmers' lives have been impacted with its family as well as animal health camps, an emphasis on public utilities such as bus shelters in rural areas, drinking water, tanks, sanitary facilities, school playgrounds, maintaining parks, and tree plantations across highways. It has implemented specialized farmer training programmes, as well as watershed development projects in a drought-prone region in Maharashtra and has extended scholarships to students in the fields of agriculture and engineering. Its *Prerna* project aims at imparting life-skills such as stitching, sewing, needlework, toy-making, courses in interiors, beauty, performing arts, elocution, and computer studies for underprivileged girl-children. 'India is set to emerge as an economic juggernaut in the 21st century,' Chairman Saroj Kumar Poddar has promised. 'We are confident that our group, under the Adventz banner, will play a key role in this transformation.'

The Aditya Birla Group: A Premium Global Corporation

A US $40 billion corporation, the Aditya Birla Group is in the League of Fortune 500. It is anchored by an extraordinary force of over 133,000 employees, belonging to 42 nationalities. The Aditya Birla Group has been ranked 4th in the world and 1st in Asia Pacific in the 'Top Companies for Leaders' study 2011, conducted by Aon Hewitt, Fortune Magazine and RBL (a strategic HR and leadership Advisory firm).

Over 53 per cent of the Group's revenues flow from its overseas operations. It operates in 36 countries.

Globally, the Aditya Birla Group is:

- A metals powerhouse, among the world's most cost-efficient aluminium and copper producers. Hindalco-Novelis is the largest aluminium rolling company. It is one of the 3 biggest producers of primary aluminium in Asia, with the largest single location copper smelter
- No.1 in viscose staple fibre
- No.1 in carbon black
- The 4th largest producer of insulators
- The 5th largest producer of acrylic fibre
- Among the top 10 cement producers globally
- Among the best energy efficient fertilizer plants
- The largest Indian MNC with manufacturing operations in the USA

In India:

- A top fashion (branded apparel) and lifestyle player
- The 2nd largest player in viscose filament yarn
- The largest in the chlor-alkali sector
- Among the top 3 mobile telephony companies
- A leading player in life insurance and asset management
- Among the top 2 super-market chains in the retail business
- Among the top 10 BPO companies

Beyond business

- Reaches out to 7 million people in 3,000 villages annually in India through the Aditya Birla Centre for Community Initiatives and Rural Development, spearheaded by Mrs. Rajashree Birla
- Focuses on: health-care, education, sustainable livelihood, infrastructure and espousing social reform
- Runs 42 schools which provide quality education to 45,000 children. Of these, over 18,000 children receive free education
- Its 18 hospitals tend to more than a million villagers
- Ongoing education, healthcare and sustainable livelihood projects in Philippines, Thailand, Laos, Indonesia, Egypt, Korea and Brazil
- Set up the Aditya Birla India Centre at the London Business School

Transcending the conventional barriers of business because we believe it is our duty to facilitate inclusive growth.

ADITYA BIRLA GROUP

Taking India to the World

www.adityabirla.com

Gate at JPL Plant, Tamnar in Chhattisgarh.

FAR LEFT: Oxygen plant, Steel Authority of India Limited, Bhilai. SAIL, one of India's public sector success stories, had dominated the country's steel industry before private sector players were permitted on the back of the economic reforms.

LEFT: Sajjan Jindal's JSW Steel has caught up with SAIL on the basis of foreign tie-ups and incorporation of newer technologies.

BOTTOM: JSW's Vijayanagar works in Karnataka; the steel major has acquired a steel plant in USA.

The Indian steel sector witnessed the entry of private players such as the Jindals and the Essar Group in the post-reforms era. Until then, the public sector Steel Authority of India Ltd (SAIL) and the country's oldest steel maker, Tata Steel, dominated the steel industry. Driven by the demand from sectors such as infrastructure, construction, automobile, and consumer durables, private players have scaled their operations and continue to add capacities. The Sajjan Jindal-led JSW Steel, through its aggressive growth strategy, foreign tie-ups, and adoption of newer technologies such as corex, has caught up with the country's largest producer, SAIL, in terms of capacity. An aggressive greenfield expansion coupled with the acquisition of ISPAT Industries Ltd has helped JSW Steel grow its capacity by over 10 times in the past nine years to 14.3 million tonnes per annum (MTPA) from 1.25 MTPA in 2003–4. Incorporated in 1994, the company has grown to $9 billion in little over 15 years.

Steel has been a major component in the country's thriving automobile sector. Tata Motors launched the upgraded Indica Vista, a sedan hatchback, in August 2011.

As part of its acquisitions in America, JSW Steel, a Sajjan Jindal enterprise, has acquired iron ore mines in Chile (and coal mines in Virginia) to supply the plant with raw material necessary for the manufacture of steel. It hopes thereby to have a certain self sufficiency in raw materials needed for manufacturing steel.

The aggressive expansion at JSW Steel assumes significance considering the company does not have any iron ore linkages in the form of captive mines. Of late, the company has faced hurdles in procuring iron ore in the aftermath of the Supreme Court ban on mining in Bellary on environmental grounds. On the other hand, Tata Steel acquired Anglo-Dutch steel maker Corus in a $7.6 billion deal, which catapulted the Indian firm into the global top 10 steel makers' league. Tata Steel is among the top 10 global steel companies and the second-most geographically diversified steel producer with manufacturing operations in 26 countries. In India, Tata Steel has doubled its capacity at Jamshedpur in the past decade from 3.4 MTPA in 2000–1 to a current capacity of over 6.8 MTPA and is expected to add another 2.9 MTPA in the near future. Tata Steel is in the process of setting up a 6 MTPA greenfield unit in Kalinganagar, Orissa, which will be operational in 2014. Essar Steel has also scaled up its operation with a current capacity of 8.6 MTPA, and is targeting a capacity of 14 MTPA. Like Tata Steel, Essar Steel and JSW Steel have also expanded their global footprint through new facilities and acquiring mineral assets. Essar has a presence in Canada and Indonesia whereas JSW Steel has expanded its presence in the Americas. It has acquired a steel plant in the US and has iron ore mines in Chili and coal mines in Virgina, USA.

One of India's earliest steel makers, Tata Steel is today ranked among the top 10 global steel companies with manufacturing operations in 26 countries.

ABOVE: Suzuki Motor Corporation acquired a majority stake of 54.2 per cent in Maruti Udyog Limited in 2002. The company has since bought out the Indian government's stake and is wholly owned by Suzuki.

TOP: Prime Minister Indira Gandhi, who oversaw the operations of Indian car manufacturer Maruti with Japan's Suzuki, hands over the keys of the first car sold by the company in 1984.

Credited with laying the foundation stone of the domestic car industry, Maruti Suzuki was formed as a joint venture between the government and Japan's Suzuki Motor Corporation in 1981. Its first car rolled out of its original Gurgaon plant in 1984. In the initial years till the government sold its stake in two phases (2003, 2007), the company faced a series of challenges over management control between the two partners. This made it tougher to get new technology and new car models for India as Suzuki did not want to part with technology rights before and was worried that the government might force it to exit. The early years saw little competition (existing only in the form of Premier Padmini and Hindustan Motors), as a result of which it captured the whole market with its models—which at times were behind what Suzuki sold in Europe and Japan. Suzuki now holds a 54.2 per cent stake in the company, while the rest are free floating shares in the market. The company has two plants—Manesar and Gurgaon—with a current combined annual capacity of 1.4 million units, and is setting up a third in Gujarat with an initial annual capacity of one million units.

Maruti Suzuki Swift was the first car to be indigenously designed by the company's engineers in India. Automobile designing courses and variants in each category now keep auto designers across automobile companies busy.

Maruti led to the modernization of car manufacturing in India, created a demand from the burgeoning middle class by offering an affordable product, and also helped set up a component supply industry through its many joint ventures. Come to 2011 and the market and industry it created is now being enjoyed by all the 10 major global automotive groups who have since set up local operations in order to be a part of the second-fastest growing auto market in the world (2010, after China). Maruti's main threat came in the form of Hyundai in 1996 when it launched its Santro, the first alternative to Maruti which was high on technology and space. Since then, competition from companies such as Ford, GM, and domestic major Tata Motors have flooded the car market, especially the small car segment (70 per cent of car sales). Even after so much competition, Maruti has been able to retain around 40 per cent of the market share.

BELOW: Tata Motors' Nano had to shift its manufacturing base from Singur in West Bengal to Sanand in Gujarat following protests about land acquisition—a challenge India will have to overcome if it is to develop key manufacturing facilities.

FACING PAGE: Maruti's Ertega and Tata's Aria are recent additions to the SUV space which has been dominated by Toyota's Innova. These utility vehicles have enjoyed great popularity among India's joint families as well as for offroading in uneven terrain.

ERTIGA
MARUTI
SUZUKI

ARIA

Hero MotoCorp, renamed from Hero Honda this year after the Munjals-owned domestic promoter Hero Group bought out Honda, did to the two-wheeler market what Maruti did to cars. Founded in 1984 with the Japanese partner, Hero MotorCorp brought reliable quality, affordable, and fuel-efficient bikes and offered an exciting alternative over the scooter/moped models offered by Bajaj, TVS, and LML. In 2011, the company was the largest two-wheeler maker globally by volumes and has now set out to chart its own destiny with a loyal customer base, heaps of cash reserves, and plans to set up its own design centre and enter international markets such as Southeast Asia, Africa, and Latin America.

Compared to the car and two-wheeler industry, the commercial vehicle space is still behind the global market and largely led by Tata Motors (over 60 per cent market share), followed by Ashok Leyland. Truck/bus models used in India are low on horsepower versus global counterparts, generations behind in design, and thus far cheaper. But things are now changing with market leader Tata and other newcomers such as Daimler, Scania, and Volvo launching new models, proving a cost benefit to truck/logistic operators (more powerful trucks, though expensive, can cover distances in shorter time and make more sense since roads are now improving).

While Tata Motors' old truck models still rule in the medium and heavy commercial vehicle segment, it has launched the new World Truck range, which has been jointly developed by Tata Motors and its two subsidiaries, Tata Daewoo Commercial Vechicle in South Korea, and Tata Motors European Technical Centre plc, UK. The company has the largest range in commercial vehicles and is the oldest player. The biggest success in recent times, however, has come from the LCV segment where it spearheaded the growth with the ACE range, by offering transporters last mile connectivity deep into cities where trucks cannot and are not allowed to go.

FACING PAGE: Pick-ups have not done well in India, but Tata's ACE LCV has been well-received for promoting last mile connectivity among transporters.

TOP: Mahindra's Scorpio has performed extremely well in events such as the Himalayan Rally as well as Desert Storm, but is also highly regarded as a city vehicle for its maneuverability.

LEFT: A line-up of jeeps from the Mahindra stable await delivery to the Trivandrum police force. Though it no longer has jeeps, the armed forces and home and defence services are major buyers of rugged terrain vehicles.

Mahindra & Mahindra (M&M) as an automotive group has come up fast in the last few years, both organically and inorganically. From being assemblers of jeeps, it now makes its own cars, two-wheelers, trucks, and even small aircraft. Among recent acquisitions are Korean SUV maker Ssangyong, Italian two-wheeler engine design firm Engines Engineering—both of which have given it a technical edge. Among Indian companies M&M boasts of the most capable R&D, which it proved with the success of the Scorpio and the premium-end XUV 500 which offers luxury features seen only in more expensive cars. With a 60 per cent share in the domestic SUV market, the company now has big ambitions to be a global auto player and has been planning an entry into the strategic US market (important for SUVs) and the highly-competitive Western European market. It is already big in South Africa and Latin America.

With economic liberalization and entry of Japanese OEMs, the Indian market started shifting to motorcycles. Bajaj Auto too shifted its focus to bikes and created its own strong R&D to weather competition. Today, Bajaj is India's second-largest bike maker. And exports over 35 per cent of its production and is India's largest exporter of motorbikes. Bajaj motorcycles are market leaders in many countries in South Asia, Africa, and Central Latin America. It is also a very profitable company with EBITDA margin hovering around 20 per cent, probably the best in the industry.

Bajaj has nourished its tie-up with Japan's Kawasaki since 1984, and the relationship has evolved from a technology tie-up to a business relationship. Bajaj has recently bought a large share in Austrian two-wheeler maker KTM and has co-developed new KTM models, which have been very successful in EU and other advanced markets.Such tie-ups will help it in getting top-level technology, though Bajaj's own R&D team is no small fry and has developed successful models such as Pulsar and Discover, unlike Hero which used Honda technology.

RIGHT: At the wheel of an early Mahindra Jeep.

FACING PAGE, *left*: Rajiv Bajaj on a Bajaj Pulsar. The two-wheeler major has a tie-up with Japan's Kawasaki and recently bought a large share in Australia's KTM, clearly signaling a shift in its focus from scooters to motorcycles. Its other brand is Discover. (bike in red and black).
Right: Bharti Airtel's growing presence around the world forms part of the brand's positioning.

Bharti Airtel is the largest telecom operator in the country both in terms of subscribers and revenues. It had nearly 240 million subscribers across 19 countries as on September 2011. Bharti Airtel's revenues in the financial year 2009–10 were Rs 38,800 crore. The company, founded by Sunil Mittal, first launched services in 1994 when it won the licence for a GSM mobile service in Delhi and its five satellite towns (called the National Capital Region). On 7 July 1995, the company launched Delhi's first GSM mobile services under the Airtel brand name. It has attracted a number of foreign investors over the years, including Telecom Italia in 1995, British Telecom in 1997, and SingTel in 2000.

In 2002, Bharti went public, completing India's first 100 per cent book building issue and got listed on the National Stock Exchange, Bombay Stock Exchange, and Delhi Stock Exchange on 18 February 2002. The stock started trading at Rs 45 per share then and today trades at close to Rs 400, giving it a market cap of Rs 1,509 billion. One of the reasons for the company's success has been its low cost business model wherein it has been able to drive profits despite operating in a market that is highly competitive with the lowest tariffs in the world. Bharti was the first operator to introduce an outsourcing model whereby it partnered with equipment vendors and system integrators to outsource its network management. IT and call-centre solutions have also been outsourced. This model has now been replicated by all the operators in India and also in other countries.

In 2009 and 2010, Bharti went international with big ticket acquisitions starting with 70 per cent stake in Warid Telecom in Bangladesh, and Zain Telecom's assets in Africa. It also started services in Sri Lanka. At present, Bharti provides GSM mobile services in all 22 telecom circles in India, Sri Lanka, Bangladesh, and 16 countries of Africa, provides telemedia services in 87 cities in India, and also offers DTH and IPTV services.

The IT majors such as Infosys ,TCS, Wipro, and others have changed the face of India's IT and software business which has been at the forefront of creating a cosmopolitan oasis in its offices in India—culturally as well as infrastructurally.

RIGHT: TCS Corporate Learning Center TVM 3, Trivandrum.

BOTTOM, *left*: A view of TCS Siruseri, Chennai.
Right: The Wipro Learning Center, Bengaluru—the talent house.

FACING PAGE, *bottom, left*: Founders of the renowned IT organization Infosys; from left, Nandan Nilekani, S. Gopalakrishnan, N.R. Narayana Murthy, K. Dinesh, N.S. Raghavan, and S.D. Shibulal–who together formed Infosys in 1981.
Middle: Multiplex at Infosys' Mysore campus.
Right: Narayana Murthy, founder promoter and former mentor of Infosys, was at the centre of a revolution that saw IT technologies—and jobs—coming to India, launching the popular phrase '*Bangalored*'.

The poster boys of the Indian IT industry like TCS have demonstrated India's outsourcing model to the world, overcoming, as they did, two rounds of global downturn—in 2001 and 2008. Helped by a vast engineering talent pool and an industry-friendly export regime back home, these global IT giants have been quick to sense the mood of global clients, tweak service offerings, re-haul business models, and even recast their own management structure, when required. Infosys, for instance, saw a change of guard earlier this year with K.V. Kamath taking over from N.R. Narayana Murthy as chairman, inducting new members to the Board, and changing its name to Infosys Ltd (from Infosys Technologies) to reflect the diverse nature of its business. Infosys—which counts Goldman Sachs and BT Group among its major clients—has a dollar revenue that grew from $545 million in 2001–2 to over $6 billion in 2010–11. It closed the last financial year with 620 clients, 6,500 projects, 64 sales offices, and 63 global development centres.

TCS—whose major customers are Citigroup, General Electric, and British Airways—today renders IT and back-office services to over 1,000 clients. TCS listed in August 2004, and between 2004–5 and 2010–11 its turnover swelled nearly four times. The company clocked $10.2 billion revenue for 2011–12. At the end of the September-quarter, TCS had over 2.54 lakh employees in 45 countries with 192 offices across the globe.

INSIGHTS AND LEADERSHIP IN INNOVATIVE TECHNOLOGY

ROLTA INC. is executing projects across a broad spectrum of industries and sectors in over 40 countries

Kamal K. Singh felicitated by Dr A. P. J. Abdul Kalam, 11th President of India, with the ™Geospatial Entrepreneurship Award on the occasion of Geospatial World Forum 2012 at Amsterdam.

In 1982, sensing that India's growth would require a technology thrust, Kamal K. Singh moved from Madhya Pradesh to Bombay. A mainframe computer was imported with considerable difficulty, and Rolta set up a data centre with ONGC as its first customer.

FIRST MOVER ADVANTAGE

In 1985, Rolta moved up the value chain of services for software projects in the US and introduced CAD, CAM, and GIS technologies in India. Today, Rolta's success lies on its ability to innovate and its ever-increasing IP repository. Rolta provides cutting-edge technology solutions in defence, homeland security, oil, gas, power, petrochemicals, government, utilities, telecom, banking, finance, insurance, healthcare, and environment segments.

ROLTA'S IP CENTRIC APPROACH

Rolta today has one of the largest pool of IPs in the geospatial arena. Its field-proven products and solutions have been successfully implemented for various applications. Rolta solutions consist of its award winning and OGC compliant Rolta Geospatial Fusion™, enterprise wide fusion of information, applications, and processes; Rolta OnPoint™, enterprise wide GIS, geospatial, and data integrator using web technologies; Rolta OnPoint Mobile™, work focused, asset-centric mobile GIS application; Rolta GeoImaging Suite, integrated system for remote sensing and image processing; Rolta Photogrammetry™, comprehensive suite of 3D digital map production solution with multi-sensory support; and Rolta Geomatica™, integrated systems for remote sensing and image processing.

Rolta cutting-edge products and solutions in defence are command and control, battlefield management system, intelligence surveillance and reconnaissance, tactical comms, digital soldier, night vision, weapon sights, mobile surveillance, and advanced photogrammetry and high-end imaging solutions. Rolta's homeland and maritime security solutions are safe city C4I, CCTNS, critical infrastructure protection, coastal security powered by Rolta CommandBridge™ technology, public safety solution for incident management and response system powered by Rolta GeoCAD™.

In the engineering domain, Rolta offers field-proven solutions from 'concept to completion' for process and power plants and for ongoing plant operations and maintenance. Rolta OneView™ is an innovative solution for extracting business intelligence from mission critical information collected from across the enterprise for various aspects of operations.

Over the years, through in-house development and strategic acquisitions, Rolta has built a rich repository of intellectual property (IP) and offers enterprise-level solutions in cloud computing, EAI,

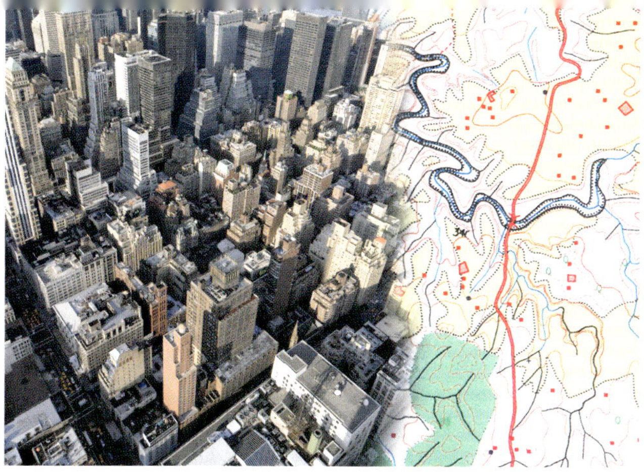

TOP, *right*: Rolta's enterprise geospatial solutions include end-to-end solutions for geospatial applications through Geospatial Fusion™.
TOP, *far right*: Rolta's defence and homeland security solutions include C4ISTAR information systems, military communications, digital soldier, and vehicle systems

BOTTOM, *right*: Rolta's engineering and enterprise solutions cover the entire lifecycle for the process industry with its OneView™ suite.
BOTTOM, *far right:* Rolta's Enterprise IT solutions are built around Rolta's IP and domain expertise.

SOA, EPM, enterprise geospatial, data integration, and business intelligence. The Rolta iPerspective Enterprise™ suite offers software components required to build a successfully integrated enterprise application stack; Rolta's CFO Impact™ solutions give cost effective and sustainable transformations of financial processes and systems; and Rolta CIO Impact™ offers a range of solutions from advisory services to IT outsourcing, providing IT resources to minimize total cost of ownership.

ACQUISITIONS/PARTNERSHIPS

Rolta has acquired technology companies like Orion Canada for enterprise wide GIS integration technology, TUSC USA for ERP, database, and business intelligence solutions on Oracle technologies, Piocon USA for field-proven solutions for improving operational efficiencies in the process, power, and manufacturing industries, WhittmanHart Consulting USA for consulting services in business intelligence, OneGIS USA for geospatial and IT solutions in mobile field force automation, ACLS Systems for field proven emergency response solutions, CommandBridge solutions from Mariner Group USA for actionable situational awareness and response for maritime security and critical infrastructure protection, assets from PCI Geomatics Canada for processing satellite imagery for environmental modelling and emergency planning and management.

Rolta has a strategic partnership with SAP to deliver their business intelligence technology platform as part of Rolta OneView™ Enterprise Suite for customers worldwide. As a Platinum level member of Oracle PartnerNetwork, Rolta bundles Oracle software components with its flagship Rolta OneView™ Enterprise Suite, for delivery to customers worldwide. Rolta has received eight prestigious Oracle Titan and Partner Excellence awards for innovative use of Oracle technologies, including one for the energy industry solution category. Rolta has partnered with GeoEye, Inc. USA, for high-resolution satellite imagery and developing innovative geospatial solutions and with P2 Energy Solutions USA for developing new solutions with Rolta OneView™ Operational Analytics suite for upstream and mid-stream oil and gas sectors. In the defence and security domain, Rolta has partnered with Thales (France), Selex Elsag (Italy), Aselsan (Turkey), Rafael (Israel), Qioptiq (UK), Controp (Israel), Sepura (UK), DAMM Cellular Systems (Denmark), DANPHONE (Denmark), NESS Technologies (Israel), and world-leading technology companies like Microsoft, ESRI, and Intergraph.

ABOVE: Kishore Biyani's Big Bazar, at the forefront of a retail revolution, is poised to benefit from the government's mandate that allows foreign investment in multi-retail formats.

TOP, *right*: Indian store In&Out is typical of the modern store format that has grown to serve urban needs, and like western countries is attached to petrol pumps— very convenient for middle class consumers.

TOP, *far right*: Godrej has entered the retail business with its Nature's Basket fresh form produce, currently restricted to only a few city locations.

RIGHT; People shopping in a department store. Organized retail in neighbourhoods are only going to grow and compliment if not compete with the unorganized sector.

FAR RIGHT: Reliance has been testing the market with its Reliance Fresh outlets, and wants to be a key player in the retail market.

FACING PAGE: A gathering of European leaders in the wake of the Eurozone crisis, which continues to impact countries around the globe.

THE ROAD AHEAD

Where the future is concerned, there is only one thing on which there is complete agreement—that it is wholly uncertain. The 2008 global financial crisis and the 2011 Eurozone crisis have left most firms worried. A problem, internal to India, is the political configurations which prevent quick decisions and rapid implementation by the government in power. Another drawback is the lack of experience with truly competitive markets. Most Indian firms have yet to come to terms with the idea that unless you constantly innovate, there will always be someone waiting to pounce on either you or your share of the market.

Then there are issues internal to the firms. Foreign investors are worried that too much executive power is concentrated in the hands of persons whose only claim to their positions is their family background. This could become acute in the next few years as investors become more savvy and demanding.

During the 1990s, a new furrow had appeared on the brows of Indian businessmen: would Indian brands survive the onslaught of the foreign ones? How would the consumer respond to the inevitable freeing of consumer good imports, then due to take place in the next decade?

Until 1991, when the Indian economy began to liberalize its trade policies, Indian brands faced no competition from foreign brands. As liberalization took hold, after a initial swing in favour of the foreign brands, the Indian consumer has regained his normal rational balance and is seeking value for money. In market after market in which foreign and Indian brands compete, he has demonstrated that what he wants is value for money. Where an Indian brand is able to provide it, he has stuck to it, much to the surprise and chagrin of foreign brands. Liberalization has not led to

a wholesale destruction of Indian brands. The key to success, Indian brand managers are realizing, is in quality and value for money. Wherever Indian companies producing branded goods have been able to provide both, they have held. Where they have not done so, the foreign brand has taken over. The Indian market is deeply layered and at every layer there can be several million consumers who make their own judgements about quality, price, brand value, et cetera. Thus, the baton of the economic race has passed into the hands of the private sector. As in all relay races, some runners will do badly, and others will have to make up for them. But, in the end, the race will have to be won. To foster this sense of destiny and to encouarge Indian firms to soar high will have to be the government's major preoccupation. It will have to be like the coach who cheers, goads, coerces, and cajoles his charges into peak performances—after all, even Cinderalla needed the witch to boost her confidence.

The author wishes to thank Business Standard *for permission to use portions from an extended essay that first appeared in the magazine.*

A BENCHMARK FOR HEALTHCARE

FORTIS is creating an Asian platform for excellence

It would be wrong to assume that it was the sale of Ranbaxy, India's largest, research-based, integrated pharmaceutical company, that was the catalyst for setting up what, in turn, has become India's—and Asia-Pacific's—fastest-growing, integrated health provider with 75 hospitals in 10 countries. 'Fortis,' executive chairman Malvinder Singh puts it in perspective, 'started as a five-man team in a 500 sq. ft office in Delhi.'

The year was 1999, historic in more ways than one. Ranbaxy, which Malvinder and Shivinder Singh's grandfather acquired from two erstwhile business associates in the 1950s, who, unable to pay back a loan, offered him their share of the business. Their father, Dr Parvinder Singh, then nurtured Ranbaxy from the late 1960s.

Dr Singh, a disciplined and astute professional, had shared his vision of extending the business into healthcare, but passed away in 1999, leaving behind two young sons who decided they would keep the banner flying 'run Ranbaxy, get into healthcare, revive the financial services arm of the business, the whole shebang', explains executive Vice Chairman Shivinder Singh.

The young inheritors pursued an aggressive, ambitious global footprint and sold Ranbaxy in 2008 to the Japanese pharma giant for $4.6 billion. By then, the family's Fortis dream was already established with acquisitions that would follow not just in India but in countries across Asia.

The vision that has today taken them to over 12,000 beds and more than 4,000 doctors began with a hospital in Mohali, Punjab. 'Punjab was close to Delhi and patients from there were coming to the capital for their healthcare requirements', explains Shivinder; so, despite resistance, a hospital there was launched and proved successful. A second, in Amritsar, followed, by which time the brothers had realized that they needed a presence in the National Capital Region, and in 2004, a Fortis hospital was launched in Noida. But it was the acquisition, in 2005, of arguably one of India's most successful heart-care hospitals, the Escort's Heart Institute, in Delhi, that proved the catalyst. 'Escort's was the best to benchmark against,' Shivinder explains, 'it was now time the public started taking Fortis more seriously.'

'My view,' Malvinder chips in, 'was to rapidly scale up the network to get the talent the doctors and economies of scale. Profitability would be a natural outcome.' Consequently, greater efficiencies were provided—for doctors, for patient care and treatment, for bed turnarounds based on average revenue per occupied bed (ARPOB), which has since become a benchmarked scale. Patient stay at Fortis hospitals is down to 4 days against the earlier 7.2 days (reducing the bill for the patient) and revenue per bed across the chain is Rs 1 crore per bed (Rs 1.35 crore in Mohali) against the earlier average of Rs 47 lakh per bed; doctors are not required to bother themselves with administrative tasks.

In a country where 80 per cent of healthcare is privately funded but 70 per cent of the infrastructure is government-owned, Fortis mapped its footprint by acquiring 10 Wockhardt hospitals (eight operational and two greenfield) in India, in 2009, and Parkway in Singapore, in 2010. 'Wockhardt hospitals had a strong presence in the south and west, fantastic infrastructure, and one of the most grounded teams in healthcare,' says Shivinder, 'it was a good fit.' The Parkway shareholding was exited 'with good economic returns', according to Malvinder. But the Asia opportunity was huge. In 10 years, Fortis had already established a pan-Indian presence; now it was time to spread wings outside India, 'to carry the learning from the Indian experience, and then bring that experience to India.'

It was back to the excitement of 1999: Malvinder Singh shifted to Singapore, and from meetings in his apartment, in hotel lobbies, and coffee shops, the group moved on to eight acquisitions in 10 countries. Today, the international arm of Fortis's healthcare business is a little more than half its total business, growing from annualized revenue of approximately Rs 1,200 crore in March 2010 to annualized revenue of approximately Rs 5,000 crore in March 2012. The consolidated global revenues for the year 2012 were close to Rs 3,000 crore compared to Rs 1,496 crore for the year 2011, a growth of over 100 per cent.

There is little doubt that Asia's trillion dollar healthcare market is the fastest growing in the world at 5.5 per cent annually, and with Fortis facilities in Australia, Canada, Dubai, Hong Kong, India, Mauritius, New Zealand, Singapore, Sri Lanka, and Vietnam sharing technologies and skills, Malvinder insists that 'India will get huge priority and investments.'

Even as Fortis India provides a mixed formula of primary, emergency, and diagnostic support, with centres of diabetes, obesity, and chronic disease, specialty cardiac, mother-and-child hospitals, and renal care dialysis centres in neighbourhoods, Malvinder promises, 'We are mere enablers and want to create Fortis as an institution beyond us.'

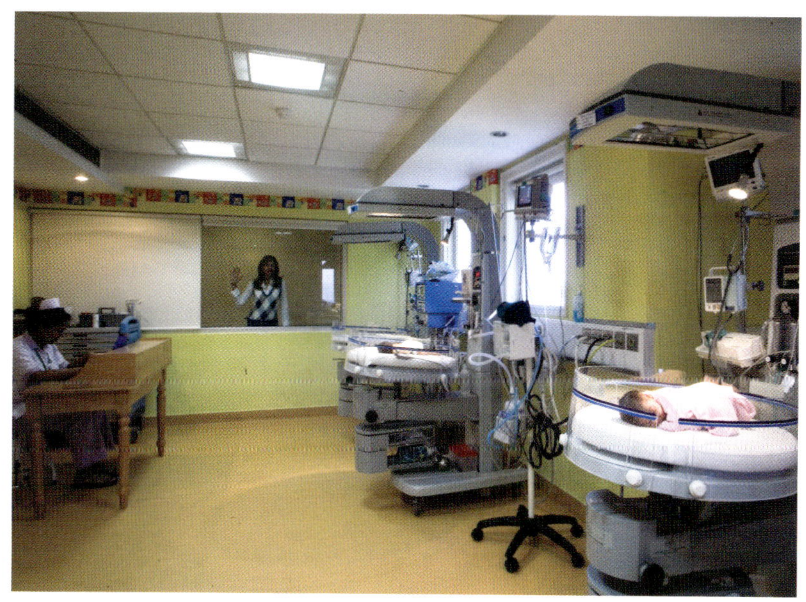

FACING PAGE: Fortis hospital (*right*) and (*left*) promoters Malvinder Singh (*standing*) and Shivinder Singh (*seated*).

ABOVE: Fortis hospitals have invested in technology, but their spread across the Asia–Pacific region has also brought global experience into its healthcare basket. They have several specialities including mother-and-child hospitals.

TOP: Doctors at Fortis hospitals do not have to fret over administrative issues, thereby increasing their own as well as the hospitals' efficiencies.

Various mall formats have been tested in the Indian market, all developed by domestic real-estate players, not all of them succesfully. DLF Emporio in New Delhi is among those that have managed to break free of the clutter with its focus on international and Indian high street brands.

Dior
VERSACE
OUT

LOUIS VUITTON
Dior

CANALI

Pipe rack at the condensate area, Mangala Processing Terminal (MPT). The Mangala field—considered to be the largest onshore hydrocarbon find in India in last two decades— was discovered in January 2004. It constitutes one of Cairn India's key assets in Rajasthan which is crucial for the nation.

Multinationals in India
A DYNAMIC PERSPECTIVE

4

VIKRAM SINGH MEHTA

Nationalized in 1976, the Burmah Shell Group had first launched its service stations in the 1930s, and in 1955 it commissioned what was then India's largest refinery. It is currently the only international company to retail fuel in India. Pictured here, Shell service station, Bangalore.

History, ideology, policy, and emotions suffuse the subject of multinational companies (MNCs) in India. Each of these factors has influenced the evolution of MNCs but none has been the definitive determinant of their current structure or position in the Indian economy. To understand how and why these companies are where they are today, these diverse and often conflicting influences have to be threaded into a composite story to contemporize our understanding of MNCs.

As chief executive officer of an energy MNC in India that has drawn on the legacy of history, faced the forces of ideology, benefitted from the economic growth of the country, and confronted varying public emotions ranging from admiration to criticism, what strikes me is the residual suspicion that MNCs are driven singularly by profit and remain indifferent to larger societal concerns. My own experience belies this view as MNCs cannot afford to regard the 'business of business to be only business'.

Tea plantation, Munnar, Kerala. The Tata owned tea esates are part of the group's global beverages division.

FACING PAGE, *top*: The Teesta Bridge in eastern India—the spread of bridges and railways by the British aided national unification hitherto only achieved culturally. *Bottom*: A quaint post box complete with a Raj crown—the post was modernized by the British, but has today been replaced by private couriers to increase efficiency, now itself endagered by instantaneous email.

HISTORY

MNCs have operated in India for over a century. British companies were early investors in, principally, coal, railways, jute, tea, and cotton textiles. European companies followed and their presence was important but never as substantive. Siemens laid the telegraph line between Calcutta and London; Phillips Electronics established a manufacturing facility for lighting systems, and the Anglo-Dutch conglomerate Unilever created the first FMCG conglomerate.

Independence marked a major discontinuity for MNCs. Prime Minister Jawaharlal Nehru was a Fabian socialist and did not trust the free market. His view was that the Russian 'command and control' system of economic planning was best suited to secure India's developmental objective. Accordingly, in 1948, his government passed an industry policy resolution that placed 'strategic' sectors like atomic energy, railways, iron and steel, telephone and telegraph, and insurance, wholly or predominantly under the purview of the state.

At an Alstom power facility. Fully 25 per cent of the world's power needs are based on Alstom technologies.

COMPANY OF THE FUTURE

ALSTOM INDIA enters its 2nd century in the country

An Alstom AGV high speed train; the company is partnering with Indian Railways' modernization programme for its rolling stock.

Alstom, globally, is a key contributor with leading positions in the markets for power generation infrastructure, power transmission, and rail transport. Across the world, Alstom boasts of 92,000 employees, with industrial and engineering sites spread across over 100 countries. Interestingly, 25 per cent of the world's electricity generation capability is based on Alstom technologies; 12.5 per cent of electricity transmission uses Alstom solutions; seven out of 10 high speed trains and one in four metro and tram trains carry the Alstom name.

Alstom's engagement with India dates back to 1911, the same year in which New Delhi was announced as its capital. Since that inception a hundred years ago, Alstom has been supporting the nation in transforming from a country working on solving developmental issues to a country that is today considered one of the fastest developing economies.

It has two R&D centres, a software technology facility at Bengaluru, Karnataka, and its Global Technology Centre in Vadodara, Gujarat, and two fully-capable boiler manufacturing units in Durgapur, West Bengal and Shahabad, Uttar Pradesh. On track is one of the largest integrated manufacturing facilities for turbine generators and auxiliaries in Mundra, Gujarat. Alstom also has one of India's largest and most-advanced hydro-manufacturing units in Vadodara, and a rolling stock traction and signalling components manufacturing unit in Coimbatore. Alstom also has a Metro & Railway Signalling Engineering and Software Centre in Bangalore, and is in the process of setting up a manufacturing facility for transport at Sri City, Andhra Pradesh, where metro coaches will be manufactured.

THE POWER STORY

Alstom's power business supplies a wide repertoire of integrated power plant equipment and services for every source of energy—coal, gas, hydro, wind, nuclear, and geothermal. Alstom India has full capabilities in engineering, manufacturing, project management, and supply of power generation equipment.

- It is the world's leading provider of clean power solutions.
- In India, it has formed strategic relationships with strong local players to bring frontline technologies to enhance the quality and efficiency of the power sector.
- Alstom supports India's economic growth through big infrastructural projects.
- Alstom has been playing a crucial role in supporting the government's vision of providing clean technologies and solutions.
- Ninety per cent of the country's aluminum smelters use Alstom's pollution control systems.
- Alstom currently has an order of supplying hydro equipment to India's biggest hydro project being developed by National Hydroelectric Power Corporation (NHPC), the 2000 MW Subansiri lower hydroelectric power plant in Assam and Arunachal Pradesh.
- Alstom globally acquired the transmission business of Areva T&D as it has tremendous synergies with Alstom's existing power business. The integration will further consolidate Alstom's portfolio to address the global power market as a total solution provider from generation to transmission.

At India's first combined cycle power plant; Alstom's range embraces all-known technologies for the manufacture of power.

A typical transport signal control room of the kind that Indian cities will require as they engage with complex commuting requirements in the 21st century

ALLY IN INDIA'S N-ASPIRATIONS

India aspires to achieve the goal of 20,000 MW electricity produced through nuclear energy by 2020, and further ramp it up to 60,000 MW by 2032. India expects to produce 25 percent of its electricity from nuclear power plants by 2050.

- Alstom, a market leader in nuclear energy, will help India in reaping the benefits of nuclear commerce, and in addressing India's concerns related to energy security and climate change.
- Alstom, along with Bharat Heavy Electricals Limited (BHEL), is already in the process of finalizing a tripartite joint-venture contract with Nuclear Power Corporation of India Ltd (NPCIL) for the transfer of technology to develop and deploy nuclear power turbines for the nuclear conventional island that generates electricity in a nuclear power plant.
- With competitive pricing, excellent references, a comprehensive product portfolio coupled with technological supremacy, the presence of Alstom in this sector will add immense value to the nuclear segment in India.

CHUGGING ON THE POTENTIAL

Alstom Transport offers a complete range of products from rolling stock, infrastructure, and information systems to services and turnkey solutions.

- Alstom Transport is dedicated to fulfilling Indian Railways' commitment of expansion in capacity and modernization of railway technology.
- It provides Linke Holfmann Bush (LHB) coaches which are used on India's current fastest trains, Shatabdi and Rajdhani.
- Alstom has been providing train control and signaling systems for the Delhi and Bengaluru Metro covering more than 100 km and 96 metro stations.
- As the Chennai Metro Rail Corporation begins implementing the Chennai Metro Rail Project, Alstom is associated with this symbol of the state capital's giant strides towards development and growth.

LINKING YESTERDAY, TODAY, AND TOMORROW

Alstom plays a significant role in contributing to society through its Alstom Foundation. Established in 2007, the Alstom Foundation champions a wide range of initiatives designed to support communities committed to improving and preserving their environment.

The projects cover the economic development of local communities while taking into account environmental concerns. Today, Alstom in India is a key social and economical contributor. It plays a vital role in bridging the demand–supply gap in the power industry through a long term capacity addition plan of more coal fired power plants and ensuring availability of spare parts, and repair and maintenance for upcoming super critical power plants in India. As Alstom begins its 'second century' in India, it understands the need to promote innovation both internally and among outside partners as part of this effort. To keep pace with rapid changes in technology and relationships with customers and outside partners, Alstom will continue to lay the groundwork for the company of the future.

The only sector left relatively untouched was the consumer goods sector, but there too the operations were constricted by licensing and bureaucratic red tape. Later, in 1956, Nehru spearheaded a second industrial policy resolution which further defined the government's intent to control the 'commanding heights' of the Indian economy. This resolution specifically identified the energy sector.

ABOVE: Narora Atomic Power Station in Uttar Pradesh began production in 1991 and is among the six operating plants of the Nuclear Power Corporation of India Limited. Its new Kudankulam plant, in Tamil Nadu, is now been developed with Russian help. However, it has been the focus of protests in Tamil Nadu caused out of fear for safety and environment concerns.

FACING PAGE: Offshore platform in the Arabian Sea, Oil and Natural Gas Commission. ONGC was set up as a state-owned enterprise by Jawaharlal Nehru against the advice of experts who had written India off as 'hydrocarban barren'. In its five decades it has set out to explore and produce oil and gas for the country.

Oil and Natural Gas Commission (ONGC) and Indian Oil Corporation (IOC) were created as 100 state-owned entities to explore, produce, refine, and market petroleum products and the incumbent MNC oil companies Burmah Oil, Burmah Shell, and Exxon-Caltex were put on notice of tightened regulation and eventual nationalization. They were also disallowed from repatriating profits and their expansion was curtailed. Coal India and National Thermal Power Corporation (NTPC) were set up to monopolize coal mining and power generation.

Nehru's ideological leanings were shared by Indira Gandhi and, indeed, the broad cadre of the Congress leadership. Profit was an 'undesirable' term and 'Indianization' became a byword of policy. The Foreign Exchange Regulation Act (FERA) was passed in 1973 which required all MNCs to bring down their foreign shareholding to below 50 per cent. This was later followed by the Monopolies and Restrictive Trade Practices (MRTP) Act which impacted the multinationals most as they were the larger groups with dominant market positions.

FACING PAGE: A vision being shaped brick by brick—Rourkela Steel Plant, SAIL. Independent India hailed the public sector to develop large projects, which were considered a national asset.

RIGHT: ONGC built its first offshore drilling platform in 1970, within five years of the first such global structure in North Sea in 1965. The picture shows the indigenously built fixed ONGC platform at Aliabet at the mouth of Narmada river.

TOP, *right*: Jawaharlal Nehru tours the Lunej discovery well in Anand, Gujarat, soon after ONGC was tasked with ensuring the energy security for India.

Some MNCs did not accept the requirements of 'Indianization'. IBM and Coca Cola refused to dilute their shareholding and left the country. Other companies like Unilever and Imperial Tobacco Company accepted the diktat and reduced their shareholding. They changed the names of their companies to Hindustan Lever and Indian Tobacco Company (ITC) respectively. Companies in strategic sectors like oil were not given any option. They were slated for nationalization—a policy decision that had broad public support because of the underlying antipathy towards large companies, especially those owned by foreigners, and partly because of the belief that during the Indo-Pak conflict of 1965 the oil MNCs had withheld supplies to Indian refineries at the behest of their parent governments. Later, in 1971, during the height of the Bangladesh crisis, the American companies were the focus of particular ire because of President Richard Nixon's decision to depute the Seventh Fleet in the Bay of Bengal. The shares of Burmah Shell, Exxon-Caltex were eventually 'purchased' by the government in 1976 and their assets transferred to two new, 100 per cent state-owned refining and marketing companies, Bharat Petroleum and Hindustan Petroleum.

ABOVE: The FMCG sector was among the few that escaped Fabian socialism, in newly independent India, though it was subject to bureaucratic whims. The situation could not be more different in post-liberalized India, with increasing space for both products and retail becoming avialable—and organized.

BELOW: Coca Cola is now in India with a big bang, as is evident by crates kept in their warehouse.

The atmospeheric and vaccum unit of Indian Oil Corporation at Paradip refinery (Odisha) under installation. Power and energy were among the industries the state reserved for itself as part of its security startegy.

LIBERALIZATION

The decade of the 1980s was a period of economic slowdown, financial crisis, and geo-politic transformations. Reeling from the aftermath of the hike in oil prices that was triggered by the Iranian Revolution of 1979 and the Iran–Iraq Gulf War in 1980–1, the Indian economy had gone into a tailspin. Inflation was in double digits, the balance of payments had critically widened, and foreign exchange reserves were severely depleted. In 1991, India had no more than two weeks' worth of imports in foreign exchange and was compelled to airlift its gold into vaults in London to secure credit. These economic pressures catalyzed major policy reforms. The licence raj was dismantled, customs duties were reduced, and the currency was devalued. Liberalization entered the government vocabulary. Sprigs of liberalization for MNCs had, in fact, already appeared in the early 1980s. Indira Gandhi came back to power in January 1980; she soon recognized that ONGC could not harness the indigenous hydrocarbon resources of the country on its own. It needed the technical expertise and financial resources of international super majors. She, therefore, reversed her earlier decision to keep the oil sector within the fold of the state-owned entities and asked the petroleum ministry to solicit international investment. A model production-sharing contract was developed and bids invited. Several contracts, including with the super majors Shell, Chevron, and Occidental, were concluded but, unfortunately, their exploration efforts were not successful. Eventually, and in accordance with the terms of the contract, they all relinquished their acreage and exited.

ओएनजीसी
ONGC
ONGC
India's energy anchor
ONGC - the Maharatna PSU, is amongst the largest E&P companies as per Platts Top 250 Global Energy companies' list. ONGC contributes 60% of India's oil and gas with cumulative production of 1,430 million metric tonnes of oil equivalent (MMToe).
ONGC has discovered six of the seven producing basins in India and holds 73% of the hydrocarbon reserves of the country. It truly is India's energy anchor.
ONGC

In the wake of liberalization, Indians have changed in the manner in which they consume products, its most obvious example being mobile telephony. While even children have taken to it almost instinctively (*above*) particularly in urban environments, in rural areas (*facing page*), it has brought the world and communications right to its doorstep—a development some consider at least as important as the spread of the railways a century ago.

The re-entry of MNCs into a sector that only a few years back had been deemed 'strategic' was a harbinger of the shifting contours of policy and ideology. A slew of micro policies directed at accelerating the return of MNCs into the country were initiated in the 1990s. The most notable of these initiatives were the National Telecom Policy of 1994 and the subsequent decision in 1995 to allow MNCs to invest up to 49 per cent equity in telecom services; the policy to permit international automobile companies to set up 100 per cent foreign-owned and managed entities; the abolition of capital controls on imports of electronic hardware and computers; the partial deregulation of the insurance sector; the replacement of FERA by FEMA and, most importantly, the streamlining of the approval process.

The result of these and other policy changes was significant. First, it increased the flow of foreign direct investment (FDI) into the country. The initial amounts were modest, averaging only US$ 4 billion per annum between 2000 and 2006, but increasing sharply thereafter. In 2007, for instance, the inflow was $17.6 billion; in 2008–9, it was $ 40 billion; in 2009–10, $41 billion, and in 2010–11, despite the subprime crisis, approximately $25 billion. It embedded MNCs into the fabric of the economy. They became an important contributor to technology, skill development, growth, and employment. Their sales revenue trebled from $40 billion in 2000 to over $120 billion in 2010, or 12.4 per cent of the total sales made by the Indian private sector.

The number of people employed by MNCs went up from 82,229 in 2000 to 3,46,833 in 2010 (approximately 14 per cent of total employment). Next, and perhaps most significant, it changed the face of the Indian economy. Billboards in every town flashed their wares; homes got crowded with foreign goods, the Ambassador car became a rarity and the ubiquitous mobile handset became a badge of identity. This makeover reflected the flow of MNC investments into, predominantly, services, computer software and hardware, telecommunications, and automobiles. Every major international automobile was now visible on Indian roads—Ford, BMW, Hyundai, Mitsubishi, Toyota, Fiat, Mercedes, Skoda, Audi, et cetera.

RIGHT: The Hyundai Sonata became one of the first luxury sedans to be assembled in India. As one of the fastest growing automobile markets, the taste for expensive sedans from small hatchbacks is growing amongts young Indians.

SONATA

A vintage Mercedes car.

Old Impala car seen at the vintage car rally, in New Delhi,March 2012.

IN R 8053

Audi R8 Coupé, the latest model to hit the Indian roads.

GROWTH PARTNER

NESTLÉ India's hundred years of creating shared value in the country

One for the record—Nestlé's promotions in 1916 in Bombay used the pomp and splendour of caparisoned elephants for the purpose.

Nestlé has been an integral part of the social fabric of India, having begun trading in imported and finished products including Lactogen, Actogen, Eledon, Nespray, and Milkmaid sweetened condensed milk and chocolates since 1912. In the century since it started, it has built a special relationship with the people of India and has been a partner in the country's growth.

SETTING ROOT

The Swiss-headquartered company has been led by its belief that investments must result in long-term sustainable growth as well as economic and social progress for the community. When the economic policies of independent India, post-1947, emphasized local production, Nestlé responded to these aspirations by forming a company in India with a sustained history of investing in the country. It set up the first factory in Moga, Punjab, in 1961. The next factory was established in Choladi, Tamil Nadu, in 1967, followed by Nanjangud in Karnataka in 1989, Samalkha in Haryana in 1993, Ponda and Bicholim, both in Goa, in 1995 and 1997 respectively, and in Pantnagar, Uttarakhand, in 2006. An eighth factory is under construction at Tahliwal, Himachal Pradesh, and investments are underway to expand capacities at almost all the existing factories.

Nestlé has committed to science-based innovation and renovation to develop products that suit the evolving needs of consumers in India. It has nutrition, health, and wellness (NHW) embedded in almost all its businesses in India, and is working to provide safe, hygienic, high quality, and taste-based products for everyday consumption that make NHW more accessible and affordable for the consumer.

Nestlé, using members of the farming community to obtain fresh milk.

A milk chilling centre in Moga, Punjab; milk farming got a boost in the region, accompanied by improvement in hygiene and technology

Nestlé India's brands reach out across generations and families with its portfolio that includes Nescafe, Maggi, Munch, KitKat, Actiplus, and Nestlé A +.

'SAANJHAPAN'

Nestlé's approach to business is to create shared value through the creation of long-term value for both society and stakeholders. This '*shared value*' or '*Saanjhapan*' about the impact of business and engagement through it goes beyond philanthropy. It reflects joint benefits and epitomizes the company's desire to create prosperity and improve the quality of life for people in an inclusive manner.

The obvious benefit the company brings to the place it operates in is the creation of direct and indirect employment. While creating economic prosperity, Nestlé India's activities help in the transfer of technology and knowledge, but it sees its greatest potential in three areas of joint value optimization with society—that is, nutrition, water, and rural development. When Nestlé started operations at its Moga factory in 1961, only about 180 farmers were willing and able to supply it milk.

Instead of investing in land and setting up its own milk farms, Nestlé created a model that provided the technology to increase produce hygienically, reduce waste, and empower the farmer economically. This pioneering extension of Nestlé Agri-services with the communities of Moga has helped to develop a vibrant milk economy with improved productivity and high quality milk production. Today, over 1,10,000 milk farmers benefit from Nestlé's expertise.

AIDING LOCAL COMMUNITIES

In recent years, Nestlé India's support to farmers for chicory cultivation is another example of technology absorption. Nestlé helped expand the cultivation and quality of chicory in different areas in India. Transfer of technology and education has expanded the area under cultivation and improved crops, while better knowledge of roasting and processing has increased yields. During the past 10 years, the number of chicory farmers benefitting from this increased from 1,000 to 7,500, and production has gone up by 600 per cent from 2,000 tonnes to 12,000 tonnes.

The Nestlé water awareness programme has reached out to the community through its water education project.

The company recently rolled out its Nescafe Plan in India to work with coffee farmers, local experts, and the Nestlé R&D Centre in France. The intent is to combine the traditional wisdom among coffee farmers in India with the benefits of modern science, help retain the characteristics of good coffee, improve the productivity and quality of coffee farms, and benefit farmers across the coffee growing areas of Karnataka, Tamil Nadu, and Kerala by making coffee farming sustainable. In the initial years, the company will train farmers who are interested while working with the others to encourage and assist them in adopting scientific methods for soil testing, balancing the use of fertilizers, and other, similar efforts.

SUSTAINING THE ENVIRONMENT

The impact of Nestlé India's work in rural development is acknowledged for its impact in helping increase yields, improving the quality of milk and other crops, and increasing farmers' incomes. Relatively less known is the work it is doing in the areas of nutrition as well as water and environmental sustainability.

Nestlé's ambition is to produce wholesome and nutritious food and beverages that also have the lowest environmental footprint. Within Nestlé India factories, there is continuous effort to improve operational efficiency, minimize consumption of natural resources, and reduce waste and emission while maximizing production. Over the past decade, not only has the company markedly improved its use of natural resources but it has also drastically reduced waste and emissions. It has created and increased awareness among the communities around its factories to help preserve the environment.

In order to create awareness in the communities about the importance of water for a good and healthy life, Nestlé has set up 'Clean Drinking Water' projects to benefit students in village schools around its factories. With every addition to the clean drinking water project, 'water education' becomes a part of the curriculum in one more village school, and more children learn about water conservation and the link between clean water, hygiene, health, and wellness.

Malnutrition in India is a complex phenomenon and is inextricably linked with illiteracy, especially female illiteracy, lack of safe drinking water and proper sanitation, ignorance, lack of awareness, and ill health. While India has shown remarkable economic development and increased prosperity, access to and understanding of balanced nutrition remains a challenge across the income pyramid. Nestlé India is constantly innovating and renovating products by using technology and its expertise in science-based nutrition to develop 'Health Plus' products for everyday consumption in India. In 2010, it launched a nutrition awareness programme across India as part of its Nestlé Healthy Kids Global Programme. The programme is structured to help students absorb basic knowledge in a practical manner. It focuses on the role of food in human bodies and how to improve the balance of nutrients in our diets. The modules specifically devote time to explain how cooking practices can improve nutrition as well as the need for food hygiene, sanitation, and physical exercise.

The ultimate expression that Nestlé believes in and endeavours to achieve is to provide 'Good Food, Good Life'. It responds to consumers' changing needs, producing safe, high quality, and nutritious products, communicating responsibly, clearly, and ethically, and with a clear approach to the business of creating shared value.

BRITANNIA
NutriChoice
KUCH HEALTHY KHAO.
Hello diabetes,
let's be friends.
facebook.com/hello.diabetes
DIABETIC FRIENDLY ESSENTIALS
Ragi
Oats
✓ Zero Added Sugar
✓ Zero Cholesterol
✓ Zero Trans Fat
✓ Extra Dietary Fibers
✓ Complex Carbohydrates

POWER PACKED
Surf

DALDA
BEST FOR ALL COOKING
डालडा

SUNLIGHT SOAP
THE PINNACLE OF PURITY
VISHNU-GARUD WAHAN
LEVER BROTHERS, LIMITED, PORT SUNLIGHT, ENGLAND

CORN FLAKES
CORN FLAKES
FROSTY FLAKES
Kellogg's
Nutri-Grain
CRUNCHY NUT CORN FLAKES

Among these MNCs, Maruti Suzuki has stood out for its success. It is the largest of the MNCs with 49.9 per cent of the passenger car market and a sales revenue of over Rs 30,000 crore. In 2010, it sold more than a million cars. Nokia has also broken significant ground. It is second to Maruti with sales of around Rs 22,000 crore. It has 62 per cent of the mobile handset market and a network of 2,00,000 distributors and retailers across the country. Vodafone has the largest market share of the mobile phone subscriber market and has invested aggressively to penetrate the market. Other successful and profitable MNCs are Unilever, Colgate, and Procter & Gamble in the FMCG sector; LG and Samsung in consumer electronics; IBM, GE, and HP in information technology, ITES software, and hardware, and Holcim in cement. Notable absentees on this list of successful MNCs are energy companies. Many of them have made substantive investments but on account of the skew in policy they have not acquired significance.

BELOW: An IBM office—not only have MNCs brought in international quality, they have also organized a more global operating environment.

BELOW, *left*: At Lafarge Home Building Centre, Kolkata. Even though entrepreneurs have been importing furniture in the high-end, most home furniture needs are met by home-grown companies that could take advantage of technological advancements in the international field. Now IKEA is in negotiation with the goverment for bringing its mass market, well-designed economic products to the Indian market

FACING PAGE: 'Indian' brands in the MNC space (HUL, ITC, Nestlé et cetera) have been localized in the manner in which they have been promoted—ranging from pricing differentials to health to, now, lifestyle.

CSR

ENERGY

LIFE SCIENCES

ENPRO

LIFE SCIENCES

MOTORS

FOOD

AGRI PRODUCTS

RETAIL

A TAKEAWAY FOR GROWTH

JUBILANT BHARTIA GROUP expands its reach from pharma and food to luxury lifestyle products and services

Brothers Shyam and Hari Bhartia have promoted conglomerate Jubilant's core businesses over a range of sectors from pharma and food to oil and aerospace

The Jubilant Bhartia Group, promoted by brothers Shyam Bhartia and Hari Bhartia, is a pharma-to-food conglomerate with a strong presence in diverse sectors like pharma and life sciences, food and retail, oil and gas, agri- and performance-polymers, and consulting services for the aerospace and oil field industries. Valued at over $3 billion, headquartered at Noida in India, it employs over 20,000 people globally (with over 1,450 in North America), and is steadfastly gaining global recognition in its various businesses.

CARING, SHARING, GROWING

The group started in 1978 with a small chemicals business which gradually transformed into India's largest integrated pharma and life sciences outsourcing firm, Jubilant Life Sciences—today among the top six global players in pharma outsourcing. It enjoys global leadership positions in several of the products it provides to its customers across 70 countries in the world.

Over the last three decades, the Jubilant Bhartia group has developed a strong presence in other sectors of food and retail, oil and gas, agri- and performance-polymers, and in consulting services. The group has three publically listed entities in India, Jubilant Life Sciences, Jubilant FoodWorks, and Jubilant Industries. The fourth entity, Jubilant Energy, is listed at AIM-London, UK.

The Jubilant Bhartia Group's vision is aimed at acquiring and maintaining global leadership positions in its chosen areas of businesses; to create new opportunities for growth in its strategic businesses; to be among the top 10 most admired companies to work for; and to achieve a return on invested capital of at least 10 points higher than the cost of capital. The group's philosophy is to identify areas of opportunity through partnering with leading international companies, facilitating their entry in India, and establishing their operations. All businesses are driven with an ambition to acquire leadership positions in the chosen areas of those businesses.

CORE BUSINESSES

Pharmaceuticals, Life Sciences, and Healthcare: Jubilant Life Sciences, the flagship venture of the group in the pharma sector, is well-recognized as an innovation-driven, integrated pharma and life sciences company providing products and services to global life sciences companies. A leading drug discovery and development solutions provider and the largest custom research and manufacturing services (CRAMS) company out of India, it has established a presence across India, North America, Europe, and China and has 10 world-class manufacturing facilities in India, the US, and Canada. The company is recognized as the world's sixth-largest pharma outsourcing player, a distinction achieved on the strength of high quality relationships with 19 out of top 20 pharma and seven out of the top 10 agrochemical companies. It has entered into multiple research collaborations with pharma companies, which has gained it the reputation of an innovator partner. Jubilant has close to 20 collaborative integrated drug discovery and development programmes with several leading global pharma companies.

Agri products and performance-polymers: Jubilant Industries Ltd is a focussed agri- and performance-polymers company, a leading producer of products for crop nutrition, crop growth, and crop protection in the agri segment. Jubilant Industries offers a wide range of performance-polymer products comprising consumer products like adhesives and wood finishes, application polymers like emulsion polymers, food polymers, and latex such as vinyl pyridine, SBR and NBR latex.

Food and retail: Jubilant FoodWorks, set up 1995, owns the master franchisee of Domino's International for India, Bangladesh, Nepal, and Sri Lanka. The company was listed on the Indian bourses in mid-2010 and has rapidly built value for its stakeholders. Jubilant FoodWorks is the fastest growing Domino's pizza country in the world with company-owned stores across India and market leadership in the organized pizza market enjoying over 50 per cent market share, and an over 70 per cent market share in the pizza home delivery segment in India. Domino's Pizza has over 400 stores in over 90 cities in India.

In 2011, the company expanded its portfolio by entering into an exclusive franchisee agreement with Dunkin' Donuts, the world's largest baked goods and coffee chain, for bringing the brand to India through a chain of company-owned Dunkin' Donuts stores. In November 2006, the group launched its TOTAL hypermarket and mall retail venture with six outlets spread over 70,000 sq. ft in Bengaluru. The hypermarkets offer the best variety and value for a wide range of products in apparel, footwear, consumer electronics and IT products, fresh food and meat, groceries, FMCG , furniture, home furnishings, et cetera.

Automobiles: Jubilant Motorworks is engaged in the sales and servicing of Audi cars through state-of-the-art showrooms in Bengaluru and Chennai.

Oil and gas: Jubilant Energy ventured into the oil and gas business in 1995 with the acquisition of a stake in a producing field in the north-eastern part of India. Jubilant Energy today has a diversified and balanced portfolio comprising of nine blocks in India, of which one is a producing field and others are in various stages of appraisal, exploration, and development.

Consulting services: Jubilant Enpro, a strategic venture business segment of Jubilant Corporation, focuses mainly on providing consulting services for aerospace and in the exploration of oil and gas, a vital Indian sector. Through its alliances with international companies, it provides business, marketing, and technical support related to oil and gas services, power and infrastructure services, and aviation related services (sales/maintenance of aircrafts and helicopters). It represents various international brands in India including Bell Helicopters.

CSR INITIATIVES TOWARDS INCLUSIVE DEVELOPMENT

The Jubilant Bhartia Group is engaged in empowering communities through its Jubilant Bhartia Foundation, a not-for-profit company that focuses on conceptualizing and implementing corporate social responsibility initiatives for its various entities. Through its 4P model of public-private-people partnership, it reaches out to 2,55,000 people in 53 villages in India.

The Foundation is engaged in taking initiatives in the areas of community development through focused projects in the area of primary education, basic healthcare, and skill development to improve the employability of youth and women. Specific projects like Muskaan for primary education of rural school children, Swasthya Prahari and Nirog Bachpan for mother and child health in rural villages, and Nayee Disha for youth and women livelihood training are running across multiple locations in India.

The Foundation aims at identifying avenues not only for making them employable but also provides employment. As an instance, the rural women trained for stitching clothes under Nayee Disha, also stitch staff uniforms at its plants. Similarly, several youth trained in communication and service skills have been employed at its Domino's and TOTAL retail stores.

apollo
A promise to protect that sets you free.
Before it is fitted on your car, an Apollo tyre has already been on a journey. Designed in global R&D labs, crafted with high-performance materials in state-of-the-art manufacturing facilities – by people who have made your safety their destination.
APOLLO TYRES WITH ***YOU-FIRST*** TECHNOLOGY.
Proven on global test tracks • Manufactured in 3 continents • Available in 118 countries
Join us on /apollotyresltd YouTube /apollotyresltd
Drive in ...
apollotyres.com
go the distance™

TOP, *left*: Metro Cash and Carry, a German grocery chain, was among the first to arrive in India—but has been limited to selling as a wholesale vendor.

TOP, *right*: Bharti Wal-Mart store, in Amritsar, Punjab. The recent policy on FDI in multibrand retail will probably see the entry of more such stores throughtout India.

FACING PAGE, *top* and *bottom*: India's retail story resembles a patchwork quilt and is made up of many disparate bits. Retail formats showing an array of luxury products and food courts in premium malls are promoted by well-known builders such as Delhi Land and Finance (DLF), promoted by K.P. Singh and his son Rajiv and daughter Pia Singh

THE UNFINISHED AGENDA

Ideology is not the obstacle it once was for MNCs. Other than the hardened ideologue, few now level the charge that MNCs are anti-national and should be constrained from expanding their presence. On the contrary, MNCs are recognized for their technological expertise, management and operating practices, and professional culture. Thousands of young people look to MNCs for their meritocratic and fair corporate culture and rank them as preferred employers. The obstacle to growth for MNCs is now political opportunism. Two examples will illustrate this point—multi-brand food retailing, and downstream oil price deregulation.

The entry of MNC supermarkets like Tesco, Wal-Mart, Metro Cash and Carry, Ikea, et cetera has been the subject of long and intense debate. The economic logic for allowing them to enter has been well documented. The current system of marketing agricultural products is inefficient and distortionary.

The farmer sells to intermediaries at razor thin margins; much of the produce is lost because of the inadequacy of storage facilities, and the quality of the product is never assured. Private sector investment in the food value chain would allow the farmer to sell directly to the retailer. That would substantially increase his earning. The creation of cold chain facilities would reduce wastage and improve quality, and this would bring multiplier benefits for the consumer. The concern that the entry of large, cash-rich MNCs would kill the small, street-corner kirana shops is exaggerated. These shops occupy a different niche and would not be driven out of business. This economic logic has not, however, had much impact on politicians whose position has shifted with the political winds and been driven by short-term interests. The opposition to MNC supermarkets is less to do with nationalism or the size of the companies, as might have been the case earlier, and more because of political opportunism.

The pricing of petroleum products is another, perhaps even more revealing, example of 'good economics' getting the short-shrift in the face of 'good' politics. The petroleum sector was among the first to be liberalized. The initial focus had been on upstream exploration and production (EP) business, but in the mid-1990s the government initiated a process for liberalizing the downstream refining and marketing segment too. It decided, however, to deregulate the sector in phases because of the political and economic sensitivity of petroleum products. In the first phase the focus was specialities—lubricants and bitumen; thereafter, LPG; then refining, and eventually and conditionally, transport fuels (that is, petrol and diesel). The idea was to bring about a 'soft landing'. The process commenced in 1994 and was completed by 1 April 2002, when through a gazette notification it was announced that the administered price regime had been dismantled; that the subsidy regime would be phased out, and that petroleum product prices would be aligned to the international market. It was also announced that the downstream petroleum market would be open to private (Indian and foreign) companies provided they met the conditions laid down in the gazette. One of those conditions was that only companies that had invested $500 million in exploration and production, refining, LNG, and pipelines, would be granted a licence to market transportation fuels. It was also stated that the playing field would be levelled for the private sector, that they would not be treated any differently from the public sector companies. The mantra was competition, efficiency, and innovation.

The response to liberalization was overwhelming. Majors such as Shell, Exxon, BP, and Total invested in the lubricants business; many set up LPG import facilities; several studied refining, but because at the time the Asia-Pacific region was long on refining capacity, no one made a commitment; and Shell secured a marketing licence for retailing diesel and petrol. Unfortunately, as with multi-brand food retailing, politics stalled the process of oil liberalization. The international price of crude oil had commenced its upward climb in 2004 and general elections were around the corner. Politicians determined that it was too risky to give oil marketing companies a free hand to set prices. They used their ownership clout to re-impose price controls and suspended the phase-out of subsidies.

ABOVE: Shell lubricants, one of key petroleum products in India, has benefitted from the petroleum industry's first phase of deregulation.

FACING PAGE: Shell was one of few companies to get a marketing licence, post-liberalization, but the petroleum sector has not been sufficiently deregulated because of political sensitivities—pictured here is the Shell LNG terminal at Hazira, Gujarat.

RIGHT: In 1976, in a wave of nationalization, the Burmah Group of Companies was taken over by the government to form Bharat Refineries—later, Bharat Petroleum Corporation Limited—and is today successful in the business of retailing gas.

FACING PAGE: The BPCL refinery in Kochi (*top*) and its an Offshore Platform (*bottom*).

This has been the situation since 2004. Public sector undertakings (PSUs) like the Indian Oil Corporation (IOC), Hindustan Petroleum Corporation Limited (HPCL), and Bharat Petroleum Corporation Limited (BPCL) are not permitted to set the price for petrol, diesel, kerosene, or LPG in line with the market, but are required to set it at a discount. In consequence, they have suffered huge losses. In 2011–12, for instance, it is estimated they will 'undercover' (a euphemism for loss) Rs 1,40,000 crore. These companies have not gone bankrupt because the government has issued them an IOU. Private companies, on the other hand, received no such IOU and have had to confront three comparably unpalatable options—either mark prices down to PSU price levels and hemorrhage cash; align prices to import parity (that is, the cost of acquisition) and lose market share; or simply exit. No private company has followed the PSU prices. Some have kept prices at import parity and lost market share (Shell), others have sold out and exited (Shell/Caltex in LPG). At the time of writing, all international and, indeed, Indian companies have put a hold on their downstream investment plans.

Politics has now permeated the upstream sector too. This is a relatively new development. The upstream sector was one of the first to be liberalized. Three rounds of international bids were carried out in the 1980s when the rest of the economy was still closed. Thereafter, the government solicited MNC investments through the acronymic NELP (New Exploration Licencing Policy). Nine rounds of bidding were carried out under NELP and the results were encouraging. Several MNCs signed contracts and some were successful. Cairn Energy, for instance, made the largest onland discovery of oil in Barmer district in Rajasthan; British Gas (along with Reliance and ONGC) arrested the declining production profile of the Panna-Tapti basin, and BP invested reportedly over $7 billion to acquire 30 per cent of Reliance's EP assets. The upstream sector was, in fact, often held up as the flag-bearer of India's open door policy.

Bharatgas

Perceptions have now begun to alter. Whether warranted or not, there is an increasing sense that this sector too is falling victim to 'good politics'. The decision to hold back the approval of Cairn Energy's sale to Vedanta for over two years, the imposition of controls on gas pricing and gas marketing in contravention of the spirit, if not the letter, of the production sharing contract, and the intervention in the operating and management practices of the MNCs created seeds of doubt that politics might prevail over economics and law in EP too. Petroleum is not the only part of the energy sector that has seen a widening divergence between de jure policy and de jure reality. The power sector has also faced a similar gap. Many early MNC investors like Enron, Congentrix, and China Light and Power exited because of this gap, and few major MNCs have invested in it since.

The underlying message is clear. Ideology and emotion are not the barriers to MNCs in India any more—it is politics. MNCs will have to walk a tightrope if involved in businesses that have a bearing on the electorate, such as food and energy. Success will come only to those that can manage this balance.

The changing face of India—an Indian Oil modern service station in the high peaks of Ladakh, catering to the needs of tourists and goods' transporters connecting the vast terriority of India.

इंडियनऑयल
IndianOil
XTRAPREMIUM
PETROL
XTRAMILE
DIESEL
SERVO
ON TOP OF THE WORLD
WELCOME

'SOFT' LEARNINGS

In the context of the altered circumstances for MNCs in India and, in particular, the importance of managing politics without compromising business objectives or business principles, there are three 'soft' learnings that MNCs should internalize. The first regards analytic methodology; the second, 'localization'; and the third, the fickleness of human emotion.

All companies have well-established and proven analytic methodologies that are process driven and quantitative. They draw on historic data with regard to volumes, prices, and margins, and are best suited for evaluating projects in markets that are mature and predictable. The challenge has been to adapt this tool to markets that are complex and transiting from regulation to liberalization. In such markets, history does not provide a useful guide and analysis depends on qualitative judgement. As a project proposal wends its way up the corporate hierarchy, any qualitative caveats and nuances often get distilled out and the top leadership falls back willy-nilly on 'hard numbers' and subjective predilections. Many MNCs failed to understand this nuance and consequently missed out on several opportunities. A good example of this is a comparative case study of an MNC decision not to invest in a refinery in India. Its studies and also those of its consultants had concluded that a greenfield refinery project in India would not meet the threshold criterion of profitability. Its conclusions were derived from projections based on past and current demand and supply data. Reliance Industries, on the other hand, undertook a similar quantitative study but overlaid that with a nuanced assessment of the Indian market, the emerging policy environment, and operating conditions. Its conclusion led to it investing in a world class refinery in Jamnagar. This refinery ended up being one of the most profitable refineries in the world during the period 2000–10.

A second lesson has to do with localization. It has always been assumed that India is a difficult place to understand and in which to operate. The key to success has, therefore, been the recruitment of a 'local' CEO and joint-venture (JV) partnerships. There is a lot of merit in this view. All else being equal, a CEO with strong market knowledge and a network of relationships can hit the ground much faster than an expatriate. A JV partner with a distribution network and established approvals minimizes the costs of entry and reduces procedural and red-tape delays. The fly in the ointment is that all is often not equal. 'Localization' is merely a means to an end—it is not an end in itself. Many MNCs, however, confused means and ends. This led to wrong appointments and incompatible partnerships. The result led to delays and, at times, their exit.

A third lesson is to never forget that public emotion towards MNCs, and especially Western MNCs, is fickle. There is no doubt that MNCs are now an accepted and integral part of public discourse. Their penetration has brought them physically into middle class homes throughout India, and most people would acknowledge that they are important contributors to economic and social development. Yet, there is a latent sense that if pushed, MNCs would place profits above principles; that they are fundamentally indifferent to larger societal issues—a view and an antipathy that is often expressed even by people of eminence. In other words, MNCs must not take public support for granted .

Nestlé's corporate social responsibility has engaged with clean drinking water, malnutrition, and hygiene issues, elements that have drawn in MNCs into the local social fabric across comunities.

HSBC
HSBC
HSBC

CONCLUSION

MNCs in India have had a long and chequered journey of twists and turns but have secured an embedded position in the Indian economy. Ideology is no longer a blocker, policy is supportive, the 'Bombay Club' has limited resonance, and MNCs are an integral member of industry federations and government think-tanks. The president of FICCI, in 2013, will for the first time in its history be the chairman of an MNC bank. That said, MNCs cannot afford to be complacent, nor wish away the legacy of history, the residual vestiges of an earlier anti-MNC era, and the inexplicable swings of public sentiment. They have also to accept the buffeting of democracy and the challenge of balancing good economics with populist politics. The multi-national company of the 21st century is not cut from the same mould as that of the 1950s and 1960s. These organizations today know that in a connected and intensely competitive world, pressure groups, and a crusading media can quickly turn moral or ethical concerns into vocal activism. They know that a singular focus on profits without regard for broader societal concerns can lead to the withdrawal of public support and the licence to grow. They know that public anger is a force that money and power cannot withstand. BP was almost brought to its knees after the Macondo oil spill in the Gulf of Mexico because of public anger. Dow got embroiled in a battle over advertising in the London Olympics because the public perceived culpability through association—it did not matter that Dow had purchased Union Carbide several years after the Bhopal tragedy. MNCs also know that corporate social responsibility is not just a social obligation—it is good business; it adds value.

FACING PAGE: Having begun its business in India in 1853 as the Mercantile Bank, the Hongkong and Shanghai Banking Corporation achieved a historic milestone when it established India's first ATM in 1987. For the first time in its history, the president of FICCI, in 2013, is the chairman of a multinational bank—HSBC's Naina Lal Kidwai *(above)*.

Larsen & Toubro has been in the business of building airports, shipyards, metros, and other large engineering projects in India since it began business in 1938 in Bombay, where it was formed by two Danish engineers, both of them committed to developing the country's engineering and infrastructure capabilities. L&T has manufacturing facilities in China, Oman, and Saudi Arabia, besides a significant presence in India.

Employees are attracted to companies that have a reputation for social development, culture, and ethics; customers and investors rank such business entities above others, and there is positive statistical co-relation between reputation and share price. Indeed, along with brand, technology, and reach, reputation is among the strongest contributors to corporate value. MNCs understand that there is no trade off between profits and principles, and whilst they cannot afford principles without profits, they cannot claim profits without principles. The issue is how this message can be communicated, how the public can be led to believe that this is not

Ranked among the best airports of the world, New Delhi's Indira Gandhi International Airport—or T3, as it is better known—caters to over 34 million passengers every year and ranks among the leading airports in the world. L&T, which helped build it, is currently engaged in building an airport in Oman.

mere rhetoric but both good business practice and a core corporate value. There can be many answers to this question, but it will only resonate with the public if built on the recognition that MNCs must now become a partner in the development of the country. It will no longer do to simply sign a cheque—MNCs will have to bring their technology, management, and marketing expertise to the table and harness it to the complementary strengths of government, Indian industry, and civic society. Only then, and over time, can MNCs claim to be part of, and in the life of, India.

ABOVE: Shiplift facility. A full-fledged shipyard at Kattupalli near Chennai, developed with help of L&T. It is India's first indigenously designed Ship Transfer System (STS). The transfer system is one of its kinds globally and has been built upon the latest technological advances in the field of mechanical and electronics engineering.

FACING PAGE, *top*: Maruti Suzuki cars await shipment. The development of private ports and a spurt in the shipping industry's reach have changed the complexion in which the import and export industries functioned post liberalization.

Located on NH-2, the 4.4 km, six-lane Delhi–Faridabad Elevated Expressway (dfskyway™), with a distinct 'Eye' shaped design for the cloverleaf interchange at Mehrauli junction, serve as an important gateway to the capital city of Delhi. Despite the challenges posed by a highly congested work area and traffic corridor, *dfskyway*™ was actually completed 23 days ahead of schedule by HCC.

Conclusion
HOPES AND CHALLENGES

OMKAR GOSWAMI

It could not have been more opportune. On 24 July 1991, the then Finance Minister Manmohan Singh concluded his first Budget speech with the words: 'As Victor Hugo once said, "No power on earth can stop an idea whose time has come." I suggest to this august House that the emergence of India as a major economic power in the world happens to be one such idea ... India is now wide awake. We shall prevail. We shall overcome.' There were many who ardently believed that it was indeed so.

Consigned as an also ran third-world country—at worst criticized for its pervasive licence-control-permit raj, and at best occasionally mentioned with a pitiful 'Oh, so many opportunities! If only ...' —we were sure that economic reforms which were as clear as day would let loose huge entrepreneurial energy that was straining at the leash.

It has been exactly so. On a scale of one to ten, where one is no reforms and ten signifies all the reforms and more, India is somewhere between five and six—more in some sectors and less in others. Yet, 21 years later, no one can doubt the enormous strides the nation has made, often along undefined, potholed paths that simultaneously go backward and sideways as these move ahead. Between 1991–2 and 2011–2, India's real GDP (that is, adjusted for inflation) has grown at a trend rate of 6.6 per cent per year. To put it in a purely factual context, there has been no country in the world, barring one, with a GDP greater than India. The country that has grown faster is China. Thus, while we certainly could have done better, there is little doubt that our growth has been substantive and, in quieter moments, worthy of discreet satisfaction.

If there is a single word that explains this growth, it has to be 'entrepreneurship'. As various chapters in this book show so well, India has been long blessed with world-class entrepreneurial talent. It needed the loosening of an encompassing and dysfunctional control hierarchy to release its animal spirits and spur growth. Consider some facts:

- The top line, that is, sales and other income, of all public limited companies listed on the Bombay Stock Exchange (BSE) increased an astounding 22 times from Rs 1,65,903 crore in 1991 to Rs 36,37,987 crore in 2011.

President Pranab Mukherjee meets a group of industry leaders in his previous role as finance minister. *from left*: Rajan Mittal, Onkar Kanwar, Pranab Mukherjee, Siddharth Birla, Y.K. Modi and Harshpati Singhania.

- Profits after tax increased 46 times—from Rs 7,948 crore in 1991 to Rs 3,63,882 crore in 2011.
- Due to various capital market reforms—a sector which has consistently improved and globalized—the market capitalization of listed companies on the BSE rose 101 times from Rs 6,75,880 crore in April 1991 to Rs 6,85,81,336 crore on end March 2011.

By any canon, these are outstanding achievements driven by the power of entrepreneurship. In fact, the story is much wider than what the listed companies suggest. It is of a growing mass of successful but unknown entrepreneurs, involved in hundreds of activities across up-country India. Automobile, tractor, scooter, and motorcycle dealerships; small yet comfortable hotels that charge around Rs 2,000 per night which are a haven for sales representatives throughout the land; shops selling mobiles, smartphones, data cards, and SIM cards; white goods stores; property developers across the land coming out of the woodworks yet unmade; salons where mothers-in-law go with their young bahus in the early afternoon to experiment with hair colouring—not hair dyeing, but hair colouring, with a streak or two.

You name an activity, and soon enough you will find hundreds of such enterprises. If there is one great thing that has thrived throughout the land, it is entrepreneurship of all kinds, blissfully devoid of caste, creed, and business royalty.

This, too, shows up in the data. Manufacturing accounted for 57 per cent of the top line of listed companies in 2011; and services 40 per cent. If we were to exclude the primary sector from national income data, manufacturing was 21 per cent in 2011, and services 75 per cent. Simply put, there are many more unlisted service enterprises that give serious heft to GDP growth—again, clear proof of the length and breadth of entrepreneurship.

Economists, true to their profession, are well-known for seeking grey clouds. Despite the permanent, nation-wide entrepreneurial upsurge that has raised the new Hindu rate of growth to 5.5 per cent or so, one cannot help but worry about four trends that are becoming prominent, each with its deleterious political, social, and economic consequences.

The first is that while poverty has reduced in urban and rural India, economic inequalities have increased. If the poor are getting better off, the middle class and the wealthy are getting far better off. In a country where the language of political and social entitlements dominates that of training for greater economic empowerment, one worries about the political consequences of such inequality.

Demographic data usually does not lie. We often talk of our 'demographic dividend' without acknowledging the huge challenges within. By 2020, there will be 251 million children between zero to nine years. Will we be able to take care of them, their health, their nutrition, and their early learning? Another 248 million will be from 10 to 19 years. What about their schooling and post-school training? And there will be 239 million between 20 and 29 years of age. Where will they get jobs? What training will situate them in a rapidly digital world? Has it even begun?

A second worry is about the spatial differences in economic development. As early as the mid-1980s, some of us were already speaking of two Indias—to the east and the west of Kanpur. It is shockingly true. If one were to classify each rural district of India according to assets and amenities available to households given in the 2001 Census (H series), the poorest districts are in Jharkhand, Bihar, Chhattisgarh, Orissa, south-eastern Maharashtra, and parts of lower Assam. Compare rural parts of districts like Ludhiana, Jalandhar, Ernakulam, and Thrissur with tragic places such as Mayurbhanj, West Singhbhum, Jamui, and Pakaur. Is it at all surprising that there is a 95 per cent correlation between such districts and forms of Maoist insurgency?

A third concern has to do with three key resources that we need to leverage in a sane and balanced manner to facilitate greater growth and more employment. These have to do with spectrum, with natural mineral resources and land. Decisions regarding all these three resources are now stuck in such deep ruts that it will need serious vision, political capital, and courage to cut the knots. Without it, it seems difficult to see how India can accelerate to a sustainable 8 per cent, leave aside 9 or 10 per cent GDP growth.

The fourth worry is the gradual resurrection of aspects of the permit raj, some of it coming through judicial interventions, occasionally even possible over-reach, some through audit observations which have stymied the executive. And some by executive action per se, based on a belief that civil servants do not get punished for creating shackles, but they can be severely censured, even incarcerated, for crafting growth-oriented reforms.

These are serious worries. Yet, as one looks back to 1991, and sees how we have progressed over the last two decades in our own chaotic way, one can say with confidence that India has it in her to continue growing. Impressively, with its democratic ethos untouched. One may have stopped dreaming of 9 per cent GDP growth, but if we manage 8 per cent over a decade, we will have more than doubled our national income. May our entrepreneurial energies be allowed to thrive. As indeed our democracy. These are our greatest blessings.

All figures quoted in the article are from Prowess, a computerized database that is the property of the Centre for Monitoring of the Indian Economy (CMIE); from the Central Statistical Organisation, Government of India; the Census of India 2001; and the UN Population Statistics.

MARKET LEADER ACROSS CATEGORIES

MODI ENTERPRISES with a wide range of interests has emerged as one of the top business houses in India

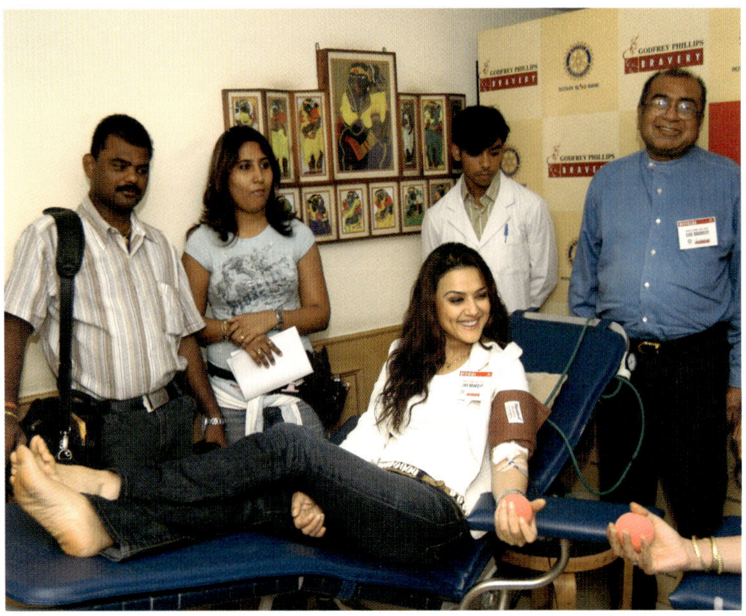

LEFT AND FAR LEFT: The Ego Thai and Lounge launched in 2002, under the Ego Restaurant Chain, has been considered favourite for a Thai cuisine fine dining experience in Delhi. This authentic Thai restaurant, with an exclusive Bar and Lounge, is frequented by the crème de la crème of Delhi.

Modi Enterprises was founded by Rai Bahadur Gujarmal Modi in 1933. Since then, the organization has grown multifold. With a turnover of over $2.8 billion, the group has a very wide range of interests, including agrochemicals, tobacco, tea and beverages, education, direct selling, network marketing and gourmet restaurants, steel, sugar, textiles, chemicals, tyres, computers, copiers, cosmetics, telecommunications, home-care, pharmaceuticals, and travel and tourism.

Employing more than 28,000 people, Modi Enterprises has emerged as one of the top business houses in India. Apart from partnering with a large number of reputed global corporations through financial and technical collaborations, it has pioneered many new businesses and has become a market leader in many categories.

The group has to its credit several pioneering projects and initiatives that have become synonymous with the rise of Indian industry. Modi Enterprises has initiated projects in different categories throughout the country: Modicare (multi-level marketing), Modi Academic International Institute (education), Twenty Four Seven (convenience stores), Colorbar (cosmetics), and cigars. Enterprises like Godfrey Phillips India and Indofil Chemicals are renowned names in the field of cigarettes and chemicals respectively.

One of the key strengths of the group is its expansive and closely-knit distribution network. For instance, Godfrey Phillips India's distribution width and penetration is among the best in the country, reaching right down to grassroot levels in the states where the group operates. The company regards its employees as its greatest asset. With the excellent employee retention ratio, the company has witnessed some of its older employees working with it for many years now.

K.K. Modi, the eldest son of Rai Bahadur Gujarmal Modi, the founder of the Modi Group of Industries, heads the Rs 4,000 crore plus diversified Modi Enterprises. He holds that the ideal of promoting entrepreneurship has helped his father to take the company to new heights. This is related to the company's another strength—its drive and determination to continue and increase its markets, both domestically and abroad.

With the Indian economy expanding rapidly, coupled with the group's plan to grow by at least 20 per cent per year, Modi Enterprises is in in a good position to increase its exports owing to its experience of working with multinational companies. With a penchant to apply Western technology more economically than is used elsewhere, it foresees itself as a truly worldwide business.

Modi Enterprises is deeply committed to giving back to society and the environment where it operates. The history of its social initiatives clearly indicates the philanthropic streak that runs through the Modi family. Besides their CSR initiatives that include the famed Godfrey Phillips Bravery Awards, women's empowerment projects that have thousands of beneficiaries, and the Modicare Foundation that promotes awareness for HIV/AIDS, the group also supports a number of educational institutions, healthcare and hospital services, spiritual and religious centres, and charitable trusts.

With its focus on people, the planet, and profits, and an abiding commitment to infuse new energy and set higher goals, Modi Enterprises continues to lead the way in multiple industries, setting benchmarks for others to follow.

EDITORS

KOKILA RANGACHARI

is a former Fellow of the Indian Council for Historical Research, New Delhi, and American Institute of Indian Studies, Chicago. She has been a former lecturer at the Indraprastha College for Women, and a former research associate at the Department of Chinese and Japanese Studies, University of Delhi. She has been associated with FICCI, New Delhi, as a senior consultant on special publications since 1998.

KISHORE SINGH

is a former editor with *Business Standard*, where he handled features and the group's magazines. A former editor of lifestyle magazines in India and abroad, editor and author of books on art, travel history, and business, a scriptwriter of documentary films, he is currently head of exhibitions and publications at premier art institution, Delhi Art Gallery.

RADHIKA SINGH

is a former model and theatre actor. She started New Delhi's first photo agency, Fotomedia, in 1987, professionalizing the sale of images in the Indian market. Since 2000, she has continued her work as an independent photo editor and curated numerous photography exhibitions in India and abroad. Her first book, *The Fabric of Our Lives: The Story of Fabindia* was published by Penguin in 2010.

VIVEK SAHNI DESIGN

started in 1993, Vivek Sahni Design (VSD) offers complete graphic design service from concept through to the final product. Experts at delicate balancing of intuitive practicality and stunning design, VSD produces work that is effective, focused, and memorable.

Vivek Sahni graduated with BA (Hons.) from Delhi University and an Associate degree in Communication Design at Parsons School of Design, New York.

Roopali Jain, senior designer at VSD, did a course in Graphic Design and Advertising from Wigan and Leigh, New Delhi. Faced with a multitude of both small and large images and material, this book has been an exercise in creativity making it contemporary and corporate.

CONTRIBUTORS

R.V. KANORIA

has an MBA from IMD, Switzerland, and did an advanced management programme from Wharton, USA, before returning to take charge of his family business in chemicals, textiles, and jute. He has headed several joint business councils, was the chair of the Commission on International Trade and Investment Policy of the International Chamber of Commerce, Paris, and part of the official Indian government delegation for the WTO inter-ministerial meetings in Seattle and Hong Kong. A past president of ICC India, he is past chairman of the Indian Jute Mills' Association and the Confederation of Indian Textile Industry, and is on the board of several companies.

DWIJENDRA TRIPATHI

was formerly Kasturbhai Lalbhai professor of business history at Indian Institute of Management, Ahmedabad. He has played a pioneering role in promoting the study of and research in business history in India. Educated at the Allahabad, Wisconsin, and Harvard universities, Tripathi has to his credit several books on Indian business history, including the monumental book *The Oxford History of Indian Business*, and a large number of papers published in reputed national and international journals. He has been general president, Indian History Congress, and is a founder editor of *The Journal of Entrepreneurship*.

R. CHAMPAKALAKSHMI

was awarded the Governor's gold medal for her M.Litt. thesis on Jainism in south India from Madras University. She has obtained her Ph.D. for her thesis on Vaishnava iconography in the Tamil country, which was later published as a book.

An associate professor at Jawaharlal Nehru University from 1982 to 1997, she has published four books and has written frequently on art, religion, society, state and urbanization in south India. She was general president of the Indian History Congress in 2010 (Delhi), and has presided over several regional history congresses

SHIREEN MOOSVI

is professor of history at Aligarh Muslim University. With 43 years of teaching experience, she has served as dean, Faculty of Social Sciences, chairman, Department of History, and coordinator, Centre of Advanced Study in History. She was secretary of the Indian History Congress (1997-2000) and has been secretary of the Aligarh Historians Society since 1998.

PURUSHOTTAM AGRAWAL

is a member of the Union Public Service Commission. He was formerly a professor and chairperson, Centre of Indian Languages, School of Languages, Literature and Culture Studies, Jawaharlal Nehru Museum, New Delhi.

ASHOK DESAI

is a consultant editor with *Business World*. As a professional economist, he specialized in industry, trade, and technology. He has been a liberal critic of Indian economic policies for the past 40 years. In 1991, when those policies led to a serious crisis, he was taken into the finance ministry, where he helped design the economic reforms for two years. He has been propagating his ideas through the press since then.

T.C.A SRINIVASA-RAGHAVAN

is a senior associate editor of *The Hindu Business Line*. He has previously worked at *Financial Express*, *Indian Express*, *Economic Times*, and *Business Standard*. He has also worked as a consultant to the history of the Reserve Bank of India, and as advisor to the director of ICRIER and the Asian Institute of Transport.

VIKRAM SINGH MEHTA

is former head of Shell-India and has written extensively in journals and newspapers on the contribution of MNCs to the Indian economy since independence, and in particular over the last two decades.

OMKAR GOSWAMI

is an economist and the chairman of CERG Advisory Private Limited, a firm specializing in corporate and economic consulting. He did his MA from the Delhi School of Economics and his D.Phil from Balliol College, Oxford. Between 1982 and 1996, Goswami taught at the Delhi School of Economics, Tufts, Harvard, Jawaharlal Nehru University, Rutgers, and the Indian Statistical Institute, Delhi. After two years as the editor of Business India, he joined the Confederation of Indian Industry as chief economist, where he worked for six years, before starting CERG Advisory in April 2004.

ACKNOWLEDGEMENTS AND PICTURE CREDITS

A large number of people have contributed to the visual bank used in the making of this illustrated volume. All efforts have been made to provide due credit, but in some cases, because of the complex nature of the production effort, oversights may have occurred. The Federation of India Chambers of Commerce and Industry (FICCI) would like to convey its gratitude to the various individuals, institutions and organizations for the research that made these pictures, illustrations and other visual material possible. FICCI would also like to thank the authors who contributed photographs from various sources for this book.

We are especially grateful to the National Museum, Fotomedia, www.indiatodayimages.com, Roli Books, Aditya Arya's India Photo Archive Foundation, Shireen Moosvi, R. Champakalakshmi, and Purushottam Agrawal for permission to use photographs from their private collection. Some visuals have been taken from *Footprints of Indian Enterprise: Indian Business Through the Ages* by FICCI (OUP 1998).

We acknowledge details of picture credits to the following:

PHOTOGRAPHERS

Aditya Patankar: pp. 103, 116, 117
Akhil Bakshi: pp. xx, xxi–xxii, xxv, 8, 112, 165, 246, 265 (2)
Amar Talwar: pp. xii–xiii, 87, 174–5, 258
Amit Pasricha: p. 56
Dinesh Khanna: pp. 81, 85, 87
Fotomedia: pp. 24 (3), 28–9, 31, 44–5, 72–3, 73, 74 75, 76–7, 77, 83, 89, 98, 116, 135, 178, 232–3
Francois Gautier: p. 113
Jnana Pravaha: pp. 3, 12 (5), 13 (4), 19, 20, 52, 86
National Museum: pp. 13, 19, 20 (2), 25, 52, 53
Sujata Kulshreshtha: pp. 70–1
Toby Sinclair: pp. 14, 48, 50, 76, 82, 196, 233
V. Muthuraman: pp. 22, 49 (2), 55, 119
www.indiatodayimages.com: pp. 43, 85 (2), 146, 161, 164 (2), 168–9 (8), 172, 189, 190, 192, 219, 221, 224 (3), 226, 242, 259, 264

COMPANIES

ACC Ltd., Ackzonobel, Aditya Birla Group, Adventz, Alstom, Ambuja Cement Ltd., Air India, Apeejay, Apollo Hospitals, Apollo Tyres, Arvind Limited, Ashok Piramal Group, Asian Paints Ltd., Audi © Audi AG, Axis Bank, Bajaj Group, Bharat Forge, Bharti Enterprises Ltd., Biocon Ltd., BPCL, Burmah Shell, Cipla, Coal India, Coca-Cola India, Dabur India, Dainik Bhaskar Group, Delegation Of The European Union To India, DLF Limited, Dr Reddy's Lab Ltd., Fortis Healthcare (India) Ltd., GMR Group, Godrej & Boyce MFG. Co. Ltd., Great Eastern Energy Corporation Ltd., GVK Power And Infrastructure Limited, HCC Ltd., HCL, HSBC, Hyundai Motor India Ltd, IMFA, India Cement, Infosys, IOC, Jaypee Group, Jet Airways, Jindal Steel & Power Ltd., JK Paper, JSW Steel, Jubilant Life Sciences Ltd., Kanoria Chemicals Ltd., KCP Ltd., Kirloskar Brothers Limited, Kotak Mahindra Bank, Lakshmi Mills, Larsen & Toubro, Lupin Ltd., Mahindra Group, Marico Ltd., Maruti Suzuki India Ltd., Max India, Mercedes ©Daimler AG, Ministry of Tourism, GOI, Modi Enterprises, MRF Ltd., MW Corp, Neemrana Hotels Pvt. Ltd., Nestle, ONGC, Piramal Healthcare, Punj Lloyd Ltd., Ramoji Group, Reliance Communications Ltd., Reliance Industries Ltd., Rolta India Ltd., Royal Enfield, RPG Enterprises, SAIL, Samsung, Samtel Group, Shree Cement Ltd., Shree Renuka Sugar, Siemens Ltd., SPIC Ltd., Sunnetwork, TAFE, Tata Central Archives, Tata Sons, The KCP Ltd., The Muthoot Group, The Oberoi Group, TVS Motor Company Ltd., Walchandnagar Industries Ltd., Wipro Ltd., Yes Bank, Zee Entertainment Enterprises Ltd.

We are extremely grateful to Textile Arts, Santa Fe, NM, USA for the use of the image on p. 53.

We acknowledge the following site for use of images of Apple 1, and IBM personal computers that appear in the book on p. 160: wikipedia.org/wiki/apple_1wikipedia.org/wiki/ibm_pc

We also wish to thank Anirudh Emani for use of Spice Jet and Indigo aircraft images, Sinkrate for Go Air, and Pete Shirk for Jet Airways that appear on p. 165, which have been taken from the Wikipedia site, and is meant for common use.

While all efforts have been made to credit photo sources, any omissions are regretted and will be amended and improved upon in subsequent editions.

Something to Chew On ! - A picture of Solid Poly Vinyl Acetate (SVPA) facility at Jubilant Industries Gajraula plant. SPVA is the major raw material for making gum base for Chewing Gum and Bubble Gum

INDEX

[Page numbers with *f* indicate visuals]

A

Aditya Birla Group 99
Adventz Group 200; *see also* Zuari Agro Chemicals
- Adventz Infraworld 203
- future prospects 203–4
- Hettich India 203
- investment and financial services 203
- Style Spa Furniture Limited 203

Agra fort, commerical activity at 61*f*
Ahmedabad business life 21–2, 59
- 'market rate' of interest 62

Aircel 163
Air India 164
Airtel 163, 218
- acquisitions 218
- DTH and IPTV services 218
- in share market 218

Akbar's return to Fatehpur Sikri 58*f*
Alam Ara 111
Alok Industries 89
Ambani, Anil 114*f*
Ambani, Dhirubhai 186*f*
Amins of Baroda 41
Andrew Yule & Co. 39, 79
Anglo-Iranian Oil Company 123
Apeejay Education Society 132
- Apeejay College of Fine Arts 133
- Rajeshwari Kala Sangam 133

Apeejay Group
- Apeejay Structurals 133
- Rolling Mills of Hindustan 133
- steel-making units 132

Apple computers 160
Armenians 23
Aruna Sugars Finance Limited 101
Arvind Mills 89*f*
Ashok Motors 143
Asian Games, 1982 188
Asian Paints 129
Aspdin, John 98
Assam Railways and Trading Company 122
Associated Cement Companies Limited (ACC) 67, 99
- ACC Cement Technology Institute 69
- Cement House 68
- CMC Centre for Infectious Diseases 69
- in community development 68–9
- indigenous cement plant 67
- medical services 69
- ready-mix concrete 68
- reason for formation 67
- Superbrand status 69
- in sustainable development 68
- utilization of industrial wastes 68
- Village Welfare Scheme 68
- workplace policy 69

Associated Chambers of Commerce and Industry of India (Assocham) 69
Astrakhan (Haji Al Tarkhan)
- Astrakhan Hindus 65
- Indian businessmen settled in 64
- mercantile significance of 64
- mid-16th century 64
- trade routes between Delhi and 65*f*

Audi 248
Aukland, George 78
Aurangzeb 27
auto industry 142–5
Ayyavole 50

B

Bachchan, Amitabh 39
Bachhraj Trading Corporation 146
Bahar, Tek Chand 60
Bajaj, Jamnalal 42*f*, 146, 146*f*, 177
Bajaj, Rahul 188*f*
Bajaj group of industries 41, 188
Bajaj Hindustan 97
Bajaj scooters 147*f*, 216–17
Bajoria, B. 82
Ballardie Thompson & Mathews 68
Balrampur Chini 97
Bananju Dharma 53
Bandra–Worli sea link, Mumbai 198–9*f*
Banias 59
Banjaras 23
Barayev, Marwari 64
Beg, Haji Zahid 21
Beg, Zahid 56
Benthall, Edward (Tom) 39
Bentinck, Lord 82
Benz, Karl 122
Berger Paints 129
Berlia, Aditya 133, 133*f*
Berlia, Neha 133, 133*f*
Berlia, Nishant 133, 133*f*
Berlia, Sushma 133, 133*f*
Berlia, Vijay 133, 133*f*
Bernier, Francois 59, 62
Bhakra Nangal Dam 66f
Bhakra Nangal project 200
Bharat Aluminium Company 141
Bharat Heavy Engineering Limited (BHEL) 148, 150
Bharat Petroleum Corporation Limited (BPCL) 268
Bhartia, Hari 261, 261*f*
Bhartia, Shyam 261, 261*f*
Bharti Airtel *see* Airtel
Bhatavdekar, Harishchandra 111
Bhatia, Rahul 164
Bhatias, Kuchchi 32
Bhira power generating station 36*f*
BIG CINEMA 114, 114*f*
bill market of Mughal empire 59–60
Bird, Sam 39
Bird & Heilger 39, 79
Bird, Paul 39
Birla, B.M. 142
Birla, Ghanshyam Das 36, 177, 179
Birla, K. K. 200
Birla Copper 141
Birlas of Rajasthan 37*f*
Bishnauth Estates 82
Biyani, Kishore 224*f*
B.K. Birla group 85
BMW 248
Bokharo Thermal Station 75*f*
Bombay Burmah Trading Company 84
Bombay Spinning and Weaving Company 32
- agreement with Cowasjee Dawar 87*f*

Borelli Tea Holdings 82

BP 267
Brihadeshwar temple, Thanjavur 50–51*f*
British Oil Engine Export 150
British textile industry 86
Bronze sculpture of Shiva 52*f*
BSNL 163
Buddhist Jatakas 04
Bureau of Industrial Finance and Reconstruction (BIFR) 79
Burmah Shell 123
Burn, Martin 39
Burn and Co. 39, 98

C

Cail-KCP Limited 106
Calcutta Electric Supply Company (CESC) 134
Caltex 123
Carr, Tagore & Co. 82
Carr, William 82
Carves, Francois 153
Catherine of Braganza 81
cellphone penetration in India 163
Cement House 68
cement industry 98; *see also* Associated Cement Companies Limited (ACC); India Cements Ltd
  Indian Cement Manufacturers' Association 98
  Porbandar plant of Indian Cement Company 98
Chaitya Hall, Ajanta 8*f*
Chalukyas 48
Chambal Fertilizers and Chemicals Limited 201
Charles II, King 81
Chellabys 21
Chetti, Malaya 22
Chetti, Suncaram 22
Chettier, Dewan Bahadur P. Somasundaram 42*f*
Chettier, Kurumuthu Thyagaraj 41
Chettiers ('Chettys') 59
Cheviot mill 79
Chevron 244
Chhotalal, Ranchhodlal 32
Chidambaram, P. 119, 193
Chilai Chettis 48
Chittirameli 50
Chitturi, Smt. Kavitha Dutt 106
Cholas 48
Cinepolis 114
City Palace, Udaipur 102*f*
Clarian 129
Clarkes 103
Coal India 241
Cognizant 161
Coimbatore, as centre of cotton production 41
coins 3*f*, 12–13*f*, 49*f*
Coke 186
Colgate 259
colonial period, Indian business during 29–44
  agency houses 30
  Birlas 36
  corporate management 33
  Dalmia-Sahu Jains 39
  Indo-British partnerships 30, 32
  Kirloskar group 40
  Kirloskars 40
  Mafatlals 39
  Seshasayees 41
  Shrirams 39
  Tatas 35
  Thapars 40–1
  Walchands 40
ColourChem 129
Connemara, Madras 103
cotton and silk masnad, 18th century 63*f*
cotton shortage, in 1860s 86
cotton trade 20*f*, 24, 32–3, 41
Courtaulds 129
Crompton Greaves 150
Crompton Parkinson Works 150
Curzon Ganges Bridge, Allahabad 83*f*

D

Daewoo 143
Dagli Committee 186
Daguerre, Louis 111
Daimler, Gottlieb 146
Daimler trucks 142
Dalmia, Seth Ram Krishna 38*f*, 39
Dalmia-Sahu Jains 39
Dasna Developers 92, 94
Davar, Cawasji Nanabhai 32, 32*f*, 86
Decentralized Distributed Generation (DDG) scheme 94
Delhi Cloth and General Mills (DCM) 39
Devchand, Kilachand 40
Dhariwal Mills 88*f*
Dhoot, Saurabh 192*f*
Dhoot, Venugopal 192*f*
DIC 129
Diesel, Rudolf 122
Dinshaw, F. E. 67, 98
Doshi, Walchand Hirachand 40
DotCom bubble, 2000 193
Drake, Edwin L. 122
DT Cinemas 114
Duff, Thomas 78–9
Dutt, V.L. 106
Dutt, M.D. 106
Dutt, V.L. Indira 106

E

earthen jar, Mohenjodaro 2*f*
East India Company 21*f*, 82
East India Company seal 30*f*
Eastman, George 111
Elgin Hotel 103
embroidery and needlework 24
Empire of Ashoka 3*f*
Engineers India Limited 148
English East India Company 22–3, 56, 60
Entegra Limited 92
  energy parks 94
  Maheshwar Hydro Electric Project (MHEP) 92–3
  renewable energy projects 93
Erivirappattana 50
Erskine, John 98
Esplanade Man 103
Essar refinery 123
Essar Steel 210
ETA Star Cement Company 99
European East India Companies 18
exploration and production (EP) business 267
Exxon 267

F

Fairhurst, G.H. 98
Federation of Indian Chambers of Commerce and Industry (FICCI) 33*f*
Fiat cars 142, 248
film industry 111
  and reforms of the early 1990s 111
Finlay, James 84
Fives Lille Cail France 107–8
flax 78
Ford motors 213, 248
Foreign Exchange Regulation Act (FERA) 241
Fortis hospitals 226–7
F.W. Heilger & Co. 39

G

Gagalbhai, Mafatlal 38*f*, 39
Gammon, J. C. 150
Gammon India 150
Gandhi, Indira 186, 244
Gandhi, Mahatma 36f, 177
Gandhi, Sanjay 143
garment production 89
Gas Authority of India 128
G.D. Bangur group 79
GE 259
Ghafur, Abdul 21
Ghafur, Mulla 56–7
Glass hubble-bubble, 17th century 19*f*
global recession 193
Gloster mill 79
GM 213
GoAir airline 164
Godfrey Phillips 285
Godrej, Adi 189f
Godrej, Ardeshir Burjorji 42*f*
Godrej, Pirojsha B. 32*f*
Godrej enterprise 41, 188
gold and silver jewellery 24
gold ear-pendant, Takshila 2*f*
Goodlass Nerolac 129
Goyal, Naresh 164
Grand Hotel, Calcutta 103
Grasim 99
Greaves Cotton 150
Greeks 2
Gujarat Ambuja Cement 99
Guptas 48
Gurunath, Rupa 100

H

handspun cotton 53*f*
Hang of China 53
hatt-tal ('market-closure') 62
hawala operators 116
Heinrich Hildebrand 146
heritage hotels 103
Hero Honda 216
Hero Motors 146
Hindalco 141
Hindalco-Novelis 141
Hindustan Copper 141
Hindustan Lever 188
Hindustan Motors 37*f*, 142
Hindustan Petroleum Corporation Limited (HPCL) 268
Hindustan Zinc 141
Hirachand, Seth Walchand 42*f*
Hirachand, Walchand 67
Holcim group 67, 99
hotel industry 103
HP 259
hundi 22
H.V. Kanoria group 79
Hydari, Sir Akbar 67
Hyundai Motors 145, 213, 248

I

IBM 186, 259
ICI 129
Idea 163
IDI 129
Imperial Chemical Industries 41
Imperial Film Company 111
Imperial Tobacco Company 41
India Cements Ltd
 acquisitions 101
 in cricket Indian Premier League 101
 Dalavoi Cement plant 101
 diversifications 101
 founders and promoters 100–1
 future strategy 101
 leadership 101
 non-conventional electric power generation 101
 production of blended cement 101
 trading and finance 101
 turnover of the company, 2011 101
Indian chintzes and textiles 18*f*
Indian enterprise, post-independence 73
 aluminium industry 141
 auto industry 142–5
 cement industry 98
 coal industry 78
 dyes, paints and printing inks industry 129
 electric power industry 134
 film industry 111
 gem-cutting industry 119
 heavy engineering industry 148
 hotel industry 103
 information and technology industry 160–1
 jewellery industry 116
 jute industry 78–9
 mineral oil industry 122–3
 motorcycle industry 146
 nonferrous metal industry 141
 peripatetic groups 153
 petrochemical industry 128
 pharmaceutical industry 131
 steel industry 98
 sugar industry 96–7
 tea industry 81–5
 television programming 111–14
 television set industry 114
 textile industry 86–92
Indian Furniture Products Limited 203
Indian history
 Ahmedabad, as trade route 21
 ancient and early medieval times 1–8
 Arab settlements 14
 during Christian Era 02
 colonial period 29–44
 commercial interaction between western India and West Asia, early times 1
 guild-like organizations 14
 Jewish settlements 14
 Kautilya's dictum 14
 major trade routes, ancient times 2, 4
 maps prepared by seafarers, 1st century CE 10–11*f*
 maritime contacts 4
 during Mauryan era 2
 migration of ethnic groups, early period 2
 Mughal period 18–27
 ports, ancient times 4, 8
 Silk Route 4, 5*f*
 sources of information 1–2, 4, 14
 in 8th and 9th centuries 14
 in 5th and 6th millenias AD 14
 trade associations 14
 voyages to Suvarna Bhumi and Suvarna Dweep 04
Indian Iron and Steel Co (IISCO) 39, 98
Indian Metals & Ferro Alloys Ltd (IMFA) 38*f*
 Bansidhar and Ila Panda Foundation (BIPF) 139
 Chinmaya Vidyalaya 139
 global progress 138
 Industrial Training Centre 139
 intervention on child and maternal health 139
 joint venture with Korea's Posco 138
Indian Oil Corporation (IOC) 123, 241, 268
Indian Petrochemicals 128
Indian private enterprise, post liberalization growth 282–3
 entrepreneurship 282–3
 market capitalization of listed companies (1991–2011) 282
 worries with 283
Indian steel sector 208, 210
India's cement industry 67
IndiGo Airlines 164
industrial policy resolutions (IPRs)
 of 1948 and 1956 177, 181
 of Chidambaram 193
 Congress attitude towards private sector, 1950s 183
 growth of companies, 1970s 183
 growth of companies, 1980s 186–8
 Mahalanobis' vision 181
 2000 onwards 193–223
 price and exchange controls and industrial licensing, 1950s 181
 private sector investments
  1950s 179
  1990s, 193
  from 1980 to 1990 186–92
information and technology industry 160–1
 airline/aviation industry 164
 satellite transmission and growth of 161
 telecommunications industry 163
Infosys 161, 196f, 221
Iranian Revolution of 1979 244
Iran-Iraq Gulf War, 1980–1 244
ISPAT Industries Ltd 208
ITC hotels 105*f*
Ivan the Terrible 64
Iyer, S.N.N Sankaralinga 100

J

Jagat Seth family 22–3
Jaguar Land Rover 143
Jain, Sahu Shanti Prasad 39
Java 4
Jay Shree Tea and Industries 85
Jeejebhoy, Sir Jamsetjee 32*f*
Jensen & Nicolson 129
Jet Airways 164
Jindal, Sajjan 208, 208*f*
Jindal Stainless 139
Jiwrajka group 89
Jobs, Steve 160
joint-stock companies 61
JPL Plant, Tamnar 206–207*f*
JSW Steel 208, 210
Jubilant Bhartia Group
 agri products and performance-polymers 262
 automobiles 262
 consulting services 262

food and retail 262
oil and gas 262
pharmaceuticals, life sciences, and healthcare 261–2
Jubilee railway bridge 77*f*
Juggilal Kamlapat of Kanpur 41
Jung, Nawab Salar 67
jute industry 78
crisis due to competition from plastics 79
early managing agents 78–9
first Indian jute mill 78
1970s 79

K
KAEFER Isoliertechnik 157
Kaikkolas 48
Kamath, K. V. 161*f*, 221
Kanchipuram 48
Kanoria Chemicals & Industries Limited
chlorine-based chemicals 126
future strategy 127
growth 126–7
manufacturing of alcohol-based intermediates 127
treatment of distillery effluents 127
'Waste to Wealth' programme 127
Karimi of Egypt 53
Kasliwal, Abhayakumar 90
Kasliwal, Mukul 92, 94
Kasliwal, Shambhukumar 90
Kasliwal, Warij 94
Kaura, Satish 115*f*
Kayasth accountant 21*f*
KCP Group
beginning 106
biotech division 108
cement division 106–7
corporate social responsibility 108
heavy engineering division 108
Heavy Engineering Unit, Tiruvottiyur 106
hospitality industry 108
ISO certification 108
KCP Biotech 106
KCP Technologies Limited 106
KCP Vietnam Industries Limited 106
Kids Patasala E.M. School 108
major divisions of 106
power division 107
Sri V. Ramakrishna Polytechnic College 108
sugar industry in Vietnam 108
Kernev, Y.M. 65
Khaitan, Brij Mohan 82, 82*f*
Khaperkheda power station 74*f*
Khatau, Dharamsey 67
Khataus of Bombay 39, 99
Khatris 59
Khushalchand 22
Kingfisher Airlines 164
Kirloskar, Lakshmanrao 40, 150
Kirloskar group 40, 150
Klopman International 90–2
Krishna and Radha, 17th century 19*f*
Krishnan, Suresh 202
Kudirai Chettis 48
Kushans 2

L
Lalbhai, Kasturbhai 38*f*
Land Rover Leyland International Holdings 143
Larpet and Co floated Assam Company 82
Larsen & Toubro (L&T) 148, 150
LG 259
liberalization era
MNCs 244
petroleum industry 267–8
Lipton 85
LML 216
locomotive and workshop logos 76f
L&T Cement Ltd 99

M
Macneills 79
Madras, 19th century 28*f*
Madras Motors 146
Madurai 48
Mafatlals 39
Magor, R.B. 82
Magor, Williamson 82
Mahajans 22
Mahalanobis, P.C. 181
Maheshwar Hydro Electric Project (MHEP) 92–3
community development programmes 93
Pandit Jasraj performance 93, 93*f*
Mahindra, Anand 145*f*
Mahindra, Keshub 42*f*
Mahindra & Mahindra (M&M) 41, 43, 145, 217
Mallaya, Vijay 164
Manrique, Sebastian 56
Maran, Dayandhi 164
Marcopolo 143
Mardia 129
Mariwala, Harsh 189*f*
Martin, Sir Acquin 98
Martin & Co. 39
Maruti Suzuki 212–13, 259
Maruti Udyog 143
Mauryan era, Indian business during 2
McleodRussel 82
Mercedes 248
Metro Cash and Carry 264
Metropolitan Hotel 103
Michet, Pierre 146
Micro inks 129
mineral oil industry 122–3
Mitsubishi 248
Mittal, Sunil 192*f*, 218
Modi, K.K. 285
Modi, Rai Bahadur Gujarmal 285
Modi Enterprises 41, 285
Modi group 41
Mody, Sir Homy 67
Mohan, Madan 39
moneylender 27
Monopolies and Restrictive Trade Practices (MRTP) Act 187, 241
Mookerjee, Sir Biren 39
Mookherjee, Sir Rajendra Nath 38*f*, 39, 98
Morarjee, Narottam 40
Morris Oxford car 142
motorcycle industry 146
Mughal amulet pendant, 18th century 25*f*
Mughal military market, miniature 18f
Mughal period, Indian business during 18–27
Banias 59
business partnerships 61
dalali (system of brokerage) 59
hatt-tal ('market-closure') 62
hundis or bills of exchange 60
long-distance trade in bulk goods 59
money transactions in villages 57
notion of a 'market rate' of interest 62
Surat merchants 57
wage-worker, system of 62
Muir, John 84
multinational companies (MNCs) in India
Alstom India 235–6
automobiles 248
Coca Cola 242
in consumer electronics 259
in FMCG sector 259
history 233
IBM 242
Imperial Tobacco Company 242
in information technology 259
and localization 272
Maruti Suzuki 259
meritocratic and fair corporate culture 264
Nestlé 254–6
number of people employed 248
post liberalization 244
public emotion towards 272, 278–9
return in 1990s 246
supermarkets 264
in telecom services 246

Unilever 242
Mundy, Peter 59
Munjal, Brijmohan Lall 146*f*
Munjal brothers 146
Murthy, N.R. Narayana 221
MW Corp 90–4
Dasna Developers 94
Entegra Limited 92–4
leadership seminar based on the 'Ontological' model 94
Maheshwar Hydro Electric Project (MHEP) 92–3
water purification and education 94
MW Infra Developers 90, 92
MW Unitexx 90–1

N

nagarattar 48
Nagarjuna Sagar Dam 107
Nagarseth 22
Naidu, G. Kuppuswamy 41, 42*f*
Naidu, P.S.G. 41
Naidu, V.R. 41
Naidu families of Coimbatore 41
Nanda, H. P. 187*f*
Narangs 41
Narayanaswami, T.S. 100
Nath, Aman 103
National Aluminium Company 141
National Jute Manufacturing Corporation 79
National Thermal Power Corporation (NTPC) 241
Neemrana Fort, 13th century 102*f*
Nehru, Prime Minister Jawaharlal 73*f*, 233
NELP (New Exploration Licensing Policy) 268
Neotia, Suresh 99
Nestle 254–6
Agri-services 255
approach to business 255
'Clean Drinking Water' projects 256
environmental sustainability 256
factories in India 254
'Health Plus' products 256
Nescafe Plan in India 256
role in cultivation and quality of chicory 255–6
Niépce, Joseph 111
Nisshin Steel 139
Nixon, Killick 67, 99
NOCIL 128
nonferrous metal industry 141
Nusli Wadia company 85

O

Oberoi, Mohan Singh 103
Oberoi hotel 103
Occidental 244
OCP Morocco 201
Oil and Natural Gas Commission (ONGC)241
Orenburg, city of 64
Orion Technology Inc. 223
Orissa Mineral Development Company 39

P

Palkhivala, Nani 67
Pallas, P.S. 65
Pallavas 48
Panda, Dr Bansidhar 138
Panda, Mrs Ila 138
Pandyas 48
paper making 24
Paradeep Phosphates Limited 201
Parekhs 21
Patel, Sardar Vallabhai 146*f*
Paul, Stya 132–3, 132*f*
Paul, Swraj 187, 187*f*
Perambul Coach Factory, Madras 72*f*
peripatetic groups 155
Periplus of the Erythrean Sea 8
petrochemical industry 128
petroleum products, pricing of 267
Phalke, Dadasaheb 111
pharmaceutical industry 131
Phillips Electronics 233
Piocon Technologies 223
Poddar, Saroj Kumar 201, 201*f*
Prashant, Shashi 192*f*
Premier Construction 40
Premier Motors 142
Premji, Asim 161*f*
pricing of petroleum products 267
printed cotton cloth, 18th century 25*f*
Procter & Gamble 259
Punj, Atul 156*f*, 157
Punj Lloyd 153
in aviation 158
early years 157
EPC (Engineering Procurement Construction) contracts 157
integrated drilling services 158
Punj Lloyd Delta Renewables 158
Punj Lloyd Infrastructure 158
social development 158

R

Raja Harishchandra 111
Rajiv Gandhi Grameen Vidyutikaran Yojana (RGGVY) 94
Ram, Bharat 186*f*
Ram, Lala Shri 38*f*, 39
Ramakrishna, Velagapudi 106
Ramanathaswamy temple,
Rameshwaram 55*f*
Ramayana reliefs
fight between Ram and Ravana 6*f*
Garuda 4*f*
Ranbaxy 226
Rashtrakutas 48
Ravi, Shashi 192*f*
Reliance Industries Limited (RIL) 186, 272, 283
Reliance Infra's thermal power station 136–7*f*
Reliance Mediaworks 114
Reliance refinery 123, 124–5*f*, 184–5*f*
Reliance telecom 163
Rilieux, Norbert 96
rock-cut caves of the Kailashnath temple complex, Ellora 1*f*
rockcut temples of Mahabalipuram 49*f*
Rohtas Industries 39
Rolta Inc. 222
acquisitions 223
engineering and software development and delivery centres 222–3
geospatial technology 222
growth 223
strategic partnerships 223
Rosen, George 179
Royal Enfield 146, 147*f*
Ruia, Shashi 192*f*
Rustomjis 21

S

Sakas 2
Sakata 129
Saklatvala N.B. 67
Sakthi Sugars 97
Saliyas 48
Samsung 114, 259
Samtel Group 114
Sarabhai, Ambalal 67
Sarabhais of Ahmedabad 41
Saran, Raghunandan 143
Sardar Sarovar Dam 152*f*
sarpech or turban ornament of Mughal origin, 17th century 62*f*, 116*f*
Sarrafs 59–60
Seal, Muthylal 30
Seksaria, Narottam 99
Sembawang Engineers & Constructors 157
Sen, S.R. 179
Seshasayee, R. 42
Seshasayee, V. 42
Seshasayees 10
Shell 244, 267
Shiv Niwas, Udaipur 102*f*
Shrirams 39
Silk Route 4, 5*f*
Simon Carves 153, 157

Singh, Parvinder 226
Singh, Kamal K. 222
Singh, Malvinder 226
Singh, Manmohan 193
Singh, Shivinder 226
Skoda 248
S. Kumars Group 90–2
Sony 114
Southern Petrochemicals Industries Corporation (SPIC) Ltd 196f
South Indian textiles 53
SpiceJet Airlines 164
Sreni and Nigama 14
Srinivasan, Chitra 100
Srinivasan, N. 100
Sri Renuka Sugar 97
Standard Oil Company 41
Standard Vacuum 123
steam engines 78
Steel Authority of India Ltd (SAIL) 208
Steelcrete 133
steel industry 98
Sterlite 141
sugar industry 96–7
  government regulations, impacts of 96–7
  production, 1930s 96
  sugar warehouse 97*f*
Sumant Moolgaokar Technical Institute, Kymore 69
Sundaram, T.V. 41
Suzuki Motor Corporation 143, 212
Svran Group 133
swords and daggers 20*f*

T

Tagore, Dwarkanath 30*f*, 82, 82*f*
Taj Mahal, Bombay 102*f*
Takshila 9*f*
Talismanic bowl 19*f*
tandas 59
Tanishq brand 119
Tata, Jamsetji N. 34*f*, 35
Tata, J.R.D. 67, 177, 179
Tata Engineering and Locomotive Company (TELCO) 142
Tata Global Beverages 85
Tata Hydro Electric Power Supply Company 35
Tata Iron and Steel Company (TISCO) 39, 98
Tata Motors 142, 213, 216
Tata Power 36, 134
Tatas 35, 67, 99, 103
TATA steel 210
Tata Steel Cement Plant 99
Tata telecom services 163
TCS 221
tea industry 81–2
  British, role in popularizing 81–2
  development of tea gardens
  in Assam 82
  major tea marketers, present times 85
  in Nilgiris 84
  story of Williamson Magor 82
  Tata Global Beverages 84–5
telecommunications industry 163
Telecom Regulatory Authority of India (TRAI) 163
television programming 111–14
terracotta statue, Harappa 2*f*
Tesco 264
Tetley 85
Texmaco Rail & Engineering Limited 200, 203
textile industry 86–92
  garment production 89
  installation of mechanical looms
  power loom firms 88, 89*f*
  knitting clusters 88
  spinning mill centres 88
  weaving mills 88
Thanjavur 48
Thanjavur temple 49*f*
Thapar, B.M. 150
Thapar, Karamchand 42
Thapars 40–1
Titan watch 118*f*
'T' logo 36*f*
Total 267
town bazaar
  Pahari (Himachal school) illustration of 27*f*
  17th century 58f
Toyo Corporation, Japan 201
Toyota 248
trading activities, early period
  agrarian regions 48
  Chola expeditions of the 11th century 50
  Chola period 48
  coin system 47
  inter-regional trade 50
  itinerant traders 50, 52
  major industries of Karnataka and Tamil Nadu 52
  Mauryan period 47
  merchant guilds, 12th–14th centuries 50
  pre-Chola period 48
Travadis 21
Triveni Engineering 97
Turner, Rustomji 30
TVS 216

U

UltraTech Cement 99
Unilever 41, 85, 233, 259
United Waters India (UWI) 94
Utkal Coal Ltd 139
Uttar Pradesh Power Corporation Limited (UPPCL) 94

V

Vakatakas 48
Veenadhara 53*f*
Vespa scooters 146
Videocon 114
Viranna, Kasi 22
Vodafone 163
Vora, Virji 18, 21, 56

W

Wacziarg, Francis 103
Wadia, Jeh 164
Wadia, Nowrosjee Nusserwanjee 42*f*
Wadia, Nusli 85*f*
Wadias of Bombay 41
Wajid, Khoja 23
Walchandnagar Industries 40
Walchands 40
Wal-Mart 264
Watson's Hotel 103
West End hotel 103
WhittmanHart Consulting 223
Wilhelm Hildebrand 146
Williamson, Captain J.H. 82
Willys jeeps 145
Wipro 161
Wozniak, Steve 160

Y

Yamuna Expressway 154–5*f*
Yavanas 8
Yule, Andrew 39

Z

Zang, Xuan 4*f*
Zaveris 22
Zoya 118f
Zuari Agro Chemicals 200
  commitment to farmers 202–3
  joint ventures 201